AMACHE

The Story of Japanese Internment in Colorado During World War II

ROBERT HARVEY

ISBN 978-0-86541-245-3 (paperback)
ISBN 978-0-86541-265-1 (digital)

Library of Congress Control Number: 2024945127

Copyright © 2024 by Robert Harvey
Third Edition
All rights reserved. No part of this publication may be reproduced, distributed, or transmitted in any form or by any means, including photocopying, recording, or other electronic or mechanical methods without the prior written permission of the publisher. For permission requests, solicit the publisher via Filter Press's website.

Filter Press, LLC
719-481-2420
www.FilterPressBooks.com

Printed in the United States of America

Publisher's Cataloging-in-Publication

Names:	Harvey, Robert, 1963- author.
Title:	Amache : the story of Japanese internment in Colorado during World War II / Robert Harvey.
Description:	[Third edition].	Filter Press, LLC [2024] Includes bibliographical references and index.
Identifiers:	ISBN: 978-0-86541-245-3 (paperback)	978-0-86541-265-1 (digital)	LCCN: 2024945127
Subjects:	LCSH: Granada Relocation Center--History.	Japanese Americans--Forced removal and internment, 1942-1945.	World War, 1939-1945--Forced removal of civilians--United States.	World War, 1939-1945--Concentration camps--Colorado--Amache.	Amache (Colo.)--History--20th century.	BISAC: HISTORY / United States / State & Local / West (AK, CA, CO, HI, ID, MT, NV, UT, WY)	HISTORY / Wars & Conflicts / World War II / General.

CONTENTS

Editorial Reviews..vii
Acknowledgments ix
Introduction..xi

Chapter 1:   The Cost of Peace..1
Chapter 2:   "The Greatest Possible Speed Is Imperative"............31
Chapter 3:   Colorado Must Do Its Duty..................................64
Chapter 4:   The Desert "Way Station" 100
Chapter 5:   Colorado's Newest City 126
Chapter 6:   "The Strange Drama" 161
Chapter 7:   "Because We Are of Different Color and Race" 201
Chapter 8:   Winning the War 234
Chapter 9:   Going Home 263
Chapter 10: Aftermath...284

Index..307

EDITORIAL REVIEWS

Harvey has done an excellent job of writing about Amache, a historical subject that needs to be repeatedly and accurately told. He has done it with solid research and great compassion.
Robert Y. Fuchigami Ed.D. University of Illinois, former Amache inmate—1942–1945, professor and author
Amache: Remembered: An American Concentration Camp

The only book on Amache that I have read that includes the historical context (economic "threat") leading up to the forced removal and imprisonment of Japanese and Japanese Americans. It is the most comprehensive document I have come across on the history of Amache.
Derek Okubo | Executive Director
Agency for Human Rights and Community Partnerships
City and County of Denver

Robert Harvey's stunning account of Japanese internment in southeastern Colorado during World War II is a remarkable piece of our state's history. Harvey's research and compelling interviews with former internees at the Amache relocation camp show the strength and resilience of people whose lives were uprooted by war hysteria. This remarkable book underscores why America can never again allow prejudice to take away human rights. When I read the original edition of Amache many years ago, I found it so moving that it inspired my novel *Tallgrass*.
Sandra Dallas, New York Times best-selling author

ROBERT HARVEY

Amache, one of the saddest and most important chapters in Colorado history, lacked book length coverage until Robert Harvey finally put together this must-read.

—Thomas J. "Dr. Colorado" Noel
professor of history,
Colorado University-Denver

Amache is a dark chapter in our history we can't afford to forget. Robert has deftly told the story in the hopes we never repeat it.

John Hickenlooper, United States Senator, Colorado

Robert Harvey's book on Amache is a must read for anyone who wishes to understand the historical context of Amache. It is a required reading for my students in the Amache Preservation Society and has been for many years. Harvey's research on Amache is extensive and accurate. The book is easy to read and we quote his work many times during our presentations on Amache.

John Hopper
Granada School Teacher
Director of the Amache Preservation Society and Amache Museum

ACKNOWLEDGMENTS

I am indebted to many for their help in creating this work.

Many hours were spent in various archives around the state to complete this project. Although many people have helped me find just the right material, four men went above and beyond. Special thanks go to David Hays in the archives of University of Colorado at Boulder Libraries, Kellen Cutsforth of the Denver Public Library, and to Frank Tapp and Matthew Mariner at the Auraria Library Archives and Special Collections Department. Without their assistance, many stories and photos would not have found their way into these pages.

John Hopper and his students also lent a great deal of time in helping me find my way around the archives at Amache. I am also appreciative of the way Hopper helped me locate new sources to interview. Your concern for those involved with Amache is evident and will never be forgotten.

I am extremely grateful to Sandra Dallas for the advice she's given me on this manuscript, and others as well. Her kindness and professionalism are an example to us all.

I'd also like to thank Kiana, Brandon, and Eva for their work in finding just the right photos and to Jessica for the time you gave to the editing process. I'm also grateful to Gary and Melissa. Without your work on digital formatting, the original work could not have been resurrected.

For the first edition of this work, I need to remember Lane Hirabayashi of University of Colorado at Boulder, Richard Rinehart of Rowman & Littlefield, and David Foxhoven who had faith in my work. For the second edition, the team at Hawes and Jenkins went above and beyond. I am grateful you've given this work new breath.

Of course, I must take a moment to thank my wife Joy and my daughters, Jessica and Eva. The three of you allowed the time needed to complete this project. I owe you.

And finally, this work would never have been written if not for the courage of those whose stories reside in its pages. To those whose lives will somehow always be touched by the events of Amache, I am thankful that you took a chance and shared your memories. This work was, from the very beginning, written for you.

I hope I shared your stories well.

INTRODUCTION

F reedom is why they come.
Hoping for opportunities not found in the land of their birth, people from all over the world come to make a new life in America.

In America, anyone can be a part of prosperity—a player in the game of democracy, a participant in the wealth of capitalism. These men and women from other lands come to America for a myriad of reasons.

For many, the sound of America's freedom rings stronger than ever. But if one listens closely, one might just be able to make out the cries of those who were wounded in this call for liberty. Throughout its history, America has been inflicted by the very wounds of injustice it has so diligently tried to exterminate.

One such period came during our country's Second World War. In the first stages of the war, Americans were seized by the fear that they might become victims of fifth column activities. Potential enemy sympathizers seemed to lurk behind every building and within every shadow. Americans began to see neighbors of different ethnic backgrounds as potential threats to democracy's foundations. Americans soon sought ways to rid themselves of these potential threats in the easiest and most convenient methods possible—concentration camps.

When one thinks of forced internment, one does usually not think of the United States. One might think of Stalin's forced labor camps. One might recall Hitler's Auschwitz and Treblinka. But the *New Encyclopedia Britannica* defines a concentration camp as an "internment center for political reasons of state security, exploitation, or punishment, usually by executive decree or military order." Few Americans today, however, remember the US concentration camps of Tule Lake and Heart Mountain. Even many historians are silent about camps such as Manzanar and Amache. However, the glaring facts of history remind us that during World War II, our democratic nation established ten such concentration camps on our soil. Although it is true that these camps never reached the barbarity found in Germany or Russia, they were—by definition—concentration camps.

During World War II, America had ten major concentration camps designed to house primarily those of Japanese descent. Spread among a handful of western and southern states, these centers were built as a means to rid America of a seemingly unsolvable problem of national security. But was internment in these camps a result of Americans trying to protect their country against enemy infiltration, or was it instead the outcome of greedy West Coast landowners and racist whites bent on purity?

The work that follows looks closely at the internment of Japanese aliens and Japanese Americans during World War II, particularly at those housed within the confines of Colorado's concentration center known as Amache.

Over ten thousand people passed through the gates of Amache during the war. In many ways, this camp was typical of America's Japanese internment centers. Within Amache's gates, people attempted to make their lives as comfortable as possible. Within its gates, children were born; fathers and mothers died. Within its gates, citizens of America were housed because of fear, greed, and prejudice.

Amache, like the other internment centers, became a stain on the fabric of America's liberty.

This is a story of an innocent people. This is a story of freedom's hypocrisy. This is the story of Amache.

CHAPTER 1

THE COST OF PEACE

The memories are still vivid.

Shigeko Hirano still recalls that fateful day like it was only yesterday. She can almost hear the sounds of shuffling papers and books that signaled the start of her day as a young girl at California's Delano Joint Union High School. Hirano loved these sounds. It was 1942, and as a freshman in high school, she finally felt grown-up. Even when older friends jokingly called her frosh, a feeling of pride would swell within her. But she couldn't help noticing the underlying current of tension and anxiety that accompanied these feelings.

For months, the fourteen-year-old Hirano had been concerned about the war overseas. Being a citizen of a country involved in such a worldwide war was terrifying. Like other Americans, Hirano had found it unbelievable that a small country like Japan could even consider attacking a powerful nation like America. Hirano was also concerned that the bombing of Pearl Harbor might affect her parents, for they were of Japanese birth. Her father had, several years before, come to America from Japan for a new lease on life. Her mother, as a young woman, had also taken the trip to America, met and married Shigeko's father, and helped her husband establish a successful business in Delano. Over the years, Shigeko's parents had become Americans in every way—in every way except citizenship.

Considered Asians by the US government, the right to citizenship had never been an option for Hirano's parents.

But fourteen-year-old Hirano didn't have these same problems. After all, she had been born in the United States. She was a citizen by birth. In fact, Hirano knew far less of Japanese culture than the American culture she had been surrounded by her entire life. She was thoroughly American in every way. And as an American, Hirano settled into another school day—the thought of her heritage never entering her mind.

But this was not to be a typical day for Hirano. It began with a simple message for one of Hirano's classmates from the school's office. These sorts of messages were not unusual. Students were often called down to the office for one reason or another. So when one of Hirano's classmates was taken from the classroom—some sort of family emergency, it was claimed—the rest of the class took it in stride and went back to their studies. However, when in thirty minutes or so another student was excused for the day, murmurs began to ripple throughout the room. Both students had been of Japanese ancestry, and both students had been called home for "family emergencies."

Throughout the day, similar messages punctuated Hirano's classes. No students other than those of Japanese heritage were called home. The entire school population began to wonder what was going on. On one of her breaks, Hirano heard a rumor that one of the students' fathers had been taken away by the FBI. But rumors like these were still highly speculative. No one was certain why these students were being called out of school en masse. So for the rest of the day, every time the door swung open with yet another message, Hirano wondered if she might be next.

Hirano's turn never came. After school, Shigeko and her older sister met outside the school for the long journey home. The day's events had filled both girls with apprehension and concern. Once at home, both girls hoped they would find out what had happened that day. But as Shigeko and her sister reached their block, their anxieties quickly turned to fear.

A strange car was in the street outside their home. Two Caucasian FBI agents met Hirano and her sister at their front door and questioned them about their whereabouts on that day. After the questioning, the two girls and their parents were instructed to step aside as the agents rifled through desks and drawers and personal belongings, searching for pieces of "evidence." Hirano was never really certain what the evidence these agents hoped to find would prove. But she was sure that something had become suddenly and terribly wrong in the life of her family.

Hirano could not have possibly envisioned the pivotal nature this day would have in her life. What had started as simply another school day had, by its end, become a dizzying nightmare of confusion and accusations. By midnight, every home owned or rented by persons of Japanese ancestry in her neighborhood would be searched. By nightfall, every Issei male in the town of Delano would be rounded up and taken away to a nearby jail. And by nightfall, it was clear that Shigeko Hirano's world, and the world of every other Japanese American in Delano, was about to be turned upside down.[1]

Those in Delano were not alone—this nightmarish scene was being played out in towns up and down the West Coast. These raids were not simply the outcome of the attack by the Japanese on Pearl Harbor.

The scene Hirano and thousands of other Japanese Americans were witnessing had been borne of racial and economic suppression and exclusion—exclusion begun decades before. To understand the story of these American citizens and their alien parents, one must look closely at the overall drama of the past—a past that pitted American against American and the desires of a majority against the constitutional freedoms of a minority.

Men and women like Shigeko's parents had been coming to Hawaii and the US mainland for decades. Japanese immigrants made their way to the United States in the late nineteenth and early twentieth centuries for much the same reasons other immigrants had come. Some sought prosperity. Others came seeking adventure. Some hoped for a fresh start. Others sought personal freedom. Some came only temporarily, hoping to make money and then to return within a few short years to Japan. Others, like Hirano's parents, came with full intentions of making America their home.

---

[1] Shigeko Hirano, personal interview, 27 January 2001.

On reaching Hawaii and the US mainland, these Japanese immigrants were given a new title—Issei (pronounced "ees-say"), meaning first-generation Japanese American. These Issei came to America expecting success. They dreamed of new businesses to market their wares or of fertile fields to raise their crops. They hoped for a quality education for their children, plenty of food and heat for their families and homes, and a fresh beginning in a new land—a land free from economic oppression. And what most of these immigrants wanted in return was simply a level playing field by which they could—through hard work and ingenuity—find personal success. Issei had heard many stories of earlier Japanese immigrants who had made the trip, stories of both humble and epic proportions. In short, immigrants from Japan came for the same reason that those from other countries had come—to live out the American dream.

And they did. The successes of Japanese immigrants coming to the United States were staggering. Within just a few decades, these immigrants became a thriving aspect of West Coast American culture. But with newfound success came a fair amount of resentment from surrounding Anglo-American communities. Americans of the West felt these Japanese aliens, with their strange appearances and customs, were arriving at the American dream far too quickly and efficiently. Competition became much too uncomfortable for established Anglo businesses. Soon, people on the West Coast began to seek ways of ridding themselves of this rivalry—this so-called immigrant problem.

The "problem" had begun in the late nineteenth century. During this period, Japanese began to immigrate to the US territory of Hawaii. Until then, the Tokugawa shogun government in Japan had crushed all attempts at immigration outside the country. But after the Meiji government came into power in the late 1860s, the Japanese were free to immigrate wherever they wished. Within a decade, thousands of Japanese immigrants flowed into Hawaii to fill a desperate need for labor there.[2]

---

[2] Rhoads Murphey, *East Asia: A New History* (New York: Addison Wesley Longman, 1997), 288.

Although the Meiji government heavily controlled this move westward, the flow of Japanese immigrants ebbed into mainland America. Within the western states of California, Washington, and Oregon, Issei found abundant labor opportunities in agriculture, lumber mills, and salmon canneries. Eventually, as the nineteenth century came to a close, Japanese aliens could even be found in inland states like Wyoming, Utah, and Colorado where they helped build railroads, mine coal, and harvest sugar beets.[3]

Immigrants were initially attracted to Colorado for economic reasons. Russell Endo, in his work entitled *Persistence of Ethnicity: The Japanese of Colorado*, remarks that "these immigrants were usually literate and ambitious individuals from rural farming areas in southern Japan." But farming wasn't what drew these immigrants to the state. As early as the late 1800s, Japanese Issei were coming to Colorado primarily as railroad laborers. Endo notes that "the total number of Issei railroad workers was never very large: in 1909 their numbers were estimated to be 400. However, railroad companies liked to use Issei labor. The Issei had a reputation for hard work and were paid less than anyone else except the Chinese."[4]

Other Issei could be found working in coalfields in southern Colorado, while still others worked for the Colorado Fuel and Iron steel mill.

Then, around 1902, Issei began to appear in the southeast Colorado counties of Otero, Bent, and Prowers. Here, they worked in agricultural areas and even became independent farmers. Western Colorado saw fewer Issei locate there. Endo writes that "a few Issei… went to western Colorado around Grand Junction and Delta. However, white hostility kept the Japanese away and in 1909 there were only twenty-five in the region working in sugar beet fields."[5]

---

[3] John M. Murrin, Paul E. Johnson, James M. McPherson, Gary Gerstle, Emily S. Rosenberg, and Norman L. Rosenberg, *Liberty, Equality, Power: A History of the American People* (Fort Worth: Harcourt Brace, 1996), 644.
[4] Russell Endo, *Persistence of Ethnicity: The Japanese of Colorado* (Boulder: Western Historical Collections, University of Colorado, 1979), 2–7.
[5] Endo, *Persistence of Ethnicity*, 2–7.

The largest concentration of Japanese immigrants, however, could be found in the youthful city of Denver. Most Issei began settling around the streets of Blake, Market, and Larimer in downtown Denver. By 1909, this area had sixty-seven Japanese businesses that included boardinghouses, supply outfitters, employment agencies, dry good stores, and grocery stores.

But the sudden influx of Issei into Colorado was met with a stiff resolve by those already there. Propaganda and agitations were common and soon the numbers of Japanese coming to Colorado began to subside.

The people of Colorado were not alone in their racial resolve. Indeed, they were only a sampling of the attitude found in the rest of the country.[6]

Those coming to America from Asian countries often were met with resistance. The right to citizenship was withheld for Issei. Anglos brought legality to this exclusion by referring to the Naturalization Statute of 1870 that stated only those of Anglo or African descent were allowed into the naturalization process.

Since Issei did not fit either description, they—like other Asian immigrants—were considered persons "ineligible for citizenship." Without the ability to become citizens of the United States, Issei were likewise ineligible to vote. Lacking legal rights and a voice in the American system of governance, Issei were powerless against segregation and exclusion.

However, the children of Issei born in America—called Nisei (pronounced "nee-say"), or second-generation Japanese Americans—were protected by the Fourteenth Amendment of the constitution as "citizens of the United States and of the state wherein they reside." On paper, Nisei—as native-born Americans—had the same rights and privileges other Americans enjoyed.

But the reality was much starker, for segregation ran rampant in cities along the West Coast. Shigeko Hirano recalls vividly the segregation policies of Delano, California, which controlled everything from housing locations to where a person could sit in movie theaters.

---

[6] Endo, *Persistence of Ethnicity*, 2–7.

Likewise, Walter Miyao remembers being segregated in an all-Japanese American school in Florin, California.[7]

Some worked around these limitations. A number of Nisei chose to return to Japan for educational opportunities. These young Americans called Kibei (pronounced "kee-bay") returned to the country of their parents. Often these young men and women returned to Japan to appease familial leaders, maintain cultural ties, and search for better educational opportunities. Kibei usually were fluent in both languages and had footholds firmly planted in both American and Japanese cultures.

In spite of the blatant lack of constitutional rights and an abundance of discrimination, Issei, Nisei, and Kibei began to make important economic and foundational footholds in America. By pooling resources, many Japanese families were able to buy substantial amounts of land and property. They established businesses and factories, supplying much of the West Coast with goods and services. Retail and wholesale outlets began to spring up in both urban and rural communities. Many Nisei—like Walter Miya who attended the University of California in Berkley as a public health specialist—trained in specialized fields.[8]

This sudden agricultural, industrial, and financial growth continued to frighten non-Asian Americans. Attempting to cap the sudden growth of Asian wealth on the West Coast, western states began passing alien land acts prohibiting the sale of land to all "ineligible aliens" (again, aimed primarily at Issei) and limiting lease contracts to no more than three years. These laws were designed to end the ownership of land by those with Japanese heritage, even though Asian landholdings constituted only a small percentage of the total West Coast landholdings. Issei often skirted around these laws by establishing ties with non-Asian partners or purchasing land under the names of their children—the Nisei—who were American citizens by birth and thus not affected by such laws.[9]

---

[7] Hirano, interview; Walter Miyao, letter to the author, 12 November 2002.
[8] Miyao, letter.
[9] Murrin et al., *Liberty, Equality, Power*, 644.

In a last-ditch effort to thwart the rising "threat" of Japanese aliens and Japanese Americans, West Coast citizens passed a new legislative act in 1924 that virtually ended the flow of Japanese immigration to the United States. This act—the Immigration Act of 1924—prohibited anyone "ineligible for citizenship" from entering America. Since only those of Anglo and African descent were considered eligible for citizenship, the new legislation was clearly aimed at Japanese and Chinese immigrants. Confident in their legal efforts to end the upsurge of immigration, West Coast anti-Asian groups waited for the moment when they would rid themselves of the Japanese problem completely.

But much to the dismay of many on the West Coast, the problem never went away. In fact, despite the presence of the 1924 Immigration Act and various Asian land laws, Issei and Nisei began to grow even more powerful throughout the 1920s and 1930s. By 1941, Japanese American holdings had grown to over $70 million in California landholdings alone.[10]

These figures represent hard work and frugality on the part of the Japanese Americans. Michi Nishiura Weglyn notes in her book *Years of Infamy* that Issei were well-known for buying strips of land previously seen as worthless lands around dams, railroads, swamplands, and desert areas—and turning them into lush agricultural sources. "The extraordinary drive and morale," Weglyn writes, "of these hard-working, frugal Issei who could turn parched wastelands, even marshes, into lush growing fields usually with the help of the entire family became legendary." Seeing this progress, Anglo competitors began claiming the Issei were buying up all the choice land in western states.[11]

And the Nisei—who were, by the 1930s, becoming old enough to compete in the workforce—had become a competitive movement within their fields of study. These faceless immigrants were no longer idle threats to just a few farmers here and there. Issei and Nisei had

---

[10] "Issei, Nisei, Kibei," *Fortune* (April 1944), 22.

[11] Michi Nishiura Weglyn, *Years of Infamy: The Untold Story of America's Concentration Camps* (Seattle: University of Washington Press, 1996), 37.

become competitive physicians, prosperous bankers, and dominate in both agriculture and commerce. Much to the dismay of many on the West Coast, both Issei and their citizen children were actually making a name for themselves in America—and with gusto.

Because of this, some Americans began dredging up old anti-Asian feelings by turning Issei and Nisei success into a Yellow Peril bent on total control of the West Coast. As many were straining under heavy financial losses to Issei and Nisei, racial tension soon grew into blind intolerance. Walter Miyao remembers that although he had accomplished all the requirements needed for a degree as a public health specialist at the University of California, he was told that he would not be allowed an internship because of his race. "Without an internship," Miyao recalls, "I was not able to find a job." With no other alternatives at hand, Miyao joined the US Army Medical Corps in October 1941.[12]

And newspapers and periodicals provided the fuel needed for such racial intolerance. For decades, Hearst Press publications had warned against the imminent Yellow Peril. Hearst's *San Francisco Chronicle*, for example, depicted Japanese Americans as spies and land-hungry villains who sought dominance over American soil. To achieve such dominance, other publications predicted the Japanese would eventually bring war to American soil.[13]

So by early December, the stage had been set. Any incident linked to Japanese imperialism—small or large—would provide the shove needed to topple the precarious racial and economic balances found on the West Coast and in Hawaii. And that shove came on the morning of December 7, 1941.

In the pristine morning air, a few Hawaiians had just begun their daily routines. Some were enjoying the quiet afforded them every Sunday morning. Others were simply taking advantage of an opportunity to rest.

---

[12] Miyao, letter.
[13] Edward H. Spicer, *Impounded People: Japanese-Americans in the Relocation Centers* (Tucson: University of Arizona Press, 1969), 45.

But the tranquility of this sleepy Pearl Harbor morning was suddenly blown apart as the dull hum of enemy aircraft pierced a tranquil sky. Within minutes, the hum turned to metallic blurs as bombers plunged toward the earth. Swooping down over the island, Japanese bombers battered American ships, planes, and bases with every ounce of weaponry they had. Soldiers and civilians alike watched as these attackers began wiping out nearly the entire US Pacific fleet. Never before had such an all-out attack by a foreign power taken place on American soil. To Americans, the bombing coupled with the same-day attack on the US air bases in the Philippines was Japanese barbarity at its highest. By nightfall, US armed forces would count a loss of over 19 ships, 188 planes, and 2,200 casualties. For a brief moment, America was sent reeling.

Lieutenant General Walter Short, the commander in chief of Pacific forces at Pearl Harbor, was caught completely unprepared by the attack. In a sudden, knee-jerk reaction, Short called for martial law throughout the Hawaiian Islands. Assets of all nationals were frozen, Issei and Nisei community leaders were taken into custody, and businesses with Japanese connections were closed. Those who could not provide proof of citizenship were automatically assumed aliens and were forbidden to withdraw money from savings accounts.

In light of such actions, the atmosphere on the islands changed drastically. The blue sky, business-as-usual climate of Hawaii became polluted—literally overnight—with the dark clouds of fear and anxiety. Suddenly, island civilians no longer had the total freedom they had enjoyed only the day before. In measures more closely resembling military rule than martial law, civilians were fingerprinted, phone calls and personal mail were censored, and nightly curfews were put into effect. In essence, the military regulated everything from the disposal of garbage to obtaining licenses and permits.[14]

Impromptu raids and arrests also followed. These sorts of raids were nothing new to the people of Hawaii. As far back as September

---

[14] Roger Daniels, "Japanese Relocation and Redress in North America: A Comparative View," in *The Mass Internment of Japanese Americans and the Quest for Legal Redress*, ed. Charles McClain (New York: Garland Publishing, 1994), 377.

6, 1939, President Roosevelt had authorized the Department of Justice to allow FBI surveillance of Japanese, German, and Italian nationals in Hawaii as well as those on the West Coast. Such surveillance was executed with the dual purpose of physical fact-finding and psychological intimidation. FBI agents, working with local law enforcement agencies, observed and kept detailed accounts of alien maneuvers. However, unlike the raids after the bombing, little or no physical force was used. No mass raids were performed. Officials claimed they were merely attempting to detect potential fifth column activities before they became physical sabotage.[15]

But such raids picked up momentum and resolution after the bombing of Pearl Harbor. Using the lists created earlier by local law officials, army and FBI authorities began in earnest to gather the Japanese nationals on the islands of Hawaii who had been previously detained or listed as "suspicious." No formal charges were needed. No notice was given. For the most part, the accusations were based on little more than ancestry, prior business connections with Japan, and leadership roles in respective communities. Suspects were rounded up and sent to the Sand Island detention center that had opened the day after the attack. These detainees would eventually be moved to mainland internment camps.[16]

On the mainland, military responses differed from those in Hawaii. Although raids and arrests also gained momentum on the West Coast, martial law was never declared. In his book *The Decision to Relocate the Japanese Americans*, Roger Daniels notes the decision to reject martial law on the West Coast was an option because the army's judge advocate general Allen W. Gullion felt that civilian courts had the ultimate say over their respective jurisdictions. Therefore, the military—regardless of any apparent necessity—had

---

[15] United States War Relocation Authority [hereafter, WRA], *Wartime Exile* (New York: AMS Press, 1975), 98.

[16] The Japanese American National Museum, *Japanese American History: An A-to-Z Reference from 1868 to the Present*, ed. Brian Niiya (New York: Facts on File, 1993), 137.

no legal footing to enforce martial law. Instead, the West Coast was designated as a theater of operations.[17]

At first glance, the theater of operations on the West Coast seemed less constraining than the martial law of Hawaii. But its domain differed from martial law because it ultimately affected the constitutional rights of only the Issei and Nisei living in the United States. In Hawaii, martial law applied to all residents, regardless of race. All civilians, regardless of ethnic background, were required to be fingerprinted and registered. Certain constitutional rights were taken from all residents of the islands, not just those of Japanese ancestry.[18]

The same was not true on the mainland. In California, Washington, Oregon, and Arizona, Japanese nationals—the overwhelming majority of enemy nationals affected under the theater of operations—were arrested because of their ancestral ties to the Empire of Japan. German and Italian nationals were arrested and imprisoned because of previously documented subversive acts—not because of their race. Ancestry was the plumb line of judgment for West Coast Japanese Americans, not previous criminal records.

Under the theater of operations domain, arrest and retention of Issei suspects fell to the FBI and local law enforcement officials. Shigeko Hirano's home was one of thousands of homes searched in the weeks and months following Pearl Harbor. Hirano and her family were powerless to do anything but watch as FBI agents emptied every drawer and cupboard in their home. The family's Philco radio (without the shortwave attachment, because they had previously been told they could keep the radio if all such attachments were removed) was taken. Cameras, toy movie projectors, and children's books written in Japanese were confiscated. The FBI agents searching Hirano's home even questioned the mother about a twenty-four-inch kitchen knife, thinking it to be a samurai sword.

"We were so scared, my sister and I," recalls Hirano. After searching her home, the FBI handcuffed Hirano's father and other promi-

---

[17] Roger Daniels, *The Decision to Relocate the Japanese Americans* (New York: J. B. Lippincott, 1975), 16.
[18] "Issei, Nisei, Kibei," 106.

nent Issei men from Delano and took them to the Bakersfield Kern County jail. "It was very convenient for [the FBI agents] because they went from one house to the next... We were all living very close to each other in this little community."[19]

As in the Hawaiian Islands, the FBI had records on most prominent Issei on the US mainland. And the weeks and months following Pearl Harbor saw the homes of these Issei ransacked by FBI and local authorities. Likewise, many Japanese nationals found bank accounts frozen and businesses closed.

Art Yorimoto recalls going to work on the day following Pearl Harbor:

> I worked as a supervisor for a wholesale produce market. As usual, I had to go in early to open up the shop. I remember I was pulling out my keys to unlock the back door of the market when I heard a voice behind me yell: "What the hell are you doing there, boy?" After telling him that I worked there, the man said: "You don't anymore" and then went on to tell me that the market had been closed because it was owned by a Japanese American.[20]

Issei businessmen, farmers, bankers, and laborers alike were rounded up and taken to local jails where they remained until transfers to federal prisons could be arranged.

Shigeko Hirano remembers trying to visit her father in one of these jails. Hoping to see him, Hirano and some of her older friends drove to the county jail where her father was incarcerated:

> It was a several story high building, and we couldn't see them. So, some of the men came to the window and they could see us. We were

---

[19] Hirano, interview.
[20] Art Yorimoto, personal interview, 18 May 2000.

shouting at them. They said, "Oh, it's okay"—my father was one of the older ones—"Hirano's okay. Tell everybody we're okay. Don't worry, we're all okay." After that, we didn't know where they were taking them. It ended up…they were eventually shipped to Santa Fe, New Mexico, and from there they went to Lordsburg, New Mexico.[21]

Hirano's father would remain isolated from his family in Lordsburg until 1944 when he was transferred to Amache.

This was the face of West Coast America in the weeks following Pearl Harbor. For Japanese Americans, these nightmarish weeks would slowly drag into months and eventually years. For the rest of America, the call of war was crying for total concentration. For most Americans, the plight of an Asian minority from the West Coast and Hawaii was not significant enough to warrant concern.

After all, there was a war going on.

Within weeks after Pearl Harbor, Americans were turning their bleak, depression-riddled country into one of astounding production and unity.

Children around the country collected cans and scrap metal for "Salvage for Victory" drives. High school boys in Buffalo, New York, turned to knitting squares needed by Red Cross workers for blankets.[22]

Women around the country baked goodies for care packages to send to Allied soldiers overseas. The *New York Times* noted one such care package included cookies with an extra-special "surprise." Unwittingly, an overzealous baker had accidentally dropped two of her diamond rings into the cookie batter as she prepared it for the troops overseas—a nice surprise for some unknowing serviceman. Although the war effort had become a priority, everyone understood

---

[21] Hirano, interview.
[22] *New York Times*, 2 January 1942, 10.

completely when the woman asked that any cookies encasing diamond rings be returned to the sender.[23]

On the surface, unity appeared to be one of the bright spots of the war effort. But in reality, the confidence brought by the united goal of victory only masked an underlying tide of ominous fear. Many Americans perceived the proximity of the West Coast and Hawaii to the Empire of Japan as far too close for comfort. The nearness of the two enemies provided too many opportunities for fifth column activists. Even President Roosevelt, in his "infamy" speech of December 8, noted that "the distance of Hawaii from Japan makes it obvious that the attack [on Pearl Harbor] was deliberately planned many days or even weeks ago." Whether Roosevelt felt this deliberately planned attack was aided by Japanese aliens is not readily clear in his address. But many military leaders did feel such aid was at least plausible. In the minds of these men, the attack by the Japanese was tightly planned and could be the first of many.[24]

The myth of a well-planned and tightly orchestrated conspiracy became a popular one outside military ranks as well. Only four days after Pearl Harbor, the *Seattle Post Intelligencer* claimed enemy aliens wishing to direct Japanese aircraft toward Seattle were setting arrow-shaped grass fires in fields south of the city. Although Washington's assistant governor later reported that the fires were the result of Anglo farmers clearing brush from their fields and were merely "coincidental," widespread panic still ensued. Rumors even circulated from San Diego to Seattle that Japanese Americans were placing ground glass in food and poisoning produce. The *Los Angeles Times* later reported test samples had proven such claims as "simply malicious and unfounded."[25]

Such fear was hardly surprising, for it had been fueled for decades by distrust, greed, and racial hatred. For years, West Coast farmers and businessmen had viewed Asian competition with disdain. Asian competition brought economic loss to once-established

---

[23] *New York Times*, 1 January 1942, 1.
[24] Franklin D. Roosevelt, speech, 8 December 1941.
[25] WRA, *Wartime Exile*, 99.

Anglo communities. Asian farmers had diminished Anglo profits by turning worthless land into productive fields. And the Asian race did not fit the model preached about on the podium of purity. By the early 1940s, the attitude of nativism had firmly replaced democracy on the West Coast. Into this inequitableness stepped a man who would eventually champion this hatred and distrust. In fact, this one man would lead the drive that—in a very brief span—would change the lives of over 110,000 Japanese Americans forever.

Lieutenant General John L. DeWitt, a sixty-one-year-old career military man, was nearing the sunset of his career. He had fought uneventfully in the Spanish-American War and was now spending his time within the bureaucracy of the army. With retirement beckoning, DeWitt desperately wished to avoid any appearance of ineptness and hoped at all costs to avoid the mistake of unpreparedness made by General Short in Hawaii. In DeWitt's mind, Pearl Harbor wasn't going to take place on his watch. So when DeWitt took command of the Western Defense Command on December 11, his stance became dogmatically guarded.

DeWitt was also a military man known for his strong racial biases. Dewitt had once complained that the ranks under him were being filled with "too many colored groups up on the West Coast." He wanted neither African Americans nor Asians under his command. In his opinion, the West Coast had "enough black-skinned people around them as it is." Likewise, he felt the Japanese population in America could not, and should not, be trusted.[26]

Although DeWitt could not deny that the vast majority of Issei and Nisei were loyal to the United States, he still adhered adamantly to the opinion that some posed a very real threat to democracy. To him, the only way to dissuade such an overpowering menace was to move it away from all points of temptation. DeWitt stood by his theory, feeling that someday it would be proven true.

But as days turned to weeks and weeks into months, America saw no sabotage by enemy aliens. To deal with this lack of activity, DeWitt was forced to take a slightly different stance by argu-

---

[26] Daniels, *Decision to Relocate the Japanese Americans*, 14.

ing that abstention was proof of fifth column activity. To summarize DeWitt's logic, the very fact that no sabotage activities had taken place or had yet been uncovered was proof that such action was about to happen. A lack of evidence merely proved such evidence existed. Roger Daniels calls DeWitt's logic a "catch-22...heads I win, tails you lose."[27]

DeWitt's catch-22 stance was most likely adopted from a December 15, 1941, statement made by Secretary of the Navy Frank Knox, which claimed "the most effective fifth-column work of the entire war was done in Hawaii with the possible exception of Norway." Although Knox's claim was never to be substantiated, DeWitt used the statement to support his earlier feelings.

Within days of Knox's statement, DeWitt and his colleagues had created a rudimentary plan in which all enemy nationals (he had not yet begun to focus on American citizens of Japanese ancestry) would be arrested and confined through an internment process. On December 19, DeWitt and his staff sent their recommended plan to general headquarters hoping to ignite some sort of reaction. DeWitt's recommendations stated:

> In view of the fact that the West Coast of the United States has now been designated and is functioning as an active theater of operations, it is recommended that action be initiated at the earliest practicable date to collect all alien subjects fourteen years of age and over, of enemy nationals and remove them to the zone of the interior.
>
> It is also recommended that these individuals be held under restraint after removal from the theater of operations in order to preclude their surreptitious return.
>
> Records indicate that there are approximately 40,000 of such enemy aliens and it is

---

[27] Daniels, *Decision to Relocate the Japanese Americans*, 14.

believed that they constitute an immediate and potential menace to vital measures of defense.[28]

The memo clearly stated the intent of DeWitt and his staff: remove enemy aliens (meaning only Japanese aliens) and place them under guard—all under the guise of America's defense.

Today, the memo to general headquarters is credited more to the efforts of DeWitt's colleagues than to DeWitt himself. Those working with DeWitt included several high-ranking military officials who had, in fact, heavily diagrammed the route to evacuation. One of DeWitt's colleagues, Major Karl R. Bendetsen, became a key architect of the evacuation plan by calling for strategic military areas in which Japanese Americans—both alien and citizen alike—could be moved. Bendetsen also called for a permit system used to monitor alien travel outside restricted areas. Bendetsen was later moved in rank to that of lieutenant colonel—and later to the rank of full colonel (all within a dizzying span of only two weeks)—to provide the clout needed to carry out such operations.[29]

Along with Bendetsen, Major General Gullion—the provost marshal general and, as such, Bendetsen's superior—worked with Bendetsen as coauthor of many of the measures of the evacuation process.

Gullion also served as a driving force in convincing Secretary of War Stimson of the need for evacuation.[30]

General Gullion heartily agreed with the evacuation of the West Coast. He had come to believe that France had fallen in part because of fifth column activities. He also strongly believed the same type of sabotage could—and given the opportunity, probably would—occur in America. Gullion highlighted these suspicions in a memorandum to the assistant secretary of war by stating, "The danger of Japanese inspired sabotage is great" and that internment should take place

---

[28] Stetson Conn, *The Decision to Evacuate the Japanese from the Pacific Coast* (Washington, DC: Center of History, U.S. Army, 1990), 127.
[29] Conn, *Decision to Evacuate the Japanese*, 139.
[30] Conn, *Decision to Evacuate the Japanese*, 146.

on a volunteer basis while restricted areas be made into "military reservations."[31]

To back the concepts put forth by Gullion and Bendetsen, the support of Assistant Secretary of War John J. McCloy was also sought. In truth, however, McCloy needed little persuasion, for he felt the removal of "dangerous" elements from society would best suit the current situation on the West Coast. In a conversation with DeWitt, McCloy remarked that:

> In spite of the Constitution, you can eliminate from any military reservation, or any place that is declared to be in substance a military reservation, anyone—any American citizen, and we could exclude everyone and then by a system of permits and licenses permitting those to come back into that area who were necessary to enable that area to function as a living community. Everyone but the Japs.

"Everyone but the Japs" seemed to be the overriding sentiment of this particular group of military leaders. DeWitt, Bendetsen, Gullion, and McCloy all worked with the same mind to map out what they saw as a valid means of solving a "military necessity."[32]

Still, DeWitt had his moments of doubt about total evacuation. Within a week of his memo to general headquarters, DeWitt confessed his doubts to Gullion regarding the internment of over one hundred thousand Japanese Americans living on the West Coast. DeWitt suggested that it might be more logistically proper to have them "watched by the police and people of the community in which they live and have been living for years." After all, he reasoned, "An American citizen is an American citizen. And while they all may not

---

[31] Daniels, *Decision to Relocate the Japanese Americans*, 16, 104.
[32] Weglyn, *Years of Infamy*, 97.

be loyal; I think we can weed the disloyal out of the loyal and lock them up if necessary."³³

But DeWitt's democratic generosity was short-lived, for within days of his conversation with Gullion, DeWitt was again driving for the complete removal of Japanese Americans from the West Coast.

Seemingly, only one high-ranking military leader held a level head—Lieutenant Delos C. Emmons. Emmons was General Short's replacement as army commander in Hawaii after the bombing of Pearl Harbor. When asked to report on findings of sabotage or fifth column activities, Emmons reported he had found none. Through careful investigations, his research had found no fifth column work by enemy aliens before, during, or after Pearl Harbor. With no proof of subversion, Emmons resolved to treat fairly all Japanese Americans who showed loyalty to the Allied war effort.³⁴

Certainly, Emmons was not a saint. At times, he doubted the loyalty of all Japanese aliens on the Hawaiian Islands. But the twentieth-century Hawaiian economy had been built primarily on the backs of immigrant Japanese. Dennis M. Ogawa and Evarts C. Fox estimate that by 1941, nearly 157,000 of the 421,000 resident civilians in Hawaii were of Japanese ancestry. Of these individuals, over 103,000 were either aliens or holding a dual citizenship. Emmons understood clearly the consequence of imprisoning all Issei nationals. If Issei were forced from the islands, the Hawaiian economy risked collapse. Faced with the possibility of at least a third of the Hawaiian population being expelled from the islands, Emmons chose to remain calm in the face of racial intolerance. In Hawaii, at least, economic necessity triumphed over national security.³⁵

On the mainland, the economic worth of Issei had never been a consideration. As the final days of 1941 faded, more and more publishers and patriotic crusaders joined the calls for evacuation. Articles began appearing in local newspapers questioning the loyalty of whites who would even consider placing the constitutional rights

---

³³ Conn, *Decision to Evacuate the Japanese*, 128.
³⁴ Daniels, *Decision to Relocate the Japanese Americans*, 27.
³⁵ Roger Daniels, ed., *Japanese Americans from Relocation to Redress* (Seattle: University of Washington Press, 1991), 135.

of Japanese Americans over American safety. *Life* magazine published an article entitled "How to Tell the Japs from the Chinese."[36] Hearst publications also found renewed vigor in their drive to exclude Japanese Americans from the West Coast. Henry McLemor, a Hearst columnist, wrote a December article blatantly void of fact:

> Everywhere that the Japanese have attacked to date, the Japanese population has risen to aid the attackers. Pearl Harbor, Manila. What is there to make the Government believe that the same wouldn't be true in California? Does it feel that the lovely California climate has changed them and that the thousands of Japanese who live in the boundaries of this state are all staunch and true Americans?
>
> I am for the immediate removal of every Japanese on the West Coast to a point deep in the interior. Herd 'em up, pack 'em off, and give 'em the inside room in the badlands.
>
> Let 'em be pinched, hurt, hungry, and dead up against it. Personally, I hate Japanese. And that goes for all of them.
>
> Let's quit worrying about hurting the enemy's feelings and start doing it.[37]

By today's standards, McLemor's comments are seen as brutally racist. But by the standards of 1941, his words echoed the hearts of far too many.

The Japanese were pictured as an inhuman race of men bent only on the destruction of those who would step into their march for power. To bolster this image, many used the events overseas as their proof. Secretary of State Cordell Hull, in a December 1941 press release, remarked that "Japan now…has taken to the Philippines the

---
[36] *Life*, 22 December 1941, 81.
[37] WRA, *Wartime Exile*, 109–110.

practices of fiendishness that she had previously demonstrated in China."[38] Indeed, the acts of Japan's government and military were rightfully regarded as barbaric and cruel. But many could not help lumping the leadership of Japan with those innocents who had found their way into America.

Such was the mindset of the press, public officials, and citizens shortly after Pearl Harbor.

And as the final days of 1941 came and went, so did the spirits of many Japanese aliens and Japanese Americans. The future looked dim. The new year held few promises.

December 1941 turned into January 1942, and New Year festivities abounded.

For some Americans, the first newspaper of the year brought headlines of the five hundred thousand celebrants who gathered on New Year's Eve to watch the ball drop outside the *New York Times* building. For Japanese Americans, it brought headlines of the forty-five aliens who were forcibly gathered up from the Japanese consulate in New York and put on a train out of town.[39]

For many Americans, the first news of the year meant updates on the latest attacks by the Japanese on Burma and Germany in Europe. To Japanese Americans, it meant new demands of surrendering firearms, cameras, shortwave-radio-receiving sets, and radio transmitters.[40]

For most Americans, the news brought glimpses of hope. For Japanese Americans, it brought dread.

The new year began much like the old one had ended. Air raid sirens sounded. Tempers flared. Reports and rumors of enemy shelling off the West Coast graced front pages around the country. Press sources furthered wartime fears with headlines like "Japs Jam American Broadcasts with False Reports" and "Nazi Officers Leading Japs, Filipinos Say."[41]

---

[38] *Alamosa Daily Courier*, 28 December 1941, 1.
[39] *New York Times*, 1 January 1942, 1, 7.
[40] *New York Times*, 1 January 1942, 1, 7.
[41] *Alamosa Daily Courier*, 30 December 1941, 1.

As newspapers carried reports about gains made by Axis troops the day before, fearful West Coast cities and towns pleaded for additional civil defense funds. Such news engulfed smaller stories such as the brutal murder of Mr. Schichiji Kikuchi and his wife, successful Japanese American ranchers, in their southern California home. Amid the news of the war overseas, a cloud of hatred for all that was Japanese began forming around the West Coast. As a result, violent attacks like those perpetrated on the Kikuchis usually were buried on page six of local newspapers.[42]

Instead, the West Coast press began to focus intensely on the campaign of removal. On January 5, John B. Hughes and other newsmen along the West Coast started a press campaign designed to pressure congressmen for the immediate evacuation of Japanese Americans—alien and citizen alike.

With this campaign, the turning point had come. The current of public opinion was changing from the exclusion of Japanese aliens only to the exclusion of all persons of Japanese ancestry—citizen or not.

"You would've thought that we bombed Pearl Harbor ourselves, by the way everyone acted toward us," recalls Tom Shigekuni. As a young Nisei, Shigekuni and his two brothers worked after school in the nursery business their father had established in the 1930s. Classmates were always harassing Tom and his two brothers. "I once got into an argument with a guy who accused me, and 'others like me' of bombing Pearl Harbor. The guy was really serious. I think most people had a hard time separating Japanese Americans from those who lived in Japan."[43]

The political and press campaigns against Issei and Nisei began to have economic effects as well. Anglo citizens were persuaded to do little or no business with persons of Japanese ancestry. Shigekuni recalls, "People eventually stopped buying flowers from our wholesale and retail places until it came to a point where we had trouble

---

[42] *New York Times*, 4 January 1942, 1, 3; 1 January 1942, 6.
[43] Tom Shigekuni, personal interview, 10 April 2000.

making a living. They might as well have thrown us in a [concentration] camp."[44]

Such campaigns for public opinion gained even more momentum when Congressman John Dies, chairman of the House Un-American Activities Committee, presented a summary of his not-yet-released "Yellow Report." He informed the press that in his report, he would provide information on fifth column activities that—if the administration had disclosed it—would have revealed Japanese plans for attacking Pearl Harbor. Although the report would never provide any conclusive evidence to support Dies's claims, it served as significant fodder for press sources in weeks to come.[45]

Joining the fray, other anti-Japanese organizations such as the American Legion and the Native Sons and Daughters of the Golden West beefed up pressure on legislators for the removal of the Japanese to interior states. Asian Americans had always been a popular target for such groups. But now, the issue of racial purity found new and heightened support by uniting economic health and ethnic cleansing with national security and American pride.[46]

The influence of Hughes, Dies, and West Coast action groups stoked the flames of racial distrust. Patriotism demanded action.

This action came when political leaders—many of whom had long ago grown tired of the West Coast commotion—began in earnest to seek a new legislative means of dealing with the "Asian problem." One such leader, Congressman Leland Ford of California, sent a memo to the secretary of war suggesting that both Issei and Nisei could be removed to inland concentration camps. Ford suggested that if Nisei really desired to show their loyalty as citizens of the United States they could do so by a willful submission to the process of being "placed in a concentration camp."[47]

Congressman Ford's feelings were representative of many in mainstream America. But Japanese Americans had already sacrificed great amounts for the war effort. When America's supply of rub-

---

[44] Shigekuni, interview.
[45] WRA, *Wartime Exile*, 116.
[46] "Issei, Nisei, Kibei," 22.
[47] Daniels, *Decision to Relocate the Japanese Americans*, 22.

ber was cut by over 90 percent because of the war in the Pacific, Japanese Americans, like other citizens, cut back on their driving and tried to make tires last until they wore out. When the need for additional sugar was increased, and the number of available farmhands decreased, many Japanese farmers converted established crops to the production of sugar beets. And when war was declared, only the ban on Japanese serving in the military could keep young, eager Nisei from enlisting in America's armed services. Now Congressman Ford was calling for all citizens of Japanese origins to prove their loyalty by exchanging established lives for ones of confinement in inland concentration camps.

In his suggestion, Congressman Ford had overlooked possibly the greatest sacrifice by Japanese Americans—community and familial bonds. When Issei, Nisei, and Kibei men who had established solid leadership roles within their respective communities were taken into custody, community morale deteriorated. Issei were bankers, landowners, and businessmen who had become necessary and established entities within their communities. Kibei were respected youth who had bridged the cultures of Japan and America. These fathers and sons, husbands and lovers, brothers and friends were vital bonds to their communities. They were the glue by which their communities stood united. When these men were ripped from their families, so, too, was the morale of their communities.

Leland Ford, as well as other Americans, missed the point. Japanese Americans were already sacrificing as much as the rest of the country—if not more. And if given the opportunity, they would offer even more to answer the call.

Japanese Americans had few allies. However, there was one man in Washington who resolutely resisted the push of West Coast legislators—the attorney general of the United States, Francis Biddle. Many saw Biddle as the bottleneck of evacuation. Biddle, who had once served as private secretary to US Supreme Court Justice Oliver Wendell Holmes, had become a respected attorney as well as a champion of civil rights. Likewise, he was known for his sluggish responses to the evacuation clamor of West Coast politicians. Biddle continually responded to such clamor by steadfastly condemning discrimination of any sort. In his opinion, if such action were ever taken, constitutional freedoms demanded it be a military matter at best.[48]

Because of these convictions, he claimed no responsibility for the evacuation process. In a letter to Roosevelt, Biddle noted:

> For several weeks there have been increasing demands for evacuation of all Japanese, aliens and citizens alike, from the West Coast states. A great many West Coast people distrust the Japanese, various special interests would welcome their removal from good farmland and the elimination of their competition... My last advice from the War Department is that there is no evidence of imminent attack and from the FBI that there is no evidence of planned sabotage.[49]

Others supported Biddle in his views. Various fair play chapters along the West Coast fought against the unconstitutionality of the racist treatment of West Coast Japanese. Likewise, Mrs. Roosevelt spoke out, saying, "I see absolutely no reason why anyone who has had a good record—that is, who has no criminal or anti-American record—should have any anxiety about his position. This is equally applicable to the Japanese who cannot become citizens but have lived here for thirty or forty years and to those newcomers who have not yet had time to become citizens."[50]

But these voices often could not be heard above the din of West Coast propaganda. Despite the doggedness of Biddle and other calming voices throughout the country, the tidal wave of pressure for evacuation eventually reached Washington. In the middle of January, President Roosevelt proclaimed that all "natives, denizens, or sub-

---

[48] *New York Times*, 21 February 1942, 1.
[49] *Personal Justice Denied: Report of the Commission on Wartime Relocation and Internment of Civilians* (Seattle: University of Washington Press, February 1983).
[50] Milton S. Eisenhower, *The President Is Calling* (Garden City: Doubleday, 1974), 100.

jects" of nations or governments at war with the United States must register with the attorney general. Biddle reluctantly responded by giving all aliens living in the United States, Puerto Rico, and the Virgin Islands over the age of thirteen the month of February to complete all necessary paperwork.[51]

On January 29, due to the continued pressure to protect vital strategic sites on the West Coast, Biddle announced the evacuation of aliens of enemy nationality from lands around electrical plants, dams, centers of military industry, and other high-profile areas. Whether Biddle liked it or not, the evacuation of the West Coast had begun.[52]

On February 2, the same day alien registrations began, FBI agents and local agents undertook spot raids on Terminal Island off the coast of California. Terminal Island was a small community in which many Japanese Americans had begun their lives in America. Fish were plentiful, and jobs abounded in this West Coast community. In a self-serving effort, the cannery on the island often helped Issei men buy jig boats and equipment for fishing in exchange for their work as fishermen. Women also worked in the cannery gutting and cleaning the latest catch.

But the new lives Issei had carved out were erased when the FBI began their sweep of the island in 1942. During their raids, agents arrested 336 Japanese American fishermen for possession of cameras, movie projectors, and handguns. The raids were certainly not a surprise. Many Issei had grown tired of the interrogations and constant surveillance. One spokesman for those arrested said the fishermen "really wanted to go to concentration camps." His odd response was clarified when the reporter explained, "They have been in suspense. Now they think they will be moved at once and will remain in one spot until the war is over."[53]

After the raids, remaining Issei and Nisei located on Terminal Island "voluntarily" moved inland after they were given forty-eight

---

[51] *New York Times*, 15 January 1942, 7.
[52] WRA, *Wartime Exile*, 109–110.
[53] WRA, *Wartime Exile*, 112–113; *Denver Post*, 3 February 1942, 3.

hours to relocate. Those who had trouble locating transportation and those who could simply not transport all their belongings out within the first twenty-four hours would often return to homes that had been plundered by Caucasians in surrounding communities. Many moved in with friends or family on the mainland. Some simply lived in makeshift housing.

At the same moment that spot raids were taking place on Terminal Island, California's state attorney general Earl Warren, the future chief justice later known for his pro-civil rights stance, was further reinforcing the need for evacuation. In a meeting with state law enforcement officers, Warren attempted to drive home the point that the state of California was not adequately prepared for the fifth column activities.[54]

The sinking of American vessels like the *San Gil* and the *Norness* off the East Coast only heightened these fears and insecurities nationwide. The constant—albeit false—reports of enemy fire off the West Coast were daily reminders of vulnerability. And many saw the sinking of *the Royal T. Frank*—an army transport vessel off the Hawaiian coast—as added proof that coastal areas needed protection.[55]

Senator Johnson of California even went as far as to state, "We haven't any protection at all on the West Coast. I see in the future another Pearl Harbor within the continental United States unless something is done to give us protection." Likewise, Representative Sheppard of California felt Biddle was "moving all too slowly in his investigation in handling of the aliens." Sheppard went on to add, "This is no time to apply civil liberties on unquestionable citizenship such as the Japanese present. No one with any knowledge of Japanese psychology can apply the complete significance of civil liberties in this case because it constitutes a national hazard."[56]

By the middle of February, the level of patience was waning among West Coast leaders. Men like Warren, Sheppard, and Johnson felt that they were surrounded by potentially dangerous fifth column

---

[54] *Los Angeles Times*, 3 February 1942, 6.
[55] *New York Times*, 15 January 1942, 1; *Denver Post*, 4 February 1942, 1; *New York Times*, 11 February 1942, 4.
[56] *New York Times*, 19 February 1942, 11; 18 February 1942, 3.

activists—and that the nation's attorney general was doing little to change the situation. Alien registrations, individual spot raids, and the evacuations of singular strategic sites were mere bandages placed on the gaping wound or sabotage. With anxiety and impatience running high, the events of mid-February picked up pace.

On February 12, the *Los Angeles Times* printed an article by the nationally syndicated columnist Walter Lippmann—an East Coast writer known and respected across the country for his liberal views. Lippmann's article disclosed his own personal findings, which agreed with DeWitt's earlier catch-22 logic. The lack of activity by Japanese Americans, Lippmann wrote, "is a sign that the blow is well organized and that it is held back until it can be struck with maximum effect."[57] A statement like this—one by a nationally respected author like Lippmann—provided the respectability West Coast journalists and editors had hoped for. Articles and editorials about the "Japanese problem" began to flood newspapers nationwide.

The day following the Lipton article, an impatient West Coast congressional delegation passed a resolution demanding the "immediate evacuation of all persons of Japanese lineage and all others, aliens and citizen alike, whose presence shall be deemed dangerous or inimical to the defense of the United States from all strategic areas." Although Biddle had already been actively evacuating such "strategic areas," the delegation was calling for, in essence, the evacuation of Japanese Americans from the majority of the West Coast.[58]

The clamor reached a peak when, on February 14, 1942, General DeWitt presented his final recommendations to Secretary of War Henry L. Stimson. In his findings, DeWitt stated that because "over 112,000 potential enemies of Japanese extraction, are at large" along the West Coast, all Japanese aliens and citizen alike should be evacuated from the coast to internment camps inland.[59]

The secretary of war was influenced greatly by McCloy, Bendetsen, and Gullion who, from the beginning, had strongly sug-

---

[57] Dillon S. Myer, *Uprooted Americans* (Tucson: University of Arizona Press, 1971), 22.
[58] WRA, *Wartime Exile*, 129
[59] WRA, *Wartime Exile*, 137.

gested the need for evacuation. DeWitt's clamor for the evacuation was simply prefaced by the urgings of these three leaders. Instead of seeing the evacuation as needless, as Attorney General Biddle had earlier stated, Stimson based his approval on the suggestions of those below him. If Stimson had taken a firm stand against evacuation, President Roosevelt might not have gone ahead with a mass evacuation order. But the recommendations approved by Stimson, along with a public outcry and hysteria coming from the West Coast, was all the information Roosevelt needed as military justification for evacuation.

The final blow came on February 19 when the president signed Executive Order No. 9066 authorizing federal troops to exclude anyone from any location as deemed necessary for national security. This executive order gave legality to exclusion. Although not specifically implied, the order was clearly aimed at Japanese Americans living in western states.

The watershed had been reached. The evacuation could now be legally enforced.

On the West Coast, racial discrimination, economic greed, and an unfounded fear had wiped clear any remaining constitutional rights.

Now Issei and Nisei were forced to step aside as someone else determined their fates.

CHAPTER 2

"THE GREATEST POSSIBLE SPEED IS IMPERATIVE"

President Roosevelt was preparing to present his first fireside chat since December 9. In his former speech, Roosevelt had spoken of the tragedy at Pearl Harbor. In this one, he would speak of unity and patriotism.

It was February 23, and for days, public interest in the president's message had run high. Newspapers had informed readers that a world map or globe would be needed to follow the president's speech. Spokesmen at Rand McNally had reported "a tremendous demand for maps in the few days prior to the president's speech." So at ten o'clock, as the president began to speak, America listened.[60]

But at the same moment that the president was sitting down at the microphone, an enemy submarine surfaced a continent away off the coast of Santa Barbara and began lobbing more than a dozen shells at the Ellwood oil refinery. Although no injuries were reported and very little damage occurred, blackouts went into effect over portions of southern California. The following day, newspapers nationwide sensationalized the uneventful attack. Though the attack was really nothing more than a weak show of force, the West Coast became

---

[60] *New York Times*, 21 February 1942, 1, 8.

engulfed in hysteria and panic—just the right conditions to support Executive Order 9066.

By the beginning of March, DeWitt was ready to flex the newly empowered muscles of Executive Order 9066. On March 2, DeWitt issued his Public Proclamation No. 1, which divided the West Coast into two military strategic areas. In Military Area No. 1, DeWitt designated the western portions of Washington, Oregon, and California, along with the southern portion of Arizona, as areas most threatened by invasion or attack from the Pacific. Military Area No. 2, the remaining eastern portions of the coastal states, was also perceived as subject to attack, but was deemed less permeable than Area No. 1.

Proclamation No. 1 was significant for two reasons. First, through it, DeWitt alluded to the possibility of forced mass evacuation from military areas. This was the first-time mention an all-out evacuation had been made. Second, in light of such forced evacuations, DeWitt suggested that all enemy aliens consider voluntary evacuation from the West Coast to points beyond militarized zones. On March 16, only two weeks after his first proclamation, DeWitt issued Public Proclamation No. 2, which established the states of Idaho, Montana, Nevada, and Utah as Military Areas 3 through 6, respectively. However, these military areas would never be subjected to the type of military control seen in Military Area No. 1, nor would they witness the same sort of mass evacuations.

With these sections carefully mapped out, DeWitt began the process of securing the coast. To follow up the initial steps, another order was issued on March 24—Public Proclamation No. 3, which established a curfew for all alien Japanese, Germans, and Italians, as well as American citizens who were of Japanese ancestry. Under the curfew, all Japanese Americans were to be found within their place of residence from the hours of 8:00 p.m. to 6:00 a.m. The curfew was effective in all military areas, and could be overridden only by special military permission or through voluntary evacuation.

Along with the curfew, DeWitt's third proclamation also established mileage restrictions mandating that enemy aliens and citizens of Japanese ancestry could travel no more than five miles away from homes or places of business. As with the curfew, special travel beyond the designated limits would be allowed only through special military authorization. Finally, Proclamation No. 3 prohibited all persons of Japanese ancestry from possessing firearms, weapons, ammunition, shortwave radios, radio transmitters, signal devices, and cameras. On this last point, the proclamation was strangely silent regarding aliens of German and Italian ancestry.

The restrictions found in Proclamation No. 3 were certainly not new to the West Coast. Enemy aliens living around Terminal Island and other strategic sites had long been subjected to them. Even the day before DeWitt's third proclamation was issued, Civilian Exclusion Order No. 1 was issued ordering all Japanese aliens and non-aliens to evacuate Bainbridge Island near Seattle. This order would be the first of 108 such civilian exclusion orders along the West Coast.[61]

But Public Proclamation No. 3 differed from earlier restrictions in three primary ways. First, DeWitt's third proclamation was designed as a broad, overriding proclamation that superseded all previous restrictions. Second, it, along with the Civilian Exclusion Order No. 1, began the chain of government and military actions that eventually stripped American citizens belonging to a particular ethnicity of their basic civil rights. No longer were Japanese American citizens living on the West Coast allowed the constitutional freedoms and rights bestowed on other American citizens. And third, the proclamation gave the widespread legal impetus needed to drive Japanese Americans away from firmly planted economic footholds.

The final result is possibly the most important in the overall picture of evacuation. West Coast businessmen, industrialists, and farmers had, for decades, been clamoring that Issei and Nisei were a threat to American economic structures. But in reality, these individuals merely wanted to take over the properties and businesses that Issei and Nisei had made so profitable. Military necessity now provided a convenient excuse to make such transactions happen.

Issei and Nisei were caught in a no-win situation. If they chose to obey the curfew and mileage restrictions, they would be limiting their lives and means of support. But if they refused DeWitt's orders,

---

[61] Daniels, *Decision to Relocate the Japanese Americans*, 54–55.

they would be branded anti-American, jailed, and later interned by force.

Frank and Terrie Masamori, Japanese Americans later interned at Poston internment camp, remember how they and other Japanese Americans were moved away from coastal regions—initially across Highway 1 and later even further inland. They also recall the curfew and the police cruising the streets at night looking for possible enemy activists. Finally, the Masamoris remember how this period began to rapidly weed out those acquaintances who were true friends and those who were not. Some simply could not, and would not, help in any way due to the fear of being labeled a Jap lover."[62]

So for Japanese Americans on the West Coast, help during this period of evacuation would not come from external sources. It was up to those who were being victimized to show their true colors. And despite great personal loss, Japanese aliens and Japanese Americans began to show their love for America in far more drastic ways than other Americans ever could.

Attempting to prove their patriotic loyalty, the vast majority of Issei and Nisei submitted to DeWitt's order peacefully. One reason for this was the attitude of civic responsibility that permeated every aspect of the war. President Roosevelt spoke clearly of this attitude in his February 23 fireside chat by listing three requirements needed for American unity during the war:

1. We shall not stop work for a single day. If any dispute arises we shall keep on working while the dispute is solved by mediation, or conciliation, or by arbitration—until the war is won.
2. We shall not demand special gains or special privileges or special advantages for any one group or occupation.
3. We shall give up conveniences and modify the routine of our lives if the county asks us to do so. We will do it

---

[62] "Amache: Patriotism Amidst Prejudice Research Project," Masamori taped interview (Boulder: Western Historical Collections, University of Colorado, 1979).

cheerfully, remembering that the common enemy seeks to destroy every home and every freedom in every part of our land.

This generation of Americans has come to realize, with a present and personal realization, that there is something larger and more important than the life of any individual or any individual group-something for which a man will sacrifice, and gladly sacrifice not only his pleasures, not only his goods, not only his associations with those he loves, but with his life itself. In time of crisis, when the future is in the balance, we come to understand, with full recognition and devotion, what this nation is, and what we owe it.[63]

Of course, Roosevelt's sentiments were not aimed directly at the Japanese American. They were, in reality, meant to unify a country with many diverse opinions. But nowhere was the pressure felt more strongly than in the lives of Japanese Americans. They were externally pressured by Americans to prove both their patriotism and their loyalty. Ironically, to be seen as loyal Americans, they had to see the war against tyranny as being more important than their own civil rights. Only by sacrificing their pleasures, goods, and lives could Japanese Americans prove their loyalty.

Besides the external pressure of patriotism, Japanese Americans also found intense pressure within its own group of supporters. Patriotism by submission had long been supported by the Japanese American Citizens League (JACL)—a controversial organization originally organized as a united front against anti-Asian intolerance. By the time of America's entry in the war, the league had become recognized as a politically conservative and primarily Nisei-led action group. In the past, it had unequivocally supported the US government in its economic and social ties to the Japanese Empire. In short, its stance had always been, and would always remain, 100 percent pro-American.

---

[63] *New York Times*, 24 February 1942, 4.

But when the Japanese Empire suddenly attacked American soil, the JACL found itself in a precarious position. If it supported the constitutional rights of Japanese Americans—thus rejecting the concepts of voluntary evacuation curfews and mileage restraints—it might appear unpatriotic and pro-Japanese. But if it supported submission to governmental orders and proclamations, the rights it had fought for decades to gain would be lost.

Naturally, JACL leaders stressed their concern about how such measures would affect Japanese American businesses and property. They asked for governmental moratoriums until the end of the war. They also stressed the need for all enemy alien groups to be subjected to these restrictions—not just those of Japanese American heritage.

But in the end, the JACL threw its full support behind DeWitt's proclamations—even the process of evacuation. In a statement to the press in late February 1942, Mike Masaoka, national secretary of the JACL, stated:

> We have just issued a statement to our sixty chapters in 300 communities throughout the United States. We have instructed them to continue cooperating with our government in whatever action may be necessary for the public welfare, just as we have consistently urged the Japanese nationals to cooperate with our government in the past. We have advised our 20,000 members not to become overly alarmed and panicky. It is difficult for us to conceive that our government, with its vaunted heritage of democratic ideals, would break down the equality that has always existed between its citizens and discriminate against one bloc of them. We trust that the sacrifices which all of us may be called upon to make will create a greater and more unified America when we have won the war.[64]

---

[64] *New York Times*, 21 February 1942, 6.

Ironically, the JACL became one of the leading causes for not resisting the proclamations of DeWitt and his staff. Most Issei and Nisei followed the leadership of the JACL, hoping to appear loyal.

By issuing the first three proclamations, DeWitt had hoped to nudge Japanese Americans—alien and citizen alike—into the process of "voluntary" evacuation. Even from a military standpoint, the logistical quagmire of moving 110,000-plus people from their West Coast homes to points inland was a nightmarish concept at best. The cost of forced evacuation, coupled with a lack of available manpower, made a military-led movement inland even less appealing. However, if Issei and Nisei voluntarily moved to inland states, all these burdens would be placed on the individual evacuee family.

In essence, West Coast officials had hoped for a repeat of Hawaii. After Pearl Harbor, Japanese Americans living on the Hawaiian Islands voluntarily moved away from exclusion areas. Most evacuees moved willingly, and little military manpower was needed. But what military and governmental officials did not understand was that there were vast differences between Japanese Americans in Hawaii and those on the mainland.

First, the distance of relocation was far greater on the mainland than in Hawaii. Hence, the cost of evacuation would prove much greater to move across several states on the mainland than moving just across the island, as in Hawaii.

Next, there was not a substantial support base for mainland Issei and Nisei. To voluntarily relocate, a Japanese American family, both in Hawaii and on the mainland, had to acquire a "sponsor" who would provide faithful accountability and find permanent employment for evacuees. On the Hawaiian Islands, a web of family and friends spreading throughout the islands closely bound the Japanese culture. On the Islands, close proximity and shared experiences provided the friends and relatives needed for sponsors and employment outside militarily restricted areas.

The same was not true for the vast majority of mainland Issei and Nisei. Most mainland Japanese Americans had few relatives outside militarily restricted areas. The need for these familial bonds was important, not only because of sponsorship and employment, but also because many Issei had had their bank accounts frozen within days of the attack on Pearl Harbor. Without access to funds, most could not pay for moves inland.

Finally, mainland evacuees often found racial discrimination extremely high in the areas into which they moved. Racial discrimination was not as apparent in Hawaii because Issei and Nisei made up a large portion of the culture. Although some instances of racism did occur in the Hawaiian territory, it was far less abundant than that which took place in mainland America.

This racial discrimination became even more acute as inland states realized DeWitt's intentions of moving the "Japanese problem" inland. Arizona's governor, Sidney P. Osborn, said the alien problem was "equally as serious in Arizona as it is in California, Oregon, and Washington," and that in no way would his state serve as "a dumping ground for the problem." Likewise, Idaho's governor, Chase A. Clark, and Oklahoma's governor, Leon C. Phillips, both said the people of their states would most likely not be willing to work with—or in competition against—Japanese Americans. Governor Phillips even noted that his citizens only supported forced evacuation if "concentration camps" were built to hold evacuees.[65]

In Nevada, vigilante mobs lined the state's western border to form a human roadblock that forced Japanese Americans back to the West Coast.[66] The state of Colorado produced groups of sugar beet and potato farmers who led drives to keep the "Japs out of Colorado." The director of Colorado's publicity bureau even remarked that planned relocations of Japanese Americans from California into his state would "ruin Colorado as a tourist attraction."[67]

Still, despite the overwhelming hurdles, a few Japanese Americans found enough nerve to venture inland during the voluntary evacuation period. Some moved to Utah and found work in Keetley Farms, an agricultural colony started by Japanese Americans for the sole purpose of voluntary relocation. Others moved to states

---

[65] *New York Times*, 2 March 1942, 8.
[66] Daniels, *Decision to Relocate the Japanese Americans*, 55.
[67] *Denver Post*, 14 February 1942, 4.

like Idaho and Colorado where, despite concerted local efforts to keep them out, volunteer evacuees found work in sugar beet and potato fields and other agricultural endeavors.

Leo Goto remembers that his family came to Colorado because of the state's reputation for accepting people of Japanese ancestry. "We relocated to Colorado as a family in the spring right after Pearl Harbor. It was still winter [in Colorado]. We had family that had farms here between Brighton and Fort Lupton... My parents and six children and two cousins came over in a pick-up truck and a trailer. The pick-up and the trailer were covered with everything we were able to load into it, plus ten people."[68]

As voluntary evacuees approached the state of Colorado, military personnel and state police stopped each party at checkpoints to verify their destinations. Unlike some states, Colorado did not discourage evacuees from entering the state at these checkpoints. However, these meetings with military personnel could still be quite frightening. Goto recalls vividly his father's reaction to one of these checkpoints:

> As we were coming over Loveland Pass, the military had set up road checks to make sure who we were. So, we were stopped there, and my cousin—who was about probably nine or ten years old at the time—got out to see what was happening. My father was very nervous because of the military. So as soon as we cleared passage, we left the top of Loveland Pass and came down. But we also left my cousin at the top. So, the military and their jeeps finally caught up with us at Georgetown and returned my long-lost cousin.[69]

Henry Sumikawa's family found a sponsor in Delta, Colorado, who would take them. Sumikawa's family had farmed around Delta

---

[68] Leo Goto, personal interview, 17 February 2001.
[69] Goto, interview.

only a few years before and had made many friends in that small farming community. They moved to California in hopes of better fortunes. But after given the choice to voluntarily relocate, they chose to move back to Delta under the sponsorship of an old friend, Ms. Harding. "You had to have someone who would more or less promise to watch over you," Sumikawa recalls. "We didn't work for Ms. Harding—we pretty much led our own lives. Our family was lucky because we knew someone back east."[70]

Like Sumikawa, Yoshimi Watada's family found a sponsor in Colorado after being forced to relocate. Watada recalls that in late January 1942, the FBI approached her father. "I remember my sisters huddling together in the back room whispering 'the FBI men are here to take our father away.'"[71] The FBI approached Watada's father primarily because of his aggressive stance in organizing and building the local Buddhist church.

After given only twenty-four hours to make a decision to move inland, Watada's father—a successful local farmer—decided to leave California for Colorado. "My father had lived in Colorado before so he had contacts there," Watada recalls. "After we decided to move to Colorado, we had to go out to the field to bury our guns and cameras because we were told we could not take them with us. Then, in the middle of the night, we packed up our things onto our tiny little truck and began to leave California."[72] Watada's fourteen-year-old brother drove a truck loaded with the family's belongings so that her mother—who was seven months pregnant—could care for the children in the family car driven by the father. As part of a small caravan, the Watadas and four other families made their way to Colorado.

Even though her family had a sponsor in Colorado, Watada remembers it wasn't an easy trip eastward:

> The place we were heading for in Colorado wasn't ready yet, so my father took us to a place in

---

[70] Henry Sumikawa, personal interview, 23 March 2000.
[71] Yoshimi Watada, personal interview, 28 February 2000.
[72] Watada, Y., interview.

> Oklahoma owned by a guy who used to sell him seed. He let us stay in his horse barn for about five months—until the beginning of July. We slept on the hay. Oh, it was terrible—I remember bed bugs and the smells of the barn. My mother was about to have the baby and the hospitals in Oklahoma would not admit Japanese, so a friend of my mother came and took her back to Colorado ahead of us. That was a rough time for me. I was in a strange school and a strange place without my mother. I remember crying every day because she had to leave us behind.[73]

Watada and her siblings finished the 1942 school year in Oklahoma. Then, in early July, her father continued on to the Rocky Ford area in Colorado where they, and the other families in their caravan, began work as farm laborers.

Ruth Yamauchi, a Nisei from California who would eventually be relocated in an internment camp, also recalls the concerted effort to move her family to Colorado. "Our family had learned that Colorado was the only state in the country that welcomed the Japanese. This was solely due to the efforts of Governor Carr who opened his state to [the] persecuted. My family jointly decided to [also] move my mother and my two younger sisters…to Denver so they would not have to be sent to detention camps."[74]

Still, despite stories like these, the total number of voluntary evacuees moving inland remained small. The most authoritative estimates show that no more than nine thousand Japanese Americans moved from their homes voluntarily. DeWitt felt the number had to be more. So by the end of March, he traded his hopes of voluntary relocation for those more drastic. The cost and logistics of such a move would no longer matter. In DeWitt's mind, forced evacuation was the only remaining way of securing the West Coast. To do

---

[73] Watada, Y., interview.
[74] Ruth Yamauchi, personal interview, 10 December 1999

so, DeWitt would need the help of a nonmilitary agency. And this agency was about to be created by the president for just such an occasion.[75]

On March 18, as the period of voluntary relocation was underway, President Roosevelt signed Executive Order 9102 establishing the War Relocation Authority (WRA). The purpose of the WRA was to formulate a program that would help relocate Japanese Americans under Executive Order 9066. By providing the necessary financial aid and housing accommodations, it was hoped that evacuees would find an easier path to interior states. The WRA was to supervise all activities of the evacuees while "safe-guarding the public interest in the private employment of such persons."

To head the new agency, Roosevelt wanted a humanitarian with few political ambitions who could steer the controversial program of evacuation smoothly into fruition. The man he chose for the job was Milton Eisenhower.

Milton Eisenhower—the youngest brother of General Dwight D. Eisenhower—was born in 1899 in Abilene, Kansas. Eisenhower had lived a simple but somewhat impoverished youth. After graduating from Kansas State College in 1924, Eisenhower took a position at the US consulate in Edinburgh, Scotland. However, within two years, Eisenhower was brought back to the United States where he was hired to work in the Office of Information at the Department of Agriculture. Eisenhower eventually worked his way up to director.

As director, Eisenhower was frantically trying to keep up with the demands at the Department of Agriculture. In early March, he had flown to Tennessee on a peacekeeping tour to resolve conflicts between states involved in the Tennessee Valley Authority and various federal agricultural and conservation agencies. With all the programs Roosevelt's administration had created during the depression era, Eisenhower was busier than ever. But while in Tennessee, Eisenhower received notice that the president needed him back in Washington immediately. Hopping the next flight to Washington, Eisenhower

---

[75] Daniels, *Decision to Relocate the Japanese Americans*, 55.

hoped that his new assignment would be one in which he would not need to board another plane.

Once in Washington, Eisenhower made his way to the Oval Office. Eisenhower had met with the president many times before and had grown to respect him greatly as both a leader and a person. However, as Eisenhower entered Roosevelt's presence, he was taken aback by what he saw. Before him sat a haggard, somber man not resembling the man he had expected to see. "In all my previous work with him," Eisenhower remarked, "I had never seen him without his jaunty air. No matter how difficult the problem, he was buoyant, smiling, and confident. Now, as he studied the paper before him, his face lacked color, his lips were a tight grim line, and as he looked up at me, I saw his eyes were bloodshot."[76]

Looking up from the papers he was reviewing, the president bluntly stated his directive:

> Milton, your war job, starting immediately, is to set up a War Relocation Authority to move the Japanese-Americans off the Pacific coast. I have signed an executive order that will give you full authority to do what is essential. The Attorney General will give you the necessary legal assistance and the Secretary of War will help you with the physical arrangements. Harold [Harold Smith, Roosevelt's budget director] will fill you in on the details of the problem.[77]

After a brief pause, Roosevelt again looked up at Eisenhower from the papers he had again returned to and added, "And, Milton... the greatest possible speed is imperative."[78]

Eisenhower was sorely unprepared for the amount of political hostility he would face in his new role of director of the WRA.

---

[76] Eisenhower, *The President Is Calling*, 95.
[77] Eisenhower, *The President Is Calling*, 95.
[78] Eisenhower, *The President Is Calling*, 95.

Eisenhower, like the majority of Americans who did not live on the West Coast, knew little of the Japanese American situation. Like some, he had heard of the immediate roundup of enemy aliens. Like some, he had heard of DeWitt's theory of fifth column work that could eventually lead to an invasion on mainland America by imperial Japan. And like most, he had heard of various congressmen holding hearings on the need to evacuate all those of Japanese ancestry from the coast.[79]

"When I assumed my new duties," Eisenhower would recall in later years, "I did not know what events had transpired between December 7, 1941, and mid-March 1942 that led President Roosevelt to make his evacuation decision. Indeed, it was not until years later, when historians reconstructed those events and wove them together into a coherent chronology, that I fully understood the situation I stepped into in March 1942."[80]

Eisenhower, as leader of the WRA, was now given a job never before seen in the history of the United States. His first task was to figure out what to do with a large number of people who, by no fault of their own, were considered a threat to the nation. As the WRA began selecting sites for relocation centers in interior states, experiments at the assembly center in Portland, Oregon, were underway to determine the feasibility of placing the evacuees in a "work corps." But the work corps experiment, in Eisenhower's words, "was a failure." He suspected that the work corps experiment failed partly because the men in Portland's assembly center did not want their participation in a work program to be construed as a desire to remain evacuated and partly because of "considerable and understandable bitterness among those in the centers—particularly among the men in the age group from which most of the volunteer workers could be expected to come."[81]

Besides having to solve the problem of evacuation, Eisenhower had to deal with the incessant cries of West Coast congressmen and

---

[79] Eisenhower, *The President Is Calling*, 96.
[80] Eisenhower, *The President Is Calling*, 98.
[81] Eisenhower, *The President Is Calling*, 121.

businessmen. In fact, throughout his term as director for the WRA, Eisenhower would serve more as a lightning rod for criticism than as director of relocation. From anti-Japanese organizations on the West Coast, he was pressured to speed up evacuation proceedings. From governors of interior states, he was pressured to keep evacuees out of central and mountain regions. And from those sympathetic to the plight of Japanese Americans, he was pressured to find occupational and living arrangements that fostered civil rights and human decency. Faced with these unworkable demands, Eisenhower tried to bring all sides together.

Like DeWitt, Eisenhower had initially hoped Issei and Nisei would voluntarily move inland by way of individual sponsors. Concentration camps were never part of the WRA's initial plans. Both Eisenhower and the WRA had initially envisioned their role in this process as one of financial aid and supervisory support. Eisenhower had hoped the WRA could make use of fifty to seventy-five small Civilian Conservation Corps (CCC) camps found in inland states. From these camps, it was hoped evacuees would clear brush, develop land, plant crops, and manufacture items for the war effort. The WRA would help evacuees find this employment and would provide emotional and economic support. And the government would provide the paychecks like it had in earlier CCC operations during the depression. In essence, the WRA hoped to be the middleman in the relocation process.[82]

But in late March, Eisenhower—as well as the entire Japanese American community—received an irreversible blow. On March 27, DeWitt issued Public Proclamation No. 4, which prohibited the voluntary movement of aliens and citizens of Japanese heritage from Military Area No. 1. Though blanketed under the guise of "military necessity," in reality the order was a method of speeding up the evacuation process. DeWitt had grown tired of the slow pace of voluntary relocation. Because Japanese Americans were neither willing nor able to move inland through their own resources, Proclamation No. 4 authorized forced military removal of alien and citizen Japanese alike.

---

[82] Eisenhower, *The President Is Calling*, 119.

In DeWitt's plan, the physical movement of evacuating over 110,000 people from military areas along the West Coast would fall to the military, but the orchestration of it would fall to Eisenhower's WRA. With his fourth proclamation, DeWitt denied Japanese Americans access to voluntary relocation. Forced mass evacuation had officially begun.

Interior states resisted the concept of forced evacuation. In a conference of ten western states held on April 7, 1942, Eisenhower received blow after blow from governors who flatly stated that their states would not become dumping grounds for the problems of West Coast states. Eisenhower later recalled that:

> I was prepared to outline my idea for establishing small inland camps on the model of Civilian Conservation Corps camps that would serve as staging areas for the evacuees as they were moved into private jobs as soon as possible and could resume something like a normal life away from the Western Defense zone. I was prepared to discuss policies about prevailing wages, health care, and other factors. But I could get no further. The governors literally began shouting at me.
>
> One governor shouted: "If these people are dangerous on the Pacific coast they will be dangerous here! We have important defense establishments, too, you know." Another governor walked close to me, shook his fist in my face, and growled through clenched teeth: "If you bring the Japanese into my state, I promise you they will be hanging from every tree." Some governors demanded that the evacuees be kept under armed guard.[83]

---

[83] Eisenhower, *The President Is Calling*, 118.

In the conference, only one governor—Ralph Carr of Colorado—maintained that aiding evacuees was the civic responsibility of American citizens. The remaining nine states adamantly refused to allow large numbers of Asian Americans to relocate within their borders unless they were confined within concentration camps. Eisenhower left the meeting frustrated and disappointed. He had hoped for greater cooperation from governors of inland states. But faced with a shortage of states needed for successful evacuation, Eisenhower was forced to concede. Calling on the Army Corps of Engineers, he began the construction of concentration camps in the six inland states of Idaho, Wyoming, Utah, Arizona, Arkansas, and Colorado as well as the West Coast state of California.

Eisenhower called the camps evacuation centers. He defended them from being called concentration camps because those inside would not be technically restricted from leaving the confines of the camps.

What to call these centers was, and continues to be, a stumbling block for many. Eisenhower's remark that evacuees were not restricted to the camps is somewhat in error. It is true that those wishing to leave for employment outside the center could do so if applications were approved. However, most found the leave process difficult at best. Those who could gain access to leave the camp usually found it difficult to obtain work and often returned to the centers from which they had come. Further, guards were always present to discourage—and shoot, if necessary—those wishing to gain freedom by any means not acceptable to the WRA.

Regardless of what the camps really represented, Eisenhower immediately began establishing a framework by which the forced evacuation of Issei and Nisei would take place. Recalling the recent failures of the Work Corps experiments in Oregon and the refusal of governors to allow evacuees to use CCC camps, Eisenhower set out to find another way of placing evacuees into work environments. This time, the WRA tried placing a small group of evacuees in farming environments in southeastern Oregon—outside the confines of an assembly center. Eisenhower recalled that "the reports of the first participants encouraged many more to apply for such work, and

WRA drew up 'seasonal leave' procedures to allow the men to leave the camps for temporary work and return when the job was finished. We insisted that the local officials guarantee the safety of the Japanese workers, pay them the prevailing wage, and provide adequate housing and transportation. The program was a success."[84]

Seasonal leaves from established relocation centers seemed to be the answer. So with a program of employment established, Eisenhower next began creating the environment in which the evacuees would live. He and his staff soon found themselves organizing schools, courts, police forces, and stores. As to the operations of the centers, Eisenhower noted that "positions in the evacuation centers were filled by evacuees themselves where possible."[85]

Evacuees would run the centers.

But what reimbursement should evacuees receive for the work they performed in the relocation centers? "In a press conference, I said we were considering prevailing wages for all positions," Eisenhower recalled. "This brought a storm of protest from members of Congress, who demanded that pay not exceed that provided for privates in the army. Politically, we had to accept this."[86] Evacuees who once owned business, ranches, farms, and industry now would be forced to accept pay in the form of free living quarters, free food, and free education, and army pay that would cover only small living expenses.

Eisenhower and his staff worked through the spring and into summer on the framework of relocation. But by mid-June, word had reached President Roosevelt that—in the words of Secretary of Interior Harold Ickes—Eisenhower had grown "sick of the job." With a host of governmental opportunities open, Roosevelt asked Eisenhower to take over as Elmer Davis's associate director in the Office of War Information. Just as quickly as he had begun, Eisenhower was out of his role as director of the WRA.

Eisenhower never came to grips with his assignment at the WRA. Although his role in the evacuation of Japanese Americans

---

[84] Eisenhower, *The President Is Calling*, 121–122.
[85] Eisenhower, *The President Is Calling*, 121–122.
[86] Eisenhower, *The President Is Calling*, 121–122.

would simply be that of creator, he would always be haunted by the fact that he was the one chosen to preside over its initial days.[87]

Of this episode in American history, Eisenhower later lamented:

> I believe to this day that most of the evacuation could have been avoided had not false and flaming statements been dinned into the people of the West Coast by irresponsible commentators and politicians. There was surely some underlying and latent dislike for Japanese in that part of the country and that provided fuel for ignorance, intolerance, and bigotry to spread like fire.
>
> The evacuation of Japanese-Americans from their homes on the coast to hastily constructed assembly centers and then to inland relocation centers was an inhuman mistake. Thousands of American citizens of Japanese ancestry were stripped of their rights and freedoms and treated almost like enemy prisoners of war. Many lost their homes, their businesses, and their savings. For 120,000 Japanese the evacuation was a bad dream come to pass.
>
> How could such a tragedy have occurred in a democratic society that prides itself on individual rights and freedoms? How could responsible leaders make such a fateful decision.[88]

With Eisenhower's transfer to the Office of War Information, a new WRA leader was needed. When Roosevelt initially asked Eisenhower to provide an adequate replacement, he could give no immediate reply. But within days, Eisenhower had found his replacement in Dillon S. Myer. Myer had worked with Eisenhower at the

---

[87] Stephen Ambrose, *Milton S. Eisenhower: Educational Statesman* (Baltimore: John Hopkins University Press, 1983), 64, 66.
[88] Eisenhower, *The President Is Calling*, 124–125.

Department of Agriculture in the past and had even helped select WRA staff members. In Eisenhower's mind, Myer would be the perfect director for the WRA.

Eisenhower approached Myer about the possibility of heading up the WRA. Myer asked if Eisenhower really felt he was the right person for the job. "Yes," came Eisenhower's reply. "If you can do the job and sleep at night." Myer, feeling he could do both, agreed to take the position—if Roosevelt would approve it. On June 16, Eisenhower recommended Dillon Myer to Roosevelt. Myer was officially appointed head of the WRA the following day. From this point on, the name of Dillon Myer would be forever linked with the internment of Japanese Americans during World War II.[89]

As construction of evacuation camps began in interior states, Japanese Americans who had stayed in prohibited areas on the West Coast suddenly found themselves forced from homes and businesses. By April 1942, evacuation notices began appearing on West Coast storefronts and street corners. The "reception center" at Manzanar—located in the Owens River Valley, 220 miles northeast of Los Angeles—was the first to open as an assembly center.

The initial flow of evacuees into Manzanar marked the beginning of one of the greatest of its kind in the history of the United States. Evacuees of all professions and stages of life came to Manzanar. Soon, other West Coast centers also began to open. Called reception or assembly centers, these facilities were primarily meant to house evacuees until more permanent facilities could be constructed inland.

Like those evacuees who would eventually be relocated in Colorado's Amache, all West Coast Japanese Americans were instructed to pack only what they could carry and report to control centers where they would be registered and assigned WRA numbers. From these control centers, evacuees would be sent to the assembly center nearest their home. Some were given only a few days to settle their affairs, while others were given up to a couple of weeks.[90]

---

[89] Myer, *Uprooted Americans*, 3.
[90] John Tateishi, *And Justice for All: The Oral History of the Japanese American Detention Camps* (Seattle: University of Washington Press, 1984), xxi.

"We were ordered by the local army command to evacuate within thirty days," Amache evacuee Robert Ichikawa recalls. "My father sold everything in the house for $21. Each of us carried a suitcase with all of our worldly possessions. Our family could not consider relocating from the West Coast because we could not afford it. Our neighbor took us to the Methodist Church on the corner of 35th St. and Normandy Ave., where we loaded onto a bus and [placed] our luggage onto trucks."[91]

Some were grateful for the evacuation. Fumiye Nishizaki of Amache remembers that "some people were really mad about it, but we were afraid of the outside people, too. Because they threw rocks at us, they called us 'You Japs.' I've been through that. Before when we were outside, I was afraid of that. I encountered all that—so much anti-Japan [sentiment]. I experienced too much of that already. So, I felt that being away from there was better for me. I was afraid, really."[92]

But for most, the process of being forced out of settled lives was shattering. "I was in sixth grade at the time," Yoshi Tanita of Amache recalls. "It was really confusing. I would salute the flag in school every day and say the pledge of allegiance. I thought I was an American citizen. But overnight it all changed. Suddenly I realized that I really wasn't considered an American after all."[93]

But what Tanita experienced was nothing compared to what her parents were going through. "When they first came to the U.S.," Tanita recalls of her parents:

> No language, no job, they were discriminated against. Just as they began working, then came the depression. And then when they were coming out of the depression, then came the war and they got wiped out again. Then they were put into camps with guards—like we were spies or

---
[91] Robert Ichikawa, letter to the author, 2 June 2000.
[92] Fumiye Nishizaki, personal interview, 27 February 2001.
[93] Yoski Tanita, personal interview, 11 May 2000.

> something. I mean I never thought of myself as anything other than an American. Then to be discriminated against so much, you know. Then having to start all over again after camp. If it were me, I don't think I could have done it.[94]

Once evacuee families had stored, sold, or given away their belongings, they found their way to the nearest civil control center where each person received instructions about the evacuation process and "assistance" in selling or storing any remaining property. All names were also recorded and a WRA number was given to each member of the family. Amache evacuee George Hirano remembers that assigned numbers written on cardboard tags were attached to the lapel and baggage of every evacuee—old and young alike.[95]

Most walked or rode the bus to the control centers, carrying only the few pieces of luggage allowed. From the control centers, evacuees were taken to assembly centers. "We were one of the first ones into the assembly camps," recalls Amache evacuee Harry Shironaka. "All we were allowed to take was one bag for each person. Later on, I heard of some people who were allowed to bring a bedroll along, too, but we didn't have that luxury."[96]

By the time of his entrance into the assembly camp, the newly married Shironaka had sold all his possessions except what could fit into two medium-sized travel bags. The army had ordered the evacuees to travel light to avoid the problem of providing on-site storage facilities. According to the evacuation notices hung around the cities, only bedding and linens, toiletries, extra clothing, and essential personal effects were allowed into the centers. All these items were to be securely packaged, tied, and plainly marked with the name of the owner. The size and number of packages brought into the camp was based on what could be carried by each family member.

---

[94] Tanita, interview.
[95] George Hirano, personal interview, 4 March 2000.
[96] Harry Shironaka, personal interview, 15 July 2000.

Some, who lived in outlying areas, drove to the centers in cars and trucks—often their only remaining family possession. At this point, evacuee-owned cars and trucks were sold or given away. Most, however, had sold their cars and other possessions for what they could get. Shironaka remembers selling the new car he had just purchased for $1,000 for a take-it-or-leave-it price of $250.[97]

Evacuees in large Japanese American urban communities often found their whole neighborhood transported into the assembly centers. These men and women, boys and girls, found the process of evacuation somewhat easier than those living in isolation from other Japanese Americans. In many ways, proximity provided added support of friends and neighbors who were going through the same circumstances themselves.[98]

There were fifteen such assembly centers stationed in various places along the West Coast. These centers were simply designated holding areas to keep evacuated West Coast Japanese Americans confined until more permanent camps could be constructed. Conditions in the centers were substandard at best. Most were hastily converted horse tracks or county fairgrounds resembling barnyards and prisons more than living quarters. Those who would eventually be interned at Amache were transported from their homes to the California assembly centers of Santa Anita and Merced.

Within these two centers, Issei and Nisei alike would be housed through the summer of 1942.

Representing the largest number of evacuees of any of the fifteen assembly centers, Santa Anita housed Issei and Nisei evacuated primarily from urban areas around Los Angeles. Into this camp came lawyers, artists, doctors, gardeners, hotel and restaurant owners, business tycoons, store clerks, homeowners, and domestic servants. Some of the brightest and most successful Americans flowed into Santa Anita during the summer of 1942.

Santa Anita was a horse track that had been converted into a massive holding center. Amache evacuee Art Yorimoto remembers

---

[97] Shironaka, interview.
[98] Chez Momii, personal interview, 12 April 2000.

his father talking about the camp years before: "My father used to have a farm about five miles west of Santa Anita during World War I. He used to call the track the Santa Anita Balloon Camp because it served as a balloon observation sight. A division of soldiers would send a balloon up and practice observation maneuvers from just above the camp."[99]

But the Yorimoto family would see the camp from a very different perspective. Although it had served many purposes in past lives, Santa Anita opened as an assembly center on March 27, 1942, and remained open until October 27 of the same year. At its peak, the center held nearly 19,000 people and obtained the reputation of having some of the worst living conditions of any of the assembly centers.[100]

In preparation for the evacuees, barbed wire was placed atop eight-foot-high fencing around the perimeter of the grounds. Searchlights and military guards with 30-caliber water-cooled machine guns (pointed toward the evacuees) sat atop towers placed at even intervals along the exterior fence. At the entrance of the center, army personnel were posted to check authorization passes of those who wished to deliver personal items from the outside. Inside the fence, civilian guards and evacuees hired as police roamed the grounds. The location of the exterior military guards and the direction in which their weapons pointed made evacuees understand the center was not designed to protect but rather to imprison those inside.[101]

The primary housing of Santa Anita consisted of army-type barracks constructed of wood and tar paper atop the track's black asphalt parking lot. Each barrack was divided into small rooms that varied in size. "The rooms were extremely cramped," recalls Amache evacuee Tom Shigekuni who had a ten-by-twenty-foot room. "If you wanted to get to the bed on the other side of the room you had to

---

[99] Yorimoto, interview.
[100] Yorimoto, interview.
[101] Yorimoto, interview.

crawl over the other beds—It was that crowded! There wasn't even room to stand up. I ended up outside most of time."[102]

The walls of the barracks didn't reach the ceiling. At night, sound filtered through the cracks, making sleep difficult at best. Like many others, Amache evacuee Chez Momii's family hung sheets from the ceiling to deaden the sounds and provide privacy.[103]

The army also converted the track's horse stables into temporary dwellings. Before internment, these enclosed horse stables consisted of wooden stalls situated behind long breezeways. After conversion, the stalls and adjoining breezeway would become small rooms—one breezeway room in front of each stall. Art Yorimoto, who lived with his family in one of these converted rooms, recalls that "if you lived in a room built out of the stable part, you had to walk through the room of the couple living in the breeze-way just to get to the outside. There wasn't much privacy."[104] Yorimoto notes that because they went into the center with a small son and a six-month-old daughter, they were given both the room in the stall, as well as the breezeway room.

Most evacuees remember the smell. The army had cleaned and whitewashed the rooms before the evacuees arrived, but the saturated smell of urine, manure, and hay still hung heavily in the air. The intense summer heat made it even more difficult to disguise the odorous past of the stable. "I don't know which was worse, the size of the rooms or the smell of the horses," Yorimoto adds. "No matter how you clean it up, a stable's a stable."[105]

Next to the horse stall were the grandstands and racing oval. These were left intact by the army and were utilized as workstations and schools.

Unlike the Santa Anita center, where evacuees were mostly from the Los Angeles area, the Merced assembly center housed Japanese Americans from urban and rural areas in northern California—areas including Sacramento, Merced, and Sonoma counties. The camp

---

[102] Shigekuni, interview.
[103] Momii, interview.
[104] Yorimoto, interview.
[105] Yorimoto, interview.

opened in early May 1942 and reached a peak of about 4,500 people. Within the confines of Merced were some of the most industrious and ingenious individuals on the West Coast.

Fumiye Nishizaki had been married to her husband, Tono, for six years when they were taken to the Merced assembly center. Tono Nishizaki was a young Issei who had been educated in the United States; Fumiye was a young Nisei woman. Tono worked as an insurance salesman; Fumiye owned a small grocery store in Los Angeles. When evacuation orders came, Tono quit his job and Fumiye sold her store.

Hoping to elude evacuation, Fumiye and Tono decided to go north to Winters, California. "They told us we might not have to go if we moved there," remembers Fumiye. "That's what they told us. Well, there were so many rumors, we should not have believed everything. There were so many rumors—you'd be surprised. Everybody was taken in by the FBI and all this, we were very scared. We just took a suitcase and a few things... We were up there a month or two and then we had to go into Merced."[106]

Before the evacuation order, Merced served as a county fairground. Like Santa Anita, Merced's army-built wood and tar paper barracks featured walls with wide gaps at the top that allowed noise to pass freely from living quarter to living quarter. Barbed wire and eight-foot-high fences with intermittently placed guard towers, machine guns, and spotlights surrounded the center's grounds.

Nishizaki recalls Merced as being just another "tar paper camp. It was so hot. It was in central California and it was very hot." The mess halls were "okay," remembers Nishizaki. "It was clean, for a place—you know, you can't expect anything. But I still couldn't eat any Spam, until recently. Because they used to serve Spam in big slices and not even cooked... That was awful. I couldn't even look at Spam."[107]

Amache evacuee Sets Sumikawa also recalls the climate of Merced, "The heat in the camp was terrible. But the Japanese are

---

[106] Nishizaki, interview.
[107] Nishizaki, interview.

quite creative. I remember people used to put wet newspaper on the floor to cool the rooms down. We also devised a lot of outdoor activities that allowed us to be outside more."[108]

Japanese Americans attempted to make an inevitable situation tolerable. Adopting the expression "Shikataganai"—"It cannot be helped"—most Issei and Nisei resigned themselves to make the best of their incarceration. As Sets Sumikawa noted earlier, the people of Merced organized outdoor activities like dances, arts and crafts classes, and baseball teams to pass the time. Within the confines of the barbed wire fences, many created new lifelong friendships while resuming and cementing old ones. Instead of focusing on their evacuation and imprisonment, instead of spending their time dwelling on the armed guards and the oppressive heat, Issei and Nisei made the most of their summer spent inside these assembly centers.[109]

"We met in Merced," recalls Amache evacuee Emory Namura. Namura and his wife, Tae, met in the Merced assembly center in the summer of 1942. "We went to the same junior college and even graduated at the same time, but neither of us had heard of the other until Merced." Tae laughs. "He was only twenty-one when he went into camp, even though he says he was twenty-two. We met on a blind date. There were dances and stuff at the camp, but I think we mostly just hung around together."[110]

Ironically, the assembly centers also brought about new freedoms. Robert Ichikawa recalls that "life in the assembly center, for our family, was easy—they didn't have to worry about putting food on the table. Social life for the teenagers was not too bad. We made new friends and attended dances."[111]

But with these freedoms came the breakdown of traditional family values. Fathers no longer faced a need for employment. Mothers were no longer accountable for fixing daily meals. Children were no longer forced to attend school. And family traditions were torn apart.

---

[108] Sets Sumikawa, personal interview, 23 March 2000.
[109] Sumikawa, interview.
[110] Emory and Tae Namura, personal interview, 20 May 2000.
[111] Ichikawa, letter.

Tom Shigekuni recalls:

> Everything was pretty unstructured. Families lost a lot of the control they had over their children before the move. My mother was a strict vegetarian—she didn't believe in red meat or anything. She only ate tofu, fish, and vegetables. So, when I got into camp I was eating like everybody else and she had no control over it... I ate at whatever mess hall I wanted to eat in. I never even saw my parents except for when I came home to sleep at night. We were just a bunch of twelve-year-old guys running around, eating at whatever mess hall we felt like. They totally lost that social control over their kids.[112]

Throughout Merced and Santa Anita, mess halls were scattered about to serve three thousand to four thousand evacuees in three shifts of about one thousand people each shift. The centers had originally organized a system by which evacuees were assigned to certain mess halls. For example, evacuees with orange passes could only eat at predetermined mess halls. However, within days of the camp's opening, the meal pass system was abandoned. Without guards stationed at the mess halls to check passes, evacuees were free to choose what mess hall they wanted. Still, many went along with the original plan and ate at their assigned mess halls.[113]

Most evacuees remember the food as being high in starch and low in taste. Some meals consisted of potatoes and bologna, some of toast and boiled eggs ("with the yolk still runny," recalls Art Yorimoto), and some of whatever was available that day. Each mess hall had a basic list of foods based on standard war rationing and WRA quotas. Although the manner in which the food was prepared was left to individual evacuee chefs, meals still had to be prepared

---

[112] Shigekuni, interview.
[113] Yorimoto, interview; Henry Okubo, personal interview, 16 February 2000.

in bulk to meet the daily demand. Some chefs were able to adapt to these conditions better than others; hence, the quality of food varied from mess hall to mess hall.[114]

Long lines into the mess halls usually accompanied each meal. Once inside the barrack like halls, evacuees could count on extensive heat, dim lighting, and insect-saturated flypaper. Kana Yorimoto, an evacuee at the Santa Anita assembly center, recalls, "They used to give us bread pudding with raisins in it. I always joked that you had to wave your hand over it before you could eat. That way, what flew away were the flies and what stayed were raisins."[115]

Other camp facilities were equally unattractive. The centers' toilet facilities consisted of open rooms in which boards with holes about a foot apart were placed. No privacy partitions of any kind divided the seats. Each evacuee was given one roll of toilet paper per week and was responsible for carrying the roll back and forth from barrack to bathroom. Urinals in the men's room were long slanted tin troughs that ran into a corner cesspool. Both the men's and women's toilets resembled large multi-holed outhouses more than the public restrooms of the time.[116]

Grace Kimoto, a Merced evacuee, described the women's toilets as "a flume under 4 holes… Every 2 minutes there was water running down the inclined flume. I had to make sure I sat on the topside so I wouldn't get splashed. Ugh, just the thought of it." Likewise, Merced evacuee Shigeko Hamaka remembers, "The bathroom facilities were so crude. At the end of this thing, there was this water gushing down. It just poured down into this [large bucket] until it got heavy and then it would tip over and go 'swish.' That was how they flushed it. The first night we got there—Oh, there were women trying to pound up sheets for some sort of partition. Because this was really bad—from a home, to something like this."[117]

Showers were also communal in nature and, like the toilets, often lacked privacy dividers. The communal nature of the show-

---

[114] Yorimoto, interview.
[115] Kana Yorimoto, personal interview, 18 May 2000.
[116] Yorimoto, A., interview.
[117] Grace Kimoto, email to the author, 6 March 2000; Hirano, S., interview.

ers was especially difficult for many Issei women who found public nudity disgraceful. Some women took showers in bathing suits, while others brought shower curtains for privacy. Most, however, took showers late at night or simply endured the humiliating circumstances of showering with others.[118]

The overriding hope was to keep everybody busy. If everyone was kept busy, the WRA and military leaders hoped, evacuees would have little time to spend on lamenting over their recent evacuation. So within the assembly centers of Merced and Santa Anita, evacuees were asked to work and go to school.

At Merced, Fumiye Nishizaki remembers being selected to order clothing for the center. "They came in," Nishizaki recalls, "and we would tell them 'what do you need' and for so much they could get—I don't know how much they could order for each one. It was free. But what they sent was awful. Sears or Wards I guess—mostly Sears's Roebuck catalogs. And they'd send what they couldn't sell or we'd order a blouse and they'd send us silk, you know shiny rayon stuff and things like that—we thought they were taking advantage of us."[119]

The grandstands at Santa Anita housed a school that attempted to provide a rudimentary education for primary and secondary students. But as Chez Momii recalls, "It wasn't well attended. I thought it was great. I loved it. They taught mostly basic subjects like math and history. Every class was taught by evacuees. But I don't think many of the guys in camp bothered to show up for class a lot of the time."[120]

The primary purpose of the school was not to educate young Nisei. Like the other centers, Santa Anita and Merced saw these temporary schools as a way to keep young minds occupied during a tense and difficult period. Japanese Americans were hired as instructors for these classes. Sets Sumikawa recalls that Merced also hired Japanese American instructors for adult dance and art classes.[121]

---

[118] Yorimoto, K., interview.
[119] Nishizaki, interview.
[120] Momii, interview.
[121] Sumikawa, S., interview.

Santa Anita classes shared the grandstands with adults who produced military camouflage netting from dyed hemp. Over eight hundred evacuees worked forty-four-hour weeks constructing nets ranging in size from twenty-two by twenty-two feet to thirty-six by sixty feet. The work was hot and exhausting. Most labored eight-hour days while kneeling on the floor under the hot summer sun. For their work, each evacuee was paid eight dollars a month. In June 1942, these poor working conditions, along with dissatisfaction over food, led to a strike by the evacuees in which all eight hundred workers stopped work. By the next day, however, leaders of the project agreed to better conditions, and workers resumed production. The Santa Anita camouflage net project yielded some twenty-two thousand nets for the military over the summer of 1942—enough to offset the cost of feeding the evacuees housed in Santa Anita.[122]

Nervous anxiety filled the air in Santa Anita. Tom Shigekuni notes, "People were very tense…always accusing everyone else of being informants."[123]

Art Yorimoto recalls an incident involving an alleged informant at the center:

> I got a job as the timekeeper in the Japanese Police Department. There was one guy on my list that never came in to work. So, I [told] my chief, "This man on my list—he never shows up." So, he told me to just mark him absent if he doesn't show up. He knew who this man was—he was a Korean sent there to spy on us.
>
> Well, it must have been about two or three months later, this man came in to get his check—he wanted that pay as well as the money he was getting from the regular police department for spying. He was mad when he came in. He told me his name and said: "How come you marked

---

[122] Japanese American National Museum, *Japanese American History*, 305.
[123] Shigekuni, interview.

me absent?" I said: "Well, you never showed up for work so I counted you absent." Anyway, I found out then that he was a spy—my chief told me.[124]

Robert Ichikawa, recalling the incident, notes that, "the man who was thought to be Korean was grabbed by a group of men and chased into the so-called Government House and beaten. A large crowd gathered and the Military Police (MPs) moved in a wedge formation to remove the man. There was no rioting—just curious onlookers."[125]

According to Art Yorimoto, the men who attacked the informant were members of the camp's Japanese internal security force. Yorimoto recalls:

> The Japanese Police had it in for him and cornered him. Most of the policemen in the Japanese division were judo men. They beat him up so bad that he was almost dead. He was taken right away to the center hospital. But the Japanese doctors knew who he was and what he was doing in the camp, so they refused to work on him. They had to take him to the Los Angeles hospital. He lived—I think—but I never heard of him anymore. He never came back.[126]

Yet another incident at Santa Anita involved a riot between disgruntled evacuees and dishonest MPs. Every week, the civilian police department inspected the center's barracks for contraband. Some say the riot started during one of these inspections. Teenage boys—who often followed the civilian police around during these inspection periods—spotted a guard pocketing an item from the barrack he was

---

[124] Yorimoto, A., interview.
[125] Ichikawa, letter.
[126] Yorimoto, A., interview.

searching. Within minutes, the teenage boys had alerted others of the theft, and the guards found themselves being chased back to the front gate by the evacuees.

Soon the center's military guard was facing an angry and riotous crowd. With the number of those taunting and harassing the civilian guards growing larger by the minute, the military guards became eager to gain control. Unable to contact the camp's internal security chief, the military began firing machine guns at the feet of the crowd. Order was soon restored, with only minor evacuee injuries reported. The cause of the disturbance—the stealing of the item by the civilian guard—was never verified. However, the overzealous military men who fired into the crowd were replaced shortly after the incident.[127]

Throughout the spring and summer of 1942, Japanese Americans incarcerated at Santa Anita and Merced made the best of their circumstances.

By early November, most evacuees had been moved by bus and train to more permanent evacuation camps. On August 27, Colorado would see its first group of Japanese evacuees arrive at Granada. For those who came to Granada in the fall of 1942, this remote and desolate corner of Colorado would be called home.

---

[127] Yorimoto, A., interview; Minoru Tonai, personal interview, February 2000.

CHAPTER 3

COLORADO MUST DO ITS DUTY

Sacrifice was the call. Victory the goal. And the only hope of winning the war was a unified front at home.

Headlines nationwide screamed of Axis atrocities. By early 1942, German troops had in hand much of Eastern Europe and the western Soviet Union. Allied troops experienced heavy losses in battles against the Japanese in the Bataan Peninsula and Corregidor. News of the war overseas hung heavy in the psyche of American minds.

Leaders around the country responded to this news with swift calls for sacrifice. Victory through unity had become the mandate for Americans at home. Joseph B. Eastman, director of the National Office of Defense Transportation, ordered that the national speed limit be lowered to a maximum of thirty-five miles per hour to conserve tires and gasoline. Likewise, a mandatory rationing program went into effect for all rubber products. Before 1942, the major supplier for natural rubber for American consumer foods was Malaya and the East Indies of the Netherlands. But when ties with rubber producers in these areas became severed due to the war in the Pacific, Americans scrambled to fill the void. Research and production of the new synthetic materials using petroleum had begun, but new synthetic rubber products would not begin to hit the general market until well into the war.[128]

In Colorado, Mayor Stapleton of Denver and Governor Carr released statements urging Colorado citizens to curb extended trips on summer vacation and holidays. Stapleton also cracked down on the excessive use of government vehicles. Citizens of Colorado quickly and decisively arose to these calls for action. Excessive driving became tagged as a wasteful use of precious wartime materials. Tires were used until threadbare. Those who refused to ration gasoline and tires were scorned for their lack of patriotism.[129]

In addition to rationing efforts, residents of Colorado also scoured garages, basements, and storage sheds for items they could contribute to local scrap drives. Governor Carr requested that "all citizens, all businessmen, everyone, everywhere in Colorado must start scrap steel and iron to market… This is the most important single war duty in the state now. We're not appealing for donations… We want private citizens, businessmen, industrialists, and all who have scrap to get it to the dealers at once."[130]

In the summer of 1942, even scores of out-of-school children were bringing used-up, threadbare tires to gas stations around the city for a hefty reward of a penny a pound. This rubber drive was sponsored by the *Rocky Mountain News* and lasted through the months of June and July. By its conclusion, the drive had collected over one thousand tons of rubber—enough tonnage to pay for the construction of fourteen aircraft carriers.[131]

Rationing and scrap drives had also become an acceptable part of Colorado's social agenda by 1942. Social and sporting events soon became fashionable methods of raising funds for military and war relief agencies. One event at a local golf course starred Lawson Little (former National Open champion), Bob Hope, Bing Crosby, and a

---

[128] *New York Times*, 4 January 1942, 2E.
[129] *Rocky Mountain News*, 4 March 1942, 1.
[130] *Alamosa Daily Courier*, 7 February 1942, 1.
[131] *Rocky Mountain News*, 4 July 1942, 1; 11 July 1942, 8.

host of local celebrities. The event drew the largest crowd to see a golf match in Denver's history up until that time.[132]

Those who failed in any way to join the unified goal of victory were viewed as lazy and simply unpatriotic. Three boys who were given a harsh sentence at a local industrial school for their part in slashing car tires were proclaimed by the juvenile court judge as the "Hitler's youth" of Denver.[133]

These were the times of sacrifice. Rationing rubber, conserving fuel, collecting scrap for the production of weapons—all these tasks fit within the daily routines of American life. But one need was nearly impossible to meet—the labor needed for the production demands of war.

The need for ever-increasing wartime supplies both at home and overseas turned the economy around at a frantic and dizzying speed. Factories churned out war goods twenty-four hours a day. Ranchers and farmers produced additional goods for the increased consumption of war. With the onset of war, labor positions around the country had been vacated by men going overseas. This lack of laborers plagued the entire country, so creative and fresh ways of doing business as usual would need to be found. In essence, the face of America's labor would need to change, and Japanese American evacuees would soon be a part of that change.

Production shifted from cars to tanks, from stoves to guns; the demand for manpower reached a high not seen since World War I. Illinois's agricultural market alone needed seventeen thousand additional full-time workers for the 1942 growing season. The nationwide labor shortage, combined with increased production demands, forced employers to hire more women, minorities, and students to fill positions in a workforce traditionally dominated by white males.

A 1942 *Wall Street Journal* article reported, "Ohio farmers this spring will employ greater numbers of women, men with minor handicaps, youths, and college students." Although the report felt that such workforces would "probably be less efficient," these men and

---

[132] *Rocky Mountain News*, 17 August 1942, 20.
[133] *Rocky Mountain News*, 2 April 1942, 1.

women were now to be called on. The young white males who had filled the prime labor positions before were at war. As the war continued, the demand for labor increased, and the makeup of America's workforce shifted from predominately white males to females and minorities.[134]

The west also was plagued with this dire need for laborers—especially farmers and ranchers who sought creative and effective methods to fill the void. To ease labor strains, postal workers in Denver took time away from their jobs to help local farmers harvest sugar beets in 1942. Colleges around the west also allowed students to register late for the fall semester in exchange for their participation in farm production. Even in rural areas, schools were placed on six-day schedules instead of the traditional five-day schedule so students might finish the school year early and work in local sugar beet fields.[135]

These methods of meeting labor needs seemed appropriate to most. But one method of meeting the demand brought a thundering storm of controversy and criticism—the hiring of Japanese Americans voluntarily relocating from the West Coast. A few farmers and ranchers hired West Coast Japanese, but most felt that hiring a member of the "Japanese menace" meant furthering the possibility of subversive activities. One Colorado county commissioner noted that Japanese labor "could only be used for contracts that can't be filled by the use of Mexican labor." No matter how severe the labor crisis got in inland states, those holding opinions such as these felt that less dangerous methods should be used to meet rising demands for labor.[136]

Issei and Nisei who had lived, worked, prospered for years in inland communities were now also suddenly open to new and subjective prejudices. Disdain gave rise to discrimination. Anglos now began to exclude—or at the very least, keep a watchful eye on—all Americans of Japanese ancestry. Racism mandated that citizens

---

[134] *Wall Street Journal*, 20 February 1942, 6.
[135] *Rocky Mountain News*, 16 September 1942, 20; *Wall Street Journal*, 20 February 1942, 6.
[136] *Holly Chieftain*, 10 September 1942, 1.

protect their state from another "Pearl Harbor." It had now become the "responsibility" of all patriotic citizens to scrutinize the attitudes and actions and lives of Japanese Americans living in—or moving to—inland states. Those who were American by birth, those who had dedicated themselves to the ideologies of democracy, and those who had never questioned their loyalty as Americans now had to prove their resolve by means above and beyond that of the average American citizen.

Citizens of Colorado were no exception to these racist attitudes. The fear of fifth column activities within the state gave rise to a fresh and heightened sense of preparedness. Neighbors watched neighbors (providing the neighbor in question was of Japanese ancestry). Military and governmental institutions around the state beefed up their operations. Several thousand men were given the responsibility of protecting Denver's gas and water mains, power lines, bridges, and viaducts from possible fifth column activities. Likewise, it was announced that Lowery Field had beefed up its base activities and would "not be caught napping" against subversive activities or surprise air raids.[137]

Colorado and the nation were willing to set aside the rights of fellow citizens. All principles of freedom would be discarded. Americans would not be caught napping. Within Colorado, the sense of public trepidation was high. Colorado citizens feared their state would soon be opened to subversive activities if Japanese Americans were not somehow watched.

As in other states, those in Colorado allowed the emotionally charged atmosphere of war to drive their sense of democracy.

Into this highly charged atmosphere came news of a possible West Coast evacuation inland. As early as mid-February, Colorado residents had heard rumors of their state's involvement in the relocation process when the regional head of the Agricultural Department's War Board, Dewey Harman, disclosed that he had been contacted to conduct a survey of appropriate housing sites for Japanese American evacuees in Colorado. Less than a week later, Harman's report was

---

[137] *Rocky Mountain News*, 1 March 1942, 4, 6.

bolstered by a February 22 *Denver Post* report stating that supplies, bedding, and utensils had been shipped to a number of vacated CCC camps in Wyoming and Colorado. Although the Harman and *Post* reports gave no clear information where wartime evacuees would be housed, they indicated that Colorado and Wyoming were strongly considered as prime WRA center locations.[138]

But as news began to surface about evacuation and relocation, one man clearly stood above the din. Colorado's Governor Ralph Carr had staunchly expressed a willingness to do what would bring about unity amid chaos. Carr's stance had always been one of cooperation with governmental authorities. If winning the war meant allowing evacuees of Japanese ancestry within his state's boundaries, Carr would willingly do so. In a press statement in the spring of 1942, Carr noted, "We of Colorado are big enough and patriotic enough to do our duty. We announce to the world that 1,118,000 red-blooded citizens of this state are able to take care of 3,500 or any number of enemies if that be the task which is allotted to us."[139]

Carr saw the evacuation as a national crisis—one that could only be repaired through cooperation. In February, Colorado's publicity director declared that a large concentration of Japanese Americans coming into the state could hurt the state's reputation. Governor Carr responded:

> Colorado is threatened with a charge of disinclination to cooperate in essential war efforts. A suspicion of a lack of patriotism which is not deserved and which cannot be permitted to go unanswered has been raised.
>
> A few weeks ago, came rumors that alien residents of the Pacific Coast states of Japanese origin were to be evacuated and perhaps 3,500 would be sent to Colorado. From some unidentified source came another suggestion, probably

---

[138] *Denver Post*, 22 February 1942, 1.
[139] *Rocky Mountain News*, 1 March 1942, 1, 8.

born of unfriendly propaganda parentage, that California was attempting to dump a bothersome problem into Colorado's lap. The first inclination of every Colorado resident was one of resentment. There was a feeling that we did not want enemy aliens within our borders who might acquire property rights, who might compete which Colorado labor, and whose presence would be a constant menace and threat to our peaceful conditions of life.

Such actions are not only wrong in themselves, but they may find their way to Tokyo and may result in hardship or even death for Americans who are now prisoners of the enemy. There are thousands of loyal German, Italian, and Japanese citizens in this state who must not suffer for the activities and animosities of others. They are as loyal to American institutions as you and I. Many of them have been born here, are American citizens, with no connection with or feeling of loyalty toward the customs and philosophies of Italy, Germany, and Japan.[140]

Carr did not act without caution, however. In late January, he had issued an order requiring an estimated 7,800 Japanese, German, and Italian aliens to apply at post offices around the state for new certificates of identification. If stopped by state police and military troops, these identification cards would prove registration.[141]

Carr, like other citizens, also remained leery of fifth column activities, which some asserted would certainly follow the sudden influx of relocated enemy aliens. Just in case, Carr felt it would be best to locate all evacuees in areas away from dams, reservoirs, and forests—areas where fires and other forms of sabotage might affect

---

[140] *Rocky Mountain News*, 1 March 1942, 1, 8.
[141] *Alamosa Daily Courier*, 28 January 1942, 1.

essential aspects of life. He also adamantly declared that any statement of cooperation with the US government by the state of Colorado should not be viewed as "an invitation" to a West Coast Japanese population. In cooperating with the military, Carr was merely fulfilling a wartime duty. His intent was patriotic. His motivation was the call of country. Carr's true purpose for accepting Japanese Americans into his state could be summed up by his statement that "only because the needs of our nation dictate it, do we even consider such an arrangement."[142]

Today, in Denver's Sukura Square, there stands a small granite memorial, reminding passersby of Governor Carr's steadfast deeds during World War II. To many, he remains one who "had the wisdom and courage to speak out in behalf of the persecuted Japanese American minority." Carr does indeed deserve great praise for his actions of World War II. He considered evacuees to be American citizens who had been placed under a great weight of injustice. He opened the doors of his state to the process of relocation. He viewed Japanese Americans as "loyal to American institutions" as any other American citizen could claim to be.

But Carr's actions were also motivated by his sense of duty. His responses during World War II to the process of evacuation were born primarily of patriotic duty and responsibility. He was aiding the national government in its time of need.

Those voluntarily evacuating the West Coast saw very little patriotism in what they were forced to do. They left everything not because they wished to start anew, nor did they move from their homes out of a sense of duty. They did so because of the fear and intimidation they had endured on the West Coast. Local authorities had pushed too hard; federal mandates seemed too difficult to fight. Evacuees moving inland voluntarily did so because they felt they had no other choice.

Many volunteer evacuees found economic and racial oppression on their entrance into Colorado. Many who voluntarily trekked there had hoped its citizens would concur with the firm stance Governor

---

[142] *Rocky Mountain News*, 1 March 1942, 1, 8.

Carr had taken earlier in the evacuation process. Instead, they found firm resistance. Their movements were watched closely. Their very presence was barely tolerated.

Throughout the voluntary evacuation period, Colorado's newspapers sensationalized the process. Press accounts often portrayed the small flow of evacuees into interior states as a great exodus threatening to endanger both the safety and the well-being of the state. One article stated that a "sample check" by the Arizona State Patrol had indicated most Japanese Americans found traveling on US Highways 66 and 89 hoped their ultimate destination would be Colorado. Other articles in subsequent papers gave detailed accounts of caravans of Japanese Americans heading for the state.[143]

Of this influx of Japanese Americans, the *Alamosa Daily Courier* remarked, "Whether residents like it or not, Japanese aliens already are being moved to the San Luis Valley." Evacuees filling three cars traveled into the La Jara city limits in search of work. Of these migrants, opponents noted that "once here, the aliens will never be taken away, the result will be crowding out of citizen labor, ever increasing percentages of foreign students in schools, and a lowering of wage and price standards."[144]

In response to voluntary evacuation, Denver's city council members also stated they felt all evacuees should be placed under a twenty-four-hour watch. Likewise, Colorado's chapter of the American Legion asked Governor Carr to call a special session of Congress to deal with the sudden influx. The legion felt this special session should focus on enacting "laws to cope with the presence of such aliens" and the repealing of laws that allowed aliens the right to acquire land. Such action, so the legion remarked, was a necessity brought about by the events surrounding Pearl Harbor. According to an American Legion spokesman, such an attack was made "possible by aliens and quislings permitted by our laxity and complacency to be residents of and move freely about the Hawaiian Islands." Fearful such an attack

---

[143] *Rocky Mountain News*, 6 March 1942, 1; 20 March 1942, 1.
[144] *Alamosa Daily Courier*, 24 February 1942, 1.

could happen in Colorado, the American Legion became a state strong arm in the evacuation process.[145]

But there was one undisputed Colorado leader who topped even the American Legion in opposition rhetoric—Colorado's former governor and newly appointed US senator, Ed C. Johnson. Time and time again, Johnson unashamedly declared his vehement opposition to the movement of all Issei and Nisei—considered "harmless or otherwise"—into Colorado. Feeling a large population of Japanese had already settled within the state, Johnson claimed a further concentration would only give rise to trouble. "Unfortunately," Johnson remarked, "Governor Carr's address on the Japanese question is being interpreted by the Japanese people of California as an invitation to come to Colorado… I remember that as governor, I called out the National Guard when 10,000 aliens from Mexico threatened to move into Colorado to take the railroad and sugar beet field jobs from Colorado citizens."[146] Contrary to what Johnson claimed, FBI files in Denver showed that the Japanese population in Colorado had grown only to about 5,000 residents statewide by May 1942—up from a prewar figure of 3,200.[147]

Despite this opposition, Carr remained firm in his prior commitment to Eisenhower's WRA, stating that because Roosevelt and the military had established certain military zones within which certain people were to be evacuated, he would cooperate fully. To this need, Carr repeated his patriotic stance by stating, "This is a war order to avoid fifth-column activities on the West Coast. My position is that anything asked of us by the government must be done as a patriotic act."[148]

However, at one point, Carr did feel that the increased voluntary relocations into the state of Colorado was significant enough to

---

[145] *Rocky Mountain News*, 22 March 1942, 1.
[146] *Rocky Mountain News*, 30 March 1942, 3.
[147] *Rocky Mountain News*, 24 March 1942, 3.
[148] *Rocky Mountain News*, 7 April 1942, 14.

declare a state of emergency. In a March 21 letter, Carr wrote to US Attorney Thomas J. Morrisey, stating:

> You will remember that when the proposed transfer of enemy aliens from military zones first arose, it was announced by me as governor that this state would do everything to cooperate with the government and with the military forces to care for undesirables who might be brought to Colorado. This was not an invitation to anybody, however these [voluntary evacuees] who, because of war conditions, are obliged to come or who have already reached Colorado, present another question. It demands immediate action by federal authorities. Many local people want to know if they may be employing American citizens and enemy aliens. From other angles come protests wherein our people demand the immediate internment of all such persons, regardless of their status, in concentration camps where they may be closely guarded… Loose talk and wild threats are made by others which imperil our own citizens in the control of, or who may be taken prisoner by, the Japanese.[149]

But the "emergency" Carr spoke of never forced him to stray from his original position. In a March 23, 1942, statement, Carr clarified his stand by stating, "My position is the same as it has been. As one of the forty-eight states, Colorado must do its duty. I have not found one person who had thought the thing out who disagreed with me. Many of these people are American citizens, and you can't put an American citizen in jail for no cause without violating the law."[150] Although he insisted the responsibility of relocation fell solely to the

---

[149] *Rocky Mountain News*, 22 March 1942, 1.
[150] *Rocky Mountain News*, 24 March 1942, 3.

federal government, Carr never demanded that concentration camps be constructed to house evacuees. He was still willing to accept evacuees into his state, as long as federal troops were responsible for supervising their actions.

Carr had once remarked in a Boulder victory rally that he felt so strongly about allowing Japanese aliens access to Colorado employment that he would stake his entire political future on his convictions. This statement would come to haunt Carr, for his views soon became much-needed fodder for his opponents' campaigns. In his bid for state senator in 1942, Carr's adversaries—particularly Senator Johnson—portrayed the governor as a leader who refused to protect the interests of his constituents. In response, Carr replied that his actions were done simply out of patriotic duty and as such he would not debate the issue with Senator Johnson. His refusal to counterattack eventually led to an unjustified and tarnished reputation—one that would lead to the demise of his senatorial dreams.[151]

Tensions in Colorado were temporarily eased when DeWitt announced on March 25 that the voluntary influx to interior states would end in favor of a more controlled evacuation program. Likewise, Colorado's residents were relieved by the news that Milton Eisenhower had "no plans…for establishment of Japanese detention camps in Colorado." A collective sigh was heaved.[152]

But before Colorado residents could get too comfortable with these new events, news surfaced in late March that Thomas C. Clark, the WRA's alien control coordinator, was en route to Denver from San Francisco to set up a WRA command office. By the first week of April, as the flow of Japanese evacuees into Colorado from the West Coast noticeably abated (due to DeWitt's ending of the volunteer evacuation process), Colorado residents began to realize that their state would indeed become involved in the process of evacuation. And for many in the southeastern portion of the state, it would become a very real and personal involvement.[153]

---

[151] *Alamosa Daily Courier*, 12 April 1942, 1.
[152] *Rocky Mountain News*, 26 March 1942, 1.
[153] *Rocky Mountain News*, 27 March 1942, 1.

In Eisenhower's meeting with the ten governors in April 1942, only Governor Carr had remained steadfast in his willingness to cooperate. New Mexico's governor avowed he would use his "emergency police powers, if necessary" to keep Japanese Americans from entering his state. Utah's governor, Herbert B. Maw, asserted he wanted "absolute assurance that once the war is over, they'll be taken out." Likewise, Idaho's governor, Chase Clark—although agreeing to abide by the federal order—stood firm to earlier convictions of not allowing evacuees the right to own or lease land within his state's borders.[154]

The meeting of the ten states was a pivotal point in the relocation process. Because governors of interior states expressed a desire to have Japanese Americans under constant military watch, the WRA had no choice but to build centers where evacuees would be concentrated and under constant guard.

Colorado's press sources began to speculate on possible sites for such a center within their state. An article in the April 26, 1942, *Rocky Mountain News* stated that US senator Eugene D. Millikin announced unofficially that a federal internment camp would be built around Alamosa, Colorado. Other news sources reported various CCC camps around the state would be logical sites for such an internment center. The WRA had indeed considered these CCC camps—in reality, now just dilapidated relics of the Depression era gone by—as possible housing sites for evacuees. But in the spring of 1942, no one—not even Carr or Johnson—could truly be sure where a center would be built or how evacuees would be supervised. No one in Colorado could even be sure as to what extent the state would be used by the WRA.[155]

In late spring of 1942, however, Senator Johnson was approached by WRA officials and asked to submit a list of possible evacuation center sites. For these sites, the WRA had very definite stipulations. The first demand by the WRA was that the area needed to be deemed suitable in providing "work opportunities in public

---

[154] *Rocky Mountain News*, 8 April 1942, 2.
[155] *Rocky Mountain News*, 26 April 1942, 8.

works, agriculture, production, and manufacturing." Second, the WRA asked for the presence of "adequate public faculties" like roads, railways, power, and abundant water supply. Next, the area needed to be in an area void of a large concentration of Caucasians. And finally, the site needed to be far from war-industry plants and other areas inviting to saboteurs.[156]

The WRA's first requirement was aimed at aiding the nation's wartime labor demand. Although the placement of evacuees into inland states had been done under the guise of "security," the convenience of having a productive and effective source of manpower around key farming communities could not be overlooked. Federal officials saw how a substantial number of laborers thrust into the right setting could effectively repair, build, or produce anything a wartime economy demanded. Even state officials began to see these benefits. Eisenhower noted in later years, "Government officials, particularly agricultural officials from the intermountain states, began to request relocation centers in their states. Having rejected the Japanese-Americans so forcefully in early April, they were now petitioning WRA for workers. Why? To rescue farm lands that were going to ruin from lack of manpower."[157]

The WRA's second stipulation was brought about due to practicality; the center would also need to be self-sufficient. The existence of 110,000 people in government-operated camps required substantial demands for food, water, electricity, and other key elements of a city's infrastructure. By acquiring a vast tract of fertile and irrigable land, evacuees could cut food costs by growing crops and raising livestock. By sustaining the community on its own water supply, the camp would not need to be dependent on another nearby community. And by having access to roads and railways, the community could ship and receive goods and evacuees easily.

The WRA's third demand—that of locating the site away from a large concentration of Caucasians—was set up to ease tension in

---

[156] Mark M. Hayashi, "Farm Section Report," 31 December 1942, 309: 0011 L6.80, Japanese American evacuation and resettlement records, BANC MSS 67/14c, the Bancroft Library, University of California, Berkeley.
[157] Eisenhower, *The President Is Calling*, 121.

surrounding communities. By locating evacuees away from established communities, the WRA hoped to cut down on the friction an already volatile situation would produce.

The final stipulation that the camps' sites needed to be situated away from industrial areas went back to the fear of fifth column activities. The WRA did not want in any way to put evacuees into areas where national safety might be put at risk.[158]

With these demands in place, Senator Johnson was asked to find a site in his state—on public or private land—that required "a great amount of labor" for improvements and could house five thousand to six thousand evacuees. Begrudgingly, he began to do so.[159]

Many sites in southeastern and eastern Colorado were considered for the WRA evacuee site. Senator Johnson had submitted a total of fourteen sites around the state that suited the four WRA requirements. But Bent County, in particular, fought the hardest for such a center. A relocation center in their county, local officials had hoped, would provide an abundant number of laborers to construct a second dam just west of the already established Mutual Carey Irrigation Project.[160]

As the selection process was underway, the rural community of Granada seemed completely unaware that they were even considered as a possible site for a relocation center. By the middle of May, WRA officials had narrowed their choices down to two possible Colorado sites. A May 14 telegram was sent to the Missouri River division of the Army Corps of Engineers, stating:

> WAR RELOCATION AUTHORITY REQUESTS YOU DETAIL AN ENGINEER COMMA AN APPRAISER AND A MAN QUALIFIED TO PASS UPON WATER SUPPLY FOR DOMESTIC PURPOSES COMMA TO MEET MR FRED RESS AT

---

[158] Eisenhower, *The President Is Calling*, 121.
[159] *Lamar Daily News*, 23 May 1942, 1.
[160] *Lamar Daily News*, 1 June 1942, 1.

PRINCIPAL HOTEL COMMA HOLYOKE COMMA PHILLIPS COUNTY COLORADO COMMA ON TUESDAY MORNING MAY 19 FOR SITE BOARD INVESTIGATION OF PROPOSED RELOCATION AREA FOR JAPANESE EVACUEES NEAR HOLYOKE STOP ON MAY 20 SAME BOARD WILL CONTINUE TO GRANADA TO INVESTIGATE LAMAR AND XY RANCH PROPERTIES IN PROWERS COUNTY COLORADO STOP RELOCATION AREA WILL PROVIDE FOR FROM 5000 TO 10000 EVACUEES TOP [sic] REQUEST YOU WIRE MR RB COZZENS COMMA WAR RELOCATION AUTHORITY COMMA WHITCOMB HOTEL COMMA SANFRANCISCO [sic] NAMES OF PERSONS WILL MEET MR RESS AS REQUESTED END IN ABS DIV ENGR
    MATHESON N 606 PM
    END END EM
    END MS[161]

The communities of Holyoke and Granada both fit the requirements earlier set up by the WRA. Both locations had an abundance of land that could be improved by an influx of laborers. Both were spatial enough for a large concentration center. And both met the WRA's, as well as Governor Carr's, insistence that evacuees be placed away from easily sabotaged sites like forests, reservoirs, and dams.

Secrecy surrounded the selection of these two sites. Not until June 1 did an official statement from Senator Johnson reveal that

---

[161] US Army Corps of Engineers, "Engineering Survey for Japanese Relocation Settlement," 309:0119 L6.54, Japanese American evacuation and resettlement records, BANC MSS 67/14, the Bancroft Library, University of California, Berkeley.

prospects were "excellent" for establishing a camp between Holly and Lamar.[162]

In the days that followed this announcement, the buzz around Prowers County was that the camp might be located near Granada. On June 3, headlines in the *Lamar Daily News* confirmed these predictions by proclaiming, "Jap Camp to Be Located on XY Ranch East of Lamar." But in truth, the XY Ranch—located next to the town of Granada—would be only one of many parcels of land acquired by the government for the campsite. Besides the XY Ranch, the WRA would also acquire the Koen Ranch and twelve smaller private holdings.[163]

News spread around the state. The *Montrose Daily Press* reported that "Jap evacuees [would] produce food crops, build irrigation systems on Colorado project."[164] The *Rocky Mountain News* also reported that Granada was to house a camp holding at least seven thousand people due to military necessity.[165]

These parcels of land where the camp would be located were richer in history than they were in fertile soil. The XY Ranch had first gained notoriety in 1885 when Fredrick H. Harvey purchased the ranch and surrounding parcels of land for grazing purposes. Harvey, in cooperation with the Santa Fe Railway, had established restaurants called Harvey Houses along the Santa Fe that served some of the finest steaks in the west. But around the turn of the century, Harvey's business ventures began to lose profits, and his land was broken into smaller pieces and sold to various ranchers and farmers.[166]

Like the XY Ranch, the Koen Ranch had changed hands many times before being purchased by the American Crystal Sugar Company. Under this ownership, the Koen Ranch served exclusively as an agricultural outlet, with thirty farmers subleasing sections of the land from the company.

---

[162] *Lamar Daily News*, 1 June 1942, 1.
[163] *Lamar Daily News*, 3 June 1942, 1.
[164] *Montrose Daily Press*, 11 June 1942, 1.
[165] *Rocky Mountain News*, 4 June 1942, 4.
[166] Ava Betz, *A Prowers County History* (Lamar: Prowers County Historical Society, 1986), 65–66.

To get these sites, the WRA had to first condemn the land before they could purchase it. This forced farmers to sell their land at fire-sale prices to the government. This sort of "purchase" of private land for the relocation center in Colorado was different from the acquisition of other sites. Rohwer and Jerome, both in Arkansas, were located on Farm Security Administration land. Gila River and Poston in Arizona were on land leased from Indian reservations. Heart Mountain in Wyoming and Minidoka in Idaho were located on Federal Reclamation Project lands. Unlike the other camps, the 10,500 acres of the Granada site were wholly located on private lands.

Such large parcels of private lands were necessary to meet WRA requirements. Government officials saw in the Granada site over ten thousand acres of commercial farm and grazing land that included "the most productive pieces of land in the valley"—if properly irrigated. Over six thousand of these acres were already either under irrigation or could be irrigated. The water rights for the property alone were over sixty-nine feet.

Officials hoped that by locating the relocation camp in Granada, some evacuees would grow and maintain WRA crops and livestock while others would use seasonal leaves to work at already established farms around the area. Eisenhower's goal was for the Granada site to produce a vast supply of sugar beets, alfalfa, and "a wide range of truck crops" for a desperate wartime economy. Although it had been reported shortly before the camp was opened that the Granada center was selected as a possible site for a wartime industrial site, a potentially productive agricultural base had always been—and would in reality be—a major reason for the site selection at Granada.[167]

At first, Elbert S. Rule (owner of the XY Ranch) and the American Crystal Sugar Company (owner of Koen Ranch) adamantly denied any transactions between themselves and the WRA—and for good reason. John Hopper, dean of students at Granada high school, notes that, "all the land that Amache sits on—all the farmland and everything—was condemned. You have to understand that the local farmers were just coming off the dust bowl era… Then they

---

[167] *Lamar Daily News*, 5 June 1942, 1; 11 June 1942, 1.

have their land condemned, just when the weather started getting better... They weren't upset—we've talked to several families—they weren't upset with the Amache people. They were upset with the government."[168]

With such an important part of the community up in arms over the sale of land to the government, neither Rule nor American Crystal wished to be tied in name as initial sellers. Both parties even went as far as to release a June 8 press statement that denied they had even been approached by the WRA. But on June 19, the Army Corps of Engineers put an end to all rumors when an office was established in Lamar for the explicit purpose of surveying land for the relocation camp—the very land Rule and Crystal were claiming they had not sold.

Two days before the establishment of the Army Corps office at Lamar, Milton Eisenhower left his position as director of the WRA. Into the void stepped Dillon Myer. Myer saw the role of the WRA as threefold. First, the WRA had the immediate objective of removing 110,000 persons from the West Coast to points inland. Next, Myer's WRA would attempt to reestablish these evacuees into communities around the country. Finally, Myer and his staff hoped to calm the patriotic uproar of the press and politicians. Although less pressing than the first objective, the tasks of relocation and quieting inflammatory remarks would prove to be the more difficult in the life of the WRA.[169]

The tasks facing Myer could well have been what Weglyn calls "the toughest, most exasperating civilian job during the war."[170] Eisenhower had left behind only the bare skeletal formation of evacuation. Weglyn describes Myer's task as even more difficult because "multiple bunglings of the army, its working at cross-purposes with the navy, the FBI, and the War Department, the frequent abrupt and arbitrary changes in the policies of these and other governmental

---

[168] John Hopper, personal interview, 19 February 2001.
[169] Myer, *Uprooted Americans*, 32–33.
[170] Weglyn, *Years of Infamy*, 119.

agencies had served to exacerbate evacuee tension to the near-explosion point."[171]

Myer, as the new head of the WRA, was now responsible for the lives of over 110,000 evacuees. Under his leadership, some of these Japanese Americans would find their way to the small community of Granada, where they would live out the next few years of their lives. Amid the desert climate of Prowers County, evacuees would begin yet another chapter of their lives as victims of the war.

To most outsiders, Prowers County and the town of Granada seemed like a barren land with little excess other than those of extreme weather conditions and sand. But a closer look at the region's history reveals a land filled with thriving towns, hearty people, and a rich, colorful past.

The region had seen both brave pioneer and spineless coward, both saint and sinner. Skinners like George "Hoodoo" Brown and Charly Wonderly followed the ever-present buffalo herds in search of buffalo hides to "harvest." It was here, for a short time at least, that Calamity Jane lived and worked. It was through these grasslands that Cheyenne, Arapaho, Kiowa, and Comanche roamed, hunted, and lived. It was also within this hostile environment that Native American and pioneer alike died trying to survive.

Trails like the Santa Fe Trail, the New Goodnight Trail, the National Cattle Trail, and the Texas-Montana Trail dissected the county and brought a never-ending line of cattle to rail lines heading for eastern markets. Along these trails, entrepreneurial men like William and Charles Bent set up trading posts. Along these trails traveled the heartiest men and women the late nineteenth century could produce—men and women looking for fresh lives and abundant land. In the late 1800s, this area in southeastern Colorado was filled with change. But into this arena of transition came one unassuming presence that would establish permanency to the county.[172]

John Wesley Prowers came to southeastern Colorado from Missouri as a temporary employee of Indian agent Robert Miller.

---

[171] Weglyn, *Years of Infamy*, 119.
[172] Betz, *Prowers County History*, 54.

Prowers worked out of Bent's New Fort for two months, trading and distributing food and clothing to the various tribes in the area. Soon Prowers had accomplished what he had been hired for and was faced with the dilemma of finding new employment. But he quickly found work with William Bent as a freighter of goods between the Midwest and Bent's Fort along the Santa Fe Trail.

After seven seasons under Bent's employment, Prowers met and married a fifteen-year-old Cheyenne Indian princess named Amache Ochinee.

Amache was the daughter of Lone Bear, a chief of the regional Cheyenne tribe. Prowers and his new bride took up ranching in the vast grazing lands of southeastern Colorado.[173]

In 1862, Prowers and his new bride—whom he called Amy—set up ranching operations along the Caddoa Creek with a hundred head of cattle and a stout bull. For the first few years of their marriage, Prowers and Amache lived the normal, happy life of any successful ranching family. But in 1864, the brutal murder of Amache's father rocked the young couple's world. Lone Bear and hundreds of other Cheyenne were slaughtered in what would become known as Colorado's Sand Creek Massacre.

Although Amache Ochinee lived with the despair and bitterness of her father's murder, she was able to successfully straddle the two worlds in which she lived. For the rest of her life, the stately woman Prowers had married endured the changing tides of western expansion and endeared herself to the countless settlers coming to the region while still remaining a proud Cheyenne.

The property Prowers owned and worked first began as a miniscule portion of the vast Kansas territory. But in 1870, the region was organized into Bent County. Then in 1888—five years after Prowers's death—Bent County was again broken into smaller and more manageable counties. This time, one of these counties was named after Prowers—the man whose career, as Colorado author Ava Betz notes,

---

[173] Betz, *Prowers County History*, 67.

"spanned the sunset of the trading era and the dawn of the ranching industry."[174]

Prowers's name would live on in the county that bore his name. The woman Prowers had called Amy would also leave a namesake. When Issei and Nisei were evacuated to Prowers County during World War II, the center they would be housed in would be called Amache. A rather dubious honor, considering the treatment Amache's Cheyenne family had received at the hands of the militia forces in 1864.[175]

Like the county itself, the towns found within Prowers County also have rich and colorful histories. The small village of Holly, located at the eastern edge of the county, began its existence as a ranch. First established by Hiram S. Holly around 1872, the site was a popular resting spot along the Santa Fe Trail. By the early twentieth century, Holly had become known around the state as an agricultural and manufacturing community. Wheat, broomcorn, oats, and alfalfa were some of Holly's major cash crops around the turn of the century and remained as such through the World War II era. Cattle ranching also remained a mainstay for the small community.

But it was the sugar beet industry that brought fame and fortune to the town of Holly. In 1905, a small sugar manufacturing firm opened a production plant at the south end of town and decided that its corporation would be well suited if named after the town. Over the next ten years, the Holly Sugar Corporation's sugar plant provided ample employment for residents of Prowers County. Area farmers also profited from the ready market Holly Sugar supplied. Many even converted from other cash crops to sugar beets to meet the demand.

But within a few years, Holly Corporation officials began seeking larger facilities outside Colorado and started dismantling their factory at Holly. By this time, however, farmers had found the raising of sugar beets as an attractive agricultural crop and would continue to raise the crop even after Holly had moved. In fact, it would be in

---

[174] Betz, *Prowers County History*, 72.
[175] Betz, *Prowers County History*, 67–68, 71–72.

the production of sugar beets that many Japanese American evacuees would find seasonal employment around southeastern Colorado.[176]

Like Holly, the nearby town of Wiley also played an important part in the events of Granada's relocation center. Twelve miles north of Lamar, Wiley and its outlying area had been known as an agricultural base from its early days of homesteading. Wiley was so well-known for its large sugar beet output in the early 1900s that it became the site of Wiley Sugar Beet Day—an annual fair designed to promote the agricultural output of this small community. It was this strong agricultural base that needed laborers in the desperate wartime economy of World War II.[177]

But no town in Prowers County was as well-known as Lamar. Like Holly and Wiley, agriculture and ranching played a large part in the development of this town. Lamar was settled in the late 1800s when a land office was established there to meet the needs of homesteaders moving to the region.

Hoping to finance the office (as well as a post office and a railway station) with government funds, land promoter I. R. Holmes named the site after L. Q. C. Lamar, secretary of the interior for President Grover Cleveland. Taking the bait, the secretary of the interior saw to it that Holmes received the necessary funding. Holmes established the Lamar Land Office in 1886, and the town of Lamar was begun.

Soon after, businesses, hotels, banks, and commercial establishments began popping up around the infant town. With the Santa Fe Railway going through the town, passenger trains also began transporting people from back east. Stage coach routes were established that transported people to nearby railheads and communities. Soon people were branching out from Lamar across southeastern Colorado like the spokes of a wagon wheel.[178]

Farmers who had already been homesteading nearby plots found ready markets for their crops in Lamar. Over the next several

---

[176] Betz, *Prowers County History*, 308, 310.
[177] Betz, *Prowers County History*, 379.
[178] Betz, *Prowers County History*, 190–191.

decades, Lamar saw the development of such agricultural industries as the Lamar Milling and Elevator plant, the Lamar Sugar factory, and several dairies and creameries. At one point, Lamar even had an ice plant that harvested and stored ice for summer use.

When Japanese Americans began arriving in the fall of 1942, the towns of Lamar, Holly, and Wiley benefited greatly from the sudden influx of people. Town fathers quickly realized the impact an overnight community of over six thousand potential customers and laborers would have on retail establishments. Farmers saw a ready and highly qualified labor pool that would bolster a sagging wartime supply.

Oski Taniwaki touched on this subject in a letter to an outside source in January 1943. Taniwaki noted:

> The relocation of the Japanese to Colorado has been a "Godsent" gift to the hundreds of farmers, particularly in the sugar beet districts. The evacuee laborers have aided in the harvesting of this essential product. In the region of Denver, Pueblo, and particularly in the southeastern part of the state surrounding the location of the colony center, these farmers who have employed Japanese labor, frankly admitted that their relationship has been of first-class rating. It has been reported that, since the standards of living of the majority of the Japanese were much higher than those formerly hired by these farmers, the evacuee laborers have contributed to the improvement of working conditions and housing facilities in general. We are in receipt of many letters of appreciation for the excellent work done by evacuee laborers everywhere.[179]

---

[179] Oski Taniwaki, letter to C. E. Toothaker, 21 January 1943, 293:0011 L2.01, Japanese American evacuation and resettlement records, BANC MSS 67/ 14, the Bancroft Library, University of California, Berkeley.

The farming of southwestern Colorado benefited from the influx of Japanese Americans. But no other Prowers County community prospered more than the small hamlet of Granada. With its proximity lying less than a mile from the relocation center, the town and farmers of Granada gained a lot from the influx of several thousand new residents. Referring to the town of Granada, Taniwaki noted:

> On the subject of community, Granada is a small town, located on the northern border of Amache Colony, having a population of approximately 350. This town has about ten stores of a general nature and the boys from the center have ample opportunity to go there for shopping purposes in the course of their day's work. Frankly, we would say that the money spent by the evacuees at this town is supporting the merchants of this "would-be forsaken" village.[180]

Granada began its existence in 1873 when the Atchison, Topeka and Santa Fe Railway—graced with a federal grant to expand its railroad line to the Colorado territory—built a line to what was thought to be the Colorado border. The surveyor who had determined that point was wrong, and the state line would later be established farther east at Sergeant, Kansas. Nevertheless, an end-of-the-line community called Grenada (known today as Old Granada) soon became a thriving town of over 1,500 residents.

By 1876—the year of statehood—the town had become the county's second-largest community. With its access to the Santa Fe Trail and situated along the New Goodnight Trail, large numbers of homesteaders, buffalo hunters, and cattlemen began passing through, and staying in, the bustling town of Grenada. Frontier men and women relied heavily on Grenada's merchants, saloons, hotels, and dance halls for the "necessities" of life. Cattle drives to Grenada's

---

[180] Taniwaki, letter to C. E. Toothaker.

Santa Fe Railway stockyards were also a regular occurrence, often providing wild nights from passing cowpunchers.

However, Grenada's boom days began to slip away when the Atchison, Topeka and Santa Fe Railway extended their tracks westward to the city of Las Animas. As the end of the line moved westward, so, too, did many of the people who lived in or frequented the frontier town. The town also received a blow when well-known businessman Fred Harvey bought the territory surrounding the town as grazing land for his cattle stock. Without further room to grow, the city's fathers began to feel pinched.

The town's leaders were forced to move the town site of Grenada to a more open area suitable for expansion. In 1886, only thirteen years after its inception, the town was dismantled and hauled three miles west to its current site on Wolf Creek. Sensing a new lease on life, the town's fathers changed the name of their community to Granada. Yet the population of Granada would never again reach that found in its earlier days of glory. Businesses in the town changed with the ebb and flow of the times—often struggling to survive on a small clientele of farmers and ranchers. In the end, it would be agriculture and ranching—the mainstays of southeastern Colorado—that would provide the sustenance for Granada.[181]

In the fall of 1942, Granada and other communities around Prowers County were preparing for the relocation of Japanese Americans into their midst. Bruce Newman recalls his father borrowing "something like $500" to expand the drugstore he owned. Never having borrowed money before, Newman's father knew the impact such a large concentration of people could have on his business and planned big.

Newman recounts how his father arranged to get the biggest building in town—a building located on Main Street and US 50. "He arranged to get this building and constructed a soda fountain in the back," Newman recounts. "My father also managed to obtain the last truckload of sake from the West Coast."[182]

---

[181] Betz, *Prowers County History*, 52–55, 66.
[182] Bruce Newman, personal interview, 18 May 2000.

In September 1942, all whiskey and gin production had been stopped to convert machines to the production of alcohol for the war effort. A total of 128 distilleries were converted to produce over 476 million gallons of alcohol to use in butadiene, smokeless powders, and other wartime materials. This stoppage of commercial alcohol severely limited the amount of alcoholic beverages that could be sold.

Taking what he could from a supplier in Seattle, Newman's father stocked up on alcohol he thought he could use for sale to the evacuees. "We had a small warehouse behind the store where we put this sake. I remember vividly having to unload all of that and stamping it. In those days you had to hand stamp each bottle with a government stamp. It was really quite a job getting ready."[183]

In preparation for the building of the center, the nearby town of Lamar also became abuzz with activity. Lt. William "Bill" Curtis of the US Army Corps of Engineers at Albuquerque was the first noticeable presence of a relocation center to arrive at Lamar. On arrival, Curtis and a handful of employees moved desks, furniture, and office supplies into a temporary office located at the state armory building in town. Desks and blankets, mattresses and tables were taken daily to an old, abandoned grocery store.[184]

Curtis and his crew immediately began to coordinate surveying teams to lay out the camp. Private contractors from the Midwest, Colorado, and Texas in search of profitable earnings also descended on Lamar. During the remaining days of June, the Army Corps of Engineers traveled to Granada and Lamar, taking bids on the various components needed for the center. By the end of the month, the bidding dust had cleared with three major contractors taking the lion's share of the pot. Two Texas firms—Lambie, Moss, Little, and James of Amarillo, and P and S Construction Company of Houston—were awarded the building and utility contracts. Foley Electrical Company of Dodge City, Kansas, took the bid for electrical work.[185]

---

[183] Newman, interview; *Rocky Mountain News*, 1 September 1942, 1.
[184] *Lamar Daily News*, 19 June 1942, 1; 20 June 1942, 1.
[185] *Lamar Daily News*, 19 June 1942, 1; 30 June 1942, 1; 6 July 1942, 1.

Center construction began immediately. On June 29, carpenters and electricians, plumbers and laborers descended on Granada. With a deadline of August 31, a crew of nearly 1,200 frantically worked night and day to get the camp ready for occupation. The town of Granada and the construction site became a blur of activity.[186]

Bruce Newman recalls that when the crews came, things changed for the town:

> They were a big bunch of people on flatbed trucks. They set up saw mills near the rail yards and would build the wall sections in town and then transport them out on flatbed trucks to the camp. They did this until they could get workshops and electricity out there. I seem to remember the crews living in tents until the walls could be constructed. While the walls were being built in Granada, they were building water storage tanks, sewage systems, and digging wells out at the camp... They were going day and night.[187]

The *Lamar Register* reported that "much activity is in progress at our local construction site. The work is now reaching a point where it will 'make a showing.'"[188]

Soon, bars and restaurants in Lamar and Granada began to feel the effects of the sudden surge of people. Vacant homes and apartments began filling up with WRA workers and army personnel. WRA officials set up temporary offices in Lamar until more permanent quarters could be erected at the center. Bars and restaurants were suddenly filled with workers and laborers. Even the Lamar jail found a new and ample supply of visitors.

The construction of the site was the responsibility of the Army Corps of Engineers. But the coordination of facilities was under the

---

[186] *Lamar Daily News*, 7 July 1942, 1.
[187] Newman, interview.
[188] *Lamar Register*, 22 July 1942, 1.

watch of the WRA. To coordinate the task, the WRA appointed levelheaded James Lindley as director of Granada's relocation center. A native of Moberly, Missouri, Lindley had earned an undergraduate degree from the University of Oregon and a metallurgical engineering degree from the University of Arizona. Before coming to Granada, Lindley had also served as the chief engineer for the southwestern division of the Soil Conservation Service at Albuquerque.[189]

Lindley first visited the relocation site in July 1942 as land was being cleared of vegetation. Although officially stationed in Denver, Lindley set up headquarters in Lamar in July and August. His initial tasks were to hire employees and to serve as go-between to the Army Corps of Engineers.

But throughout the process of construction, Lindley had little say in how the camp should be set up. Lindley later bemoaned the fact that:

> attempts to incorporate changes felt desirable met with little or no response from the Army Engineers. A few minor changes were made such as the addition of partitions in the administrative offices and additional toilet facilities in the offices. The elimination of the proposed barbed wire fence between the evacuee quarters and the administrative area was also effected. As a compromise, a barbed wire fence was built entirely around the Military Police area.[190]

Other than these compromises, however, the Army Corps of Engineers followed their initial plans for the internment camp.

Indeed, with the arrival of the detachment of 134 enlisted men and 3 officers of the 335th MP Escort Guard Company on August 20, the center began to look more and more like an evacuation center.

---

[189] *Lamar Daily News*, 8 July 1942, 1.
[190] James Lindley, "Granada Relocation Center Final Report," 15 November 1945, 1, Special Collections: Schulz Center; University of California, Berkeley.

These enlisted men and officers would be responsible for maintaining the outer guard around the center. Evacuees would be responsible for establishing their own internal security force.[191]

By the end of August, the basic infrastructure of the internment camp was finally set up. Where sagebrush once grew, there were now rudimentary army barracks, fences, and guards. At a final cost of $4.2 million, a new roughly hewn city now stood awaiting the arrival of its residents.[192]

The barren windblown desert around Granada was about to take on a new role—a role that would impact the community—and the country—for generations to come.

---

[191] Lindley, "Granada Relocation Center Final Report," 2.
[192] Joyce E. Williams and Alice M. Coleman, *Lest We Forget* (East Rockaway: Cummings and Hathaway, 1992), 72.

Auraria Library Archives—Joseph McClelland Collection

The vast Arkansas River Valley of southeastern Colorado was viewed by WRA Officials as the perfect spot for one of the ten relocation centers.

Amache Historical Site Archives—Kameoka Collection

Dillon Myer's way station—the Granada Relocation Center

Amache Historical Site Archives—Fujita Collection

Internees were allowed only the bare necessities. The first wave of internees arrived early to help with the infrastructure of the camp.

Auraria Library Archives—Joseph McClelland Collection

In the early stages of Amache, only dirt and lumber lined the barracks. Evacuees who planted trees and gardens gradually turned these bleak surroundings into a livable state.

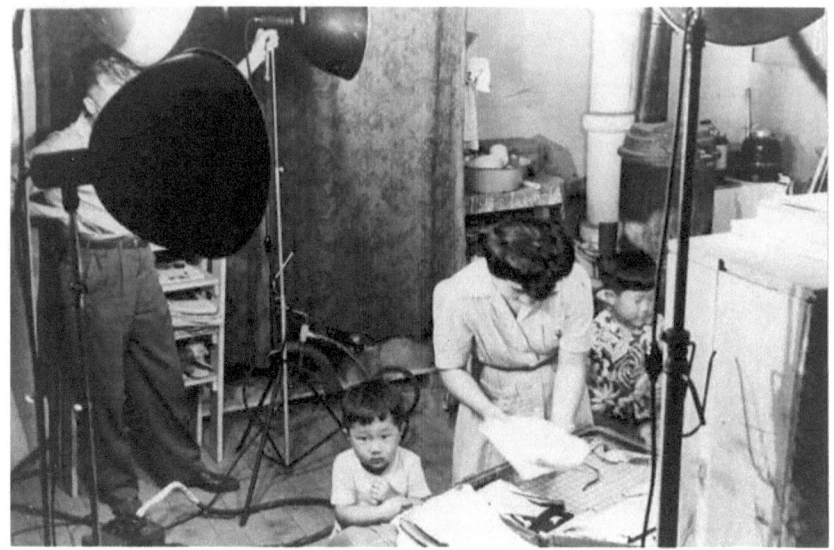

Auraria Library Archives—Joseph McClelland Collection

A look inside a typical evacuee "apartment." WRA photos were often staged to show various aspects of the camp in a more favorable light.

Amache Historical Site Archives—Kameoka Collection

Onlookers watch the inspection of the camp's fire equipment.

Amache Historical Site Archives—Ochikubo Collection

The high school at Amache held the largest concentration of students in southeastern Colorado.

Amache Historical Site Archives—Kameoka Collection

A graduating class filing into what Dillon Myer called "the most publicized and most famous high school in the United States."

Amache Historical Site Archives—Ochikubo Collection

Driving winds sweeping down from the valley forced snow and cold through the cracks of hastily constructed barracks.

Auraria Library Archives—Joseph McClelland Collection

Night falls at Amache. The guard towers that surrounded the center were said to protect those persons who would live inside its gates.

AMACHE

Amache Historical Site Archives—Kameoka Collection

In planting victory gardens, internees demonstrated their ability and patriotism in growing a wide variety of crops in the sandy soil of southeastern Colorado.

Auraria Library Archives—Joseph McClelland Collection

Determined to make the most of their experience, some evacuees turned the dry, wind-blown soil into beautiful Japanese gardens. In recent archaeological digs, Granada High School students have unearthed the garden shown.

CHAPTER 4

THE DESERT "WAY STATION"

"It was ugly," Tom Shigekuni recalls of his trip to Granada. "They put us on a train and pulled the shades down. They took us from Santa Anita, down through the center of LA, right by the Sears and Roebuck building, through the rail yards, and then up toward Utah, Wyoming, and then brought us back into Colorado... They didn't want us to look out. I don't know why—maybe they didn't want the Americans to see us or us to see the Americans. I don't know."[193]

The first carload of evacuees left the Merced assembly center on August 24 at 6:00 p.m. to help aid in the preparation of the camp. Over the next several days, larger numbers of evacuees from the Merced and Santa Anita assembly centers would begin their long, arduous journey by rail to Granada.

Through the deserts of the southwest, over the Rocky Mountains, and into Colorado traveled fathers and infants, toddlers and mothers, young boys and teenage girls. Each had experienced his or her own personal tragedies. Each was heading for a place they had never heard of or had never been to—a place that, for most, would be home for the next several years. Many had never been out

---

[193] Shigekuni, interview.

of California. Indeed, some had never even been out of their hometowns of Los Angeles, Sacramento, Walnut Grove, or Merced.

These men and women, like those headed for other centers around the country, were unsure of what lay ahead. On leaving the assembly centers, some were handed sandwiches and sack lunches by church volunteers. Some had been provided with an extra portion of food by the mess hall chefs. But these small gestures were the only niceties given for an otherwise frightening journey.

The trip itself was unpleasant. Each evacuee was instructed to pull down the shades of the windows at their assigned seats. Because of conspiracy theories, the military was leery of Japanese Americans viewing the industrial sections of the cities they passed through. Some, like Shigekuni, were told to leave the shades drawn throughout the entire length of the trip. Others were told it was only necessary while going through towns.

"I don't know what they thought we would see," says George Hirano. "We went through the most desolate parts of the country. Besides, never having been out of Sausalito, I wouldn't know what to look for anyway."[194]

The route the evacuees took was determined by which rail line had the least amount of military and commercial traffic. Some traveled through Utah, Wyoming, and Colorado, while others traveled more southerly routes. Robert Ichikawa recalls that after saying his goodbyes to the people at Santa Anita, he and his family boarded a train and headed along a southern route that passed by the Salton Sea and into Arizona and New Mexico before reaching Colorado.[195]

But no matter what route was taken, the trip to Granada usually took about three days and three nights to complete. Under normal circumstances, the trip from California to Colorado took far less time, but heavy war traffic forced the low-priority evacuee trains to sidetrack to allow those carrying materials and troops to pass. Some train personnel allowed their passengers to step off the trains—under the careful watch of the armed military guards—to stretch weary

---

[194] Hirano, G., interview.
[195] Ichikawa, letter.

muscles and to fill tired lungs with fresh air. These stops happened usually once or twice daily and only in remote, uninhabited areas.

Many, however, were not afforded this option. Forced to remain onboard for the entire duration of the trip, George Hirano remembers his ride east as a wretched experience. "We were never allowed to get off the train. I never looked out—just a law-abiding citizen." In addition, Hirano recalls that the train he traveled on was a locomotive driven by coal. "The soot would come back into our area so bad and fill our clothes and noses. We would blow our noses, and it would be black. Of course, we couldn't wash. And it was very hot. Three days of going—but not always moving—it was miserable."[196]

Like Hirano, Henry Okubo remembers his trip as being "very hot… We had to open the windows for air, but every time we did that, soot from the train's engine would come back at us."[197]

Between each car of the train—in the connecting area—stood one armed military guard who attempted to monitor any evacuee movements between cars. Guards also surrounded the platforms of every depot stop along the way. "I don't know where they thought we would go if we escaped." Okubo laughs. "We were usually in the middle of nowhere."[198]

Each train had a Caucasian doctor and two nurses onboard to take care of medical emergencies. The long, hot trip was difficult for the aged who were forced to endure the trip. Some who had been bedridden before their evacuation were under constant medical supervision throughout the ride to Amache. According to articles in the *Lamar Daily News*, every trainload of evacuees had persons who needed medical attention. Some were even rushed to the camp hospital or hospitals in surrounding communities. Evacuees must have wondered why such aged or invalid people would have ever been considered a "threat to national security."[199]

Both Pullman and passenger cars were used to transport evacuees from Merced and Santa Anita to Granada. Elderly people or

---

[196] Hirano, G., interview.
[197] Okubo, interview.
[198] Okubo, interview.
[199] *Lamar Daily News*, 8 September 1942, 1.

invalids were assigned to Pullman cars in which sleeping quarters and more comfortable surroundings were provided. Mothers and fathers with small children were also assigned to Pullman cars. All others were given seats in passenger cars. Those assigned to passenger cars were forced to remain in the rigid, upright seats to which they had been assigned. Sleeping was difficult. Travel was monotonous. Uncertain of their destination, evacuees were given no other choice but to sit and wait until the journey's end.

As a young girl, Shigeko Hirano was among those being transported to Amache. "We were put into these old—I don't know what kind of trains they were—they must have been out of service to the regular public, I don't know. They were very old and dirty. It was early September, and it was very hot."[200]

Hirano remembers distinctly the continual cries of infants. Toddlers were fussing. The elderly were uncomfortable.

> They kept telling us we couldn't look out the windows—you know all the shades were pulled. But you know these young kids would peek when the guards weren't looking. Then we would say to them "What, what's out there?" and they would say "It looks like desert. There's nothing out there. Maybe we're in Texas." We were just trying to figure out where we were going… Finally after three days, the train stopped and they said we were there… A bunch of evacuees had gone there before us and they said, "Welcome to Colorado." We said, "Oh, we're in Colorado."[201]

The general condition of the trains was usually old and worn. "They looked like they were just brought out of the moth balls," recounts Art Yorimoto. Indeed, they may have been. With the additional demand to transport military troops across the country, the

---

[200] Hirano, S., interview.
[201] Hirano, S., interview.

United States was forced to use whatever transportation they could during the war years.[202]

It was not unusual to find military troops being transported on the same trains as evacuees in the fall of 1942. Tom Shigekuni holds that the uniformed soldiers on these trains "seemed to be okay. I didn't really know where they were going. I saw them in the dining cars mostly. They weren't hostile or anything—I didn't see hostility of any kind by the soldiers. I mean, I wouldn't say they were nice to us, but they didn't bother us either. We were so used to being harassed in L.A. that I guess they just seemed okay."[203]

Meals were served to soldiers and evacuees alike in the elegant environment of the Pullman dining cars. These dining cars were in severe contrast to the hot, fly-infested assembly mess halls the evacuees had just left. "It was the first time I had ever eaten with white tablecloths and candles on the table," remarks Shigekuni. "It was really first class. But I guess there was no other way to feed us. It was quite an experience to ride on a train and eat in Pullman cars with real chinaware and with porters serving us. I thought I was really living."[204]

The first contingent of Japanese Americans from Merced arrived at Granada's station at ten forty on August 27, 1942. The majority of this group of 212 evacuees was male—only 19 women and 1 child were present. Included within this number were 36 hospital workers, 82 laborers, and 51 mess hall workers.

Due to the need for qualified workers, this first group was forced to prepare the camp for those who would follow. Lindley recalled, "This group was hand-picked at the assembly center and was composed of artisans, stenographers, clerks, cooks, and other specialists who would help the WRA organization prepare the center for the arrival of the main group."[205]

Fumiye and Tono Nishizaki were among this first contingent. "We were chosen to go first, because I didn't have any children,"

---

[202] Yorimoto, A., interview.
[203] Shigekuni, interview.
[204] Shigekuni, interview.
[205] *Lamar Daily News*, 25 August 1942, 1; Lindley, "Final Report," 2.

Fumiye Nishizaki remembers. "And the single people were also selected on the first contingent to go there—because Amache wasn't finished yet. The windows weren't in. So, the wind was just blowing and the sand was coming in. And, you know, it was a horrible place. But later on, the evacuees planted trees and it was much better. But at first it was very hard."[206]

"We were the very first ones," Nishizaki continues. "There were very few women. Myself and another couple, maybe two or three other couples. I don't know why, but we were selected to go. The men folk were helping put the windows up… They did a lot of things like that—set up the place so the others could come."[207]

Evacuees were immediately assigned to tasks of transporting supplies, unloading trucks, building tables and furniture, and preparing the camp's barracks, mess halls, and hospital. In addition to these tasks, the evacuees were also trained to check in and acclimate the next few contingents.

Of this initial group, Lindley would later complain that "although this group contained some good people who were of help to the organization, a great deal too much stress seemed to have been put on recreational activities. The majority of the group seemed to feel that their main function was to provide entertainment, games and other outlets for the many idle hours that they evidently, and rightly, envisioned."[208]

On September 3, the second trainload of evacuees—the first regular contingent—arrived at Granada. Between September 3 and September 18, eight trainloads of evacuees arrived at the Granada train station from Merced. Each carload of evacuees was slowly drawn onto a sidetrack where evacuees were taken off one carload at a time. Under the ever-present eye of the military police (MPs), evacuees disembarked the train at the station, and WRA officials verified the presence of each evacuee with the train's passenger list. Caucasian doctors and nurses were also present at each new arrival

---

[206] Nishizaki, interview.
[207] Nishizaki, interview.
[208] Lindley, "Final Report," 2.

to treat emergency medical needs. Once everyone was accounted for, the list was signed by the commanding officer in charge and by James G. Lindley, Granada project director.

Through late August and early September, evacuees arrived from the west. By September 18, 4,492 Merced evacuees had arrived at Granada's train station. Then on September 19, the flow of evacuees from Merced stopped, and evacuees from Santa Anita began to arrive. In all, six trains from Santa Anita arrived at Granada between September 19 and September 30, depositing 2,942 evacuees. Each trainload that arrived from Merced and Santa Anita carried between 452 and 557 evacuees. By the end of October, 7,567 Japanese Americans had passed through the train station at Granada on their way to the WRA relocation center.[209]

After verification proceedings were complete, Issei and Nisei and the few possessions they had with them were loaded onto WRA flatbed trucks or MP trucks, school buses, or anything else that could be scrounged for the move to the center. George Hirano recalls, "We had to climb up on the trucks and stand while they threw our belongings up to us. If you could make an analogy, I guess it would be very much like if you took cows or sheep and you put them on a truck and shoved them all together."[210]

Evacuees were loaded on trucks and buses and taken to the WRA project site—less than a mile east of town—where they and their belongings were dropped off for check-in procedures. Project Director Lindley recalls that "trains arrived, usually at night; lighting facilities were extremely sketchy, and families stumbled around in the dark, individuals often falling into excavations when being led to their quarters. Candles, with their ever-present fire hazard in this city of cardboard homes, were their only light."[211]

Once at the camp, a WRA employee met with evacuees to coordinate living arrangements for those families wishing to live next to

---

[209] James Lindley, "Quarterly Report," 30 June–30 September 1942, 3–4, 288:0123 Ll.08, Japanese American evacuation and resettlement records, BANC MSS 67/14c, the Bancroft Library, University of California, Berkeley.
[210] Hirano, G., interview.
[211] Lindley, "Final Report," 1–2.

one another and those who had no such preference. Evacuees were next given medical checkups. At this point, families were separated by males of each household going to a temporary housing station for apartment assignment, and women and children going to a laundry room to wait.

Job-placement recruiters also set up tables in the laundry room. These recruiters attempted to recruit workers for jobs found in mess halls and medical services—those jobs in need of workers immediately.

At the temporary housing stations, those considered the head of each household—mostly fathers or the oldest male in the family—were issued a registration form duplicated, as much as possible, from the previous train roster. Once the name, sex, and age of all family members were verified or listed, evacuee families were again reunited and assigned living quarters. Personal baggage, boxes, and other possessions—which had been thrown from the trucks on arrival at the projects gate—could now be claimed. Camp personnel were originally to place all evacuee belongings neatly into stacks based on the evacuees' railroad car number. However, most evacuees found their luggage randomly tossed in haphazard, unorganized heaps. Heavier possessions were often left by the rail sidings in Granada and transported later to the evacuee quarters.

Once registration was complete and the evacuees had claimed their luggage, an escort was assigned to walk each family to their newly assigned quarters called apartments. In all, the entire induction process usually took approximately two or three hours to complete.[212]

Dillon Myer felt his work in the WRA was important to the lives of evacuees. In his opinion, the camps he operated were not prison camps in any way, shape, or form. They were, instead, "way stations" in which Nisei evacuees could find food and basic shelter until they could resettle into outside communities. And for the Issei, the camps were protection from the "discrimination and race-baiting" found in communities from which they had come. In later years, Myer would

---

[212] Lindley, "Quarterly Report," 3–4; Hirano, G., interview.

even say the evacuees looked on the centers as "havens of rest and security."²¹³

To this end, crews constructed Myer's "way station" in Granada through the summer of 1942. Evacuees began to arrive in August and September. But on their arrival, many did not see the same way station that Dillon Myer had envisioned.

Tom Shigekuni remembers, "When I first saw Granada, I thought 'My God, is this it, or is this just another rest stop.' I had never seen such a desolate place in all my life. There just seemed to be no one living there. But after a while I realized there wouldn't be any one there to hassle us like they did back home, so that part of it would be okay."²¹⁴

Chez Momii is haunted by her first exposure to the project. Momii's first thoughts were "'Oh my God, we are going to live here?' It was so stark and desolate. We were so far removed from civilization."²¹⁵

Momii also recounts the arrival of her friend, Lilly Otera:

> For some reason my friend wasn't on the same train. She came a day latter, and I knew she was coming, so I met the truck when they unloaded. It was in a dust storm. Oh my gosh, her face was packed with sand and mud. Our mess halls and laundry rooms and bathrooms were not finished yet, so I had just a bucket of water in my barracks to wash her face and arms. She said, "It's no use. I have to go back outside to get to my barracks across the street." You know, being from L.A. and southern California, everything is green and the weather is nice most of the time—that was a shock.²¹⁶

---

[213] Myer, *Uprooted Americans*, 291–292.
[214] Higekuni, interview.
[215] Momii, interview.
[216] Momii, interview.

Even more of a shock was that evacuees were often moving into their barracks as carpenters were still pounding nails. Only 90 percent of basic infrastructures—items such as the sewer system, pumping systems, roads, and electrical system—had been completed. At their arrival, evacuees found only 80 percent of the center's hospital construction had been completed, while only twenty blocks had latrines, showers, and laundry rooms.

In some cases, the evacuees had to temporarily stay in overcrowded quarters until carpenters and electricians could complete their assigned rooms.

Many had to eat in cramped mess halls as only half were finished. Lindley noted that during this period, "One mess hall served as many as four blocks, 1,000 to 1,200 people, serving in three or four shifts."[217]

Matters became even more complicated when, for the first several weeks, the medical department would not designate the water in the center's tanks as potable. During this time, evacuees were forced to ration the water supply that was carted by water truck from the town of Granada. Of course, water for latrine use didn't matter, for most of the plumbing to block latrines had not yet been made. Lindley noted, "The toilets in the wash rooms were used before the water connections were made and a clean-up squad was necessary to clean up the attendant litter."[218]

For those who lived in blocks that lacked plumbing and latrines, outhouses were constructed at the rear of their blocks. Henry Okubo recalls, "When we first got there, they only had outhouses for us. I remember they were located right behind my barrack. After they got the latrines fixed up and they took away the outhouses, it was always a joke among the farmers that the corn would grow higher where the outhouses once stood. You could look out and see a difference in the height of the corn where the out-houses used to be."[219]

---

[217] Lindley, "Quarterly Report," 3–4; Lindley, "Final Report," 1–2.
[218] Lindley, "Final Report," 2.
[219] Okubo, interview.

Those who had usable latrines fared little better than those who did not. One evacuee recalls the situation in the men's toilets as "twelve guys sitting on the pot and thirty guys waiting to get in. It was a pretty ugly situation. There were just six pots in two rows, each sitting back to back."[220]

Little privacy was provided in these communal latrines. Harry Shironaka recalls, "In the men's latrine, the seats were partitioned off, but it was an automatic flush toilet. Every so often, the water came through and would take care of everyone down the drain."[221]

Shironaka adds that trips to the bathrooms at night and in the winter could be extremely uncomfortable. "If you had to go in the middle of the night when it was snowing, you just went unless you had a bucket in your room." The lack of heaters in the latrines added to the misery of these nocturnal trips to the bathroom.[222]

From Project Director Lindley's point of view, the rushed opening of the camp at Granada was a miscalculation, for he felt that "a little resentment was added to minds already filled with fear, hatred, and frustration. A little common sense in delaying the movement from the assembly centers until the relocation center was ready might have resulted in more cooperation and better understanding from the evacuees."[223]

Attempting to speed up construction of mess halls, latrines, and laundry facilities, fifty evacuees were hired as laborers by the camp's contractors. These evacuees worked the same intense hours as non-Japanese employees and were paid a similar wage. However, due to labor union contracts, only a select few were hired for construction. Evacuees were only used if no Caucasians could be found to do the work.[224]

Some evacuees also left camp immediately to work on indefinite or seasonal leaves. By October 8, 1942—a little more than a

---

[220] Shigekuni, interview.
[221] Shironaka, interview.
[222] Shironaka, interview.
[223] Lindley, "Final Report," 2.
[224] *Lamar Daily News*, 8 September 1942, 1.

month after the camp's opening—more than a thousand evacuees had gained employment outside the camp.

Others chose to remain within the camp to work or wait for better employment opportunities. Those who stayed created rudimentary living conditions by stuffing mattresses with straw, setting up cots, and hauling coal to their new living quarters.

By the end of September 1942, over 7,400 Japanese Americans had entered Amache's gates. Life at Dillon Myer's way station in Granada, Colorado, had begun.

Granada's relocation center was one of five types of governmentally controlled camps used to imprison Japanese Americans during World War II.

The first type was the assembly center where evacuees were sent immediately after removal from their homes. These centers were designed as holding areas housing evacuees until more permanent quarters could be constructed.

The second type of camp was an internment camp. Several of these camps dotted the west and south in areas like Santa Fe, New Mexico; Crystal City, Texas; Fort Lincoln, North Dakota; and Fort Missoula, Montana. Internment camps were run by the Department of Justice and had as their primary purpose the housing of enemy aliens considered risks to national security. The residents of these camps, totaling nearly seven thousand Japanese Americans, were never given the opportunity of relocation to outside areas.

The next type of camp was a segregation center that housed those deemed disloyal to the American government. Opening in late 1943, the WRA's only segregation camp was housed at the converted relocation camp of Tule Lake. Those evacuees considered "disloyal" or who answered the 1943 loyalty questionnaire negatively was transferred from the other relocation camps to Tule Lake.

A fourth type of camp was an isolation center that housed evacuees who resisted the authoritative styles of the relocation centers. The isolation center began on December 10, 1942, and was originally situated at Moab, Utah, at a former CCC camp. In early 1943, the camp was moved to an abandoned Navajo boarding school at the Leupp reservation in Arizona.

The final type of camp was the type of site located at Granada—a relocation center. There were ten such centers located in the seven states of California, Arizona, Utah, Idaho, Wyoming, Arkansas, and Colorado. In reality, relocation centers were—by their very nature—war concentration camps in which the majority of enemy nationals and Japanese Americans evacuated from the coast were held until the end of World War II. However, the WRA used the terminology of relocation center to give the appearance of temporary stations.[225]

Relocation camps were operated by the WRA and housed populations ranging from 7,500 to over 20,000 evacuees. However, the populations of these centers were somewhat fluid in nature because of the various work opportunities evacuees were offered outside.

Two of these ten relocation centers were in California. The Manzanar center, located north of Los Angeles in the Owens Valley, had a population of over ten thousand Japanese Americans. Manzanar began as an assembly center in 1942 and was converted to a relocation center in the summer of the same year.

Tule Lake, California's other relocation center, was located just south of the Oregon border in an immense dry lake bed and had a population that ranged upward to over eighteen thousand evacuees. In 1943, the center was converted from a relocation center to a segregation center that housed those evacuees from other relocation centers who were considered disloyal. Evacuees from Tule Lake who were considered loyal were given the opportunity to relocate to the Jerome relocation center in Arkansas or Colorado's Granada relocation center.[226]

Arizona also had two relocation centers located within its borders. The Gila River relocation center was situated in the southern portion of Arizona, just southeast of Phoenix. Although the center was known for its excessive heat and arid conditions, it was also the site of an extensive and productive farming program. In late April 1943, Gila River gained national notoriety when Eleanor Roosevelt

---

[225] Japanese American National Museum, *Japanese American History*, 8.
[226] Page Smith, *Democracy on Trial: The Japanese American Evacuation and Relocation in World War II* (New York: Simon & Schuster, 1995), 28–32.

visited the center to investigate charges that Japanese Americans were being "pampered."[227]

Poston, the other Arizona relocation center, was located on the Colorado Indian reservation just east of the California border. Also known as the Colorado River relocation center, the camp had the largest amount of acreage as well as one of the largest populations of interned Japanese Americans. Poston was managed by the Office of Indian Affairs until late 1943 and, as such, was the only relocation center not specifically managed by the WRA. Frank and Terrie Masamori, Japanese Americans who were evacuated to Poston, note that the heat and dust storms at Poston made life unbearable. Terrie recalls, "[Japanese Americans] make the best of every situation and try to make a better life afterwards... It happened and we made the best of it."[228]

Like California and Arizona, Arkansas also had two camps within its borders. The Rohwer relocation center in southeastern Arkansas was known for its hot, swampy living conditions. Arkansas's other relocation center, Jerome, was also a hot marshlike environment not known for its agricultural endeavors. Both Rohwer and Jerome had populations of just over eight thousand evacuees.

The other four states—Idaho, Utah, Wyoming, and Colorado—each had one relocation center located within their states' boundaries. Idaho's center—the Minidoka relocation center—was located in the southern portion of the state and had a population of just under ten thousand evacuees. Minidoka was known for its severe dust storms, frigid winters, and extreme summer temperatures.

Like Minidoka, Heart Mountain (Wyoming's relocation center) and Topaz (Utah's relocation center) were also known as locations where extreme weather conditions severely affected the lives of its evacuees. The populations of these two camps were over ten thousand and over eight thousand evacuees, respectively.[229]

---

[227] *Rocky Mountain News*, 27 April 1943, 5.
[228] "Amache: Patriotism Amidst Prejudice," Masamori taped interview.
[229] Smith, *Democracy on Trial*, 28–32.

Colorado's Granada relocation center was the smallest of all the centers. Its location amid the farm and ranch lands of southeastern Colorado made it one of the more agriculturally productive sites belonging to the WRA.

The site of the Granada relocation center overlooked the bottomlands of the Arkansas River. Situated atop an elevated portion of land about one mile southwest of the town of Granada, the site had previously been inhabited by grazing cattle, turtles, jackrabbits, rattlesnakes, and a handful of ranchers and farmers. Although most of the 10,500 acres of farmland purchased by the WRA consisted of a rich clay-type soil suitable for farming and grazing, the soil at the relocation center site was heavily laden with sand.

The Granada relocation center and all the land owned by the WRA surrounded the small town of Granada on the north, east, and west sides. Of the project's 10,500 acres, 5,000 acres would be devoted to farming operations, while over 4,500 acres would be devoted to grazing and other nonproductive idle uses. The remainder of the project's land—roughly one square mile—would be used for the relocation center in which the Japanese evacuees themselves would live.

Granada's relocation center's layout was much like the layout of the other relocation centers. Resembling an army base more than a temporary city, the center was surrounded by four-strand, double-barbed-wire fencing placed on fir posts spaced about ten feet apart. Six seven-by-seven-foot octagon-shaped watchtowers were placed at even intervals around the center. These towers—standing sixteen feet above the ground—included just enough room for one guard and a searchlight.

There were two basic portions of the camp—an operations area and a housing area. The first area—the operations area—sat at the northern part of the center and contained the administration section, a warehouse section, the center's hospital, and MP barracks. The other portion—the housing area—sat at the southern part of the camp and contained divided sections similar to city blocks on which evacuee living quarters were situated.[230]

---

[230] Lindley, "Final Report," appendix II.

AMACHE

The main gate of the center was located at the north end of the center in the operations area. Just inside this gate was a small twelve-by-twenty-foot gatehouse by which evacuees and visitors alike were made to check in. Also, by the front gate stood MP barracks and the staff mess hall. Across the street from the MP barracks was the project's farm division, transportation division, and supply offices.

Also located in the operations area was the main administration section. Consisting of three blocks, this area was just south of the main gate. The administration section included the center's post office, relocation office, employment division, office of welfare, fire department, motor pool, and administrative buildings. The center's small eleven-by-fifteen-foot two-pump gas station, as well as an eighty-by-twenty-foot garage were also in this area. A portion of the administrative area was also set aside for the housing needs of WRA staff who lived on-site.

At the northwest corner of the camp sat fifteen forty-by-one-hundred-foot warehouses where mess supplies, personal belongings, motor pool equipment, and other supplies necessary for the operation of the camp were stored. One of these warehouse buildings was reserved for use as an evacuee-operated tofu factory. At the far west end of the warehouse section was a thirty-by-ninety-seven-foot root cellar which included two twenty-by-one-hundred-foot walk-in refrigeration plants, a twenty-by-twenty-foot carpenter shop, the camp's butcher house, and the offices of the center's biweekly newspaper.[231]

At the northeastern corner of the operational area sat the center's largest complex—the hospital. Granada's relocation center hospital was typical of most army-style complexes in construction. It consisted of seventeen wings and employed hundreds of evacuees. Housing over 150 beds, the hospital was able to accommodate the majority of the camp's medical cases.

Behind, or to the south, of the operational area of the center was the housing area. This portion of the camp was divided into thirty-four blocks and was primarily devoted to the housing and living needs of the evacuees. Twenty-nine blocks of the housing area were

---

[231] "Amache," Joseph McClelland Collection, Box 1, Folder 6, Auraria Library Archives and Special Collections, Denver, 21, 24.

set aside for evacuee barracks, mess halls, and laundry facilities. The remaining blocks were used for the center's elementary school buildings, the high school, athletic fields, and the center's business district.

Streets dividing these blocks ran east-west and north-south. North-south streets were labeled alphabetically, with A positioned at the west side of the camp. East-west streets were labeled numerically, with First Street situated at the north end of the center. Hence, if an evacuee lived on a block that was bordered by G Street to the west and Eleventh Street to the north—as was the case of evacuee Henry Okubo—that evacuee would live in block 11G.

At the west side of the center were streets A, B, and C and at a slight angle to the rest of the camp. Between these streets were the main coal storage areas of the camp. From here, coal was picked up and delivered to each block where evacuees would get enough for individual use. Also, at the west side of the center sat the sewage treatment plant, a landfill, and the center's cemetery. The sewage treatment plant included an Imhoff tank, a sledge bed, and treatment ponds, all of which were used to send the treated sewage down into open ditches where it eventually found its way into Wolf Creek.[232]

"I have a friend who got his Ph.D. in chemistry after the war," recalls Tom Shigekuni.

> His job at Amache was keeping the sewer unplugged as it came out at the cesspool down there…I said, "What's your job?" (he was a senior and I was about in ninth grade). He said, "Well, I use a rake and I rake up the sewer so it doesn't clog up the gratings." I said, "What are you raking?" and he said, "Rubbers, condoms." I said, "You mean there are that many condoms flowing through there?" And he said, "Yeah, I don't know where they're getting them, but they sure have them available to these folks."[233]

---

[232] "Amache," 21, 24.
[233] Shigekuni, interview.

Shigekuni today wonders if the staff at the center was attempting to have the inmates at Amache practice birth control. Whatever the case, Shigekuni's friend went on to become a professor of chemistry at the University of California. "But he got his start raking condoms off the sewer line at Amache," Shigekuni adds. "It's almost funny."[234]

Granada's relocation camp took its water supply from four wells approximately 800 feet in depth—located on the project's property. Water was pumped from the wells by two 40-horsepower and two 50-horsepower 3-phase motors. These motors pumped in excess of 250 gallons of water per minute into a 200,000-gallon partially submerged water storage tank.

Once in the storage tank, the water was chlorinated and pumped by 40- and 50-horsepower engines to a 25,000-gallon water tower at the southern border of the camp. From this orange-and-white-checkered tank elevated to a height of 72 feet aboveground, water was sent to the center for individual and administrative use.[235]

Blocks where the evacuees lived took up the largest portion of the Granada relocation center. Each evacuee block included twelve 120-by-20-foot barracks that were subdivided into six one-room living quarters. Although these cramped, barren living quarters were given the ambiguous title of "apartment" by the WRA, they in fact held little resemblance to a typical apartment outside of camp. Stark and illuminated by only one bare bulb hanging from the ceiling, apartments came in three sizes—sixteen by twenty feet (the two units located at either end of each barrack), twenty-four by twenty (the units next to the end units), and twenty by twenty (the two units located at the center of the barrack). WRA apartments were one-story, one-room dwellings, with plain, unpainted walls. No dividers were present, unless evacuees would build them themselves.

Foundations on which the barrack walls stood were of poured concrete and stood roughly ten inches aboveground. Inside the wall foundations lay flooring made of brick atop loose dirt. Between the bricks, sand was placed to take the place of mortar.

---

[234] Shigekuni, interview.
[235] "Amache," 13, 14.

The barracks' walls sat on the concrete foundations. These walls consisted of wooden frames covered with exterior wallboard painted with tar, sand, and a beige—sometimes blue—paint. Unlike other WRA relocation camps, Amache's barracks had interior walls made of thin and often unpainted Celotex or gypsum board. Due to the haste in which the barracks were built, there were often gaps where walls joined windows and roofs. These gaps were a constant nuisance to evacuees. Regular and thorough cleanings were required due to the seasonal dust storms that often deposited sand and dirt through the cracks and onto bedding and floors. Driving winds would also force snow and rain through the cracks in the walls in the wintertime.

Entrance into evacuee apartments was through a single door that led to two separate apartments. Each apartment also had a semi-completed closet located just inside this door. Roof construction consisted of wood sheathing on wood joists covered by tar paper.[236]

Evacuees recall vividly their first experience of walking into their new living quarters. Except for the folding cots and thin mattresses the evacuees were given at induction, no furniture of any kind graced the cramped rooms. Only a small coal-burning stove, a bare light bulb hanging from the ceiling, and a sliding glass window served to break the starkness of their new living quarters. Evacuees found their apartments had no restroom, no kitchen, no dividing walls, and no running water—only a barren vacant room awaited their arrival. One electrical outlet per room gave the illusion of modern convenience.[237]

The bare light bulb and windows were never enough to keep the apartments well lit. Likewise, the small coal stove often could not keep the living quarters heated in temperatures that sometimes dipped to well below zero. Since the camp was atop a hillcrest, the cold winter winds whipped between barrack walls and into apartments, leaving little shelter from the elements.[238]

---

[236] Paul Freier, "Housing Report," 31 December 1942, 307:0011 L6.41, Japanese American evacuation and resettlement records, BANC MSS 67/14c, the Bancroft Library, University of California, Berkeley; Shigekuni, interview.
[237] "Amache," 13–14.
[238] "Amache," 13–14.

The cots provided were uncomfortable, to say the least. They were often flimsy and poorly constructed. With little or no support, the canvas cloth sagged miserably. Many evacuees found mattresses, stuffed them with straw, and placed them on top of the cots as padding. Sam and Itsako Kuruma recall finding burlap bags and stuffing them with hay for their beds. Others even preferred to place straw mattresses on top of boards placed directly on the floor. Still others, skilled in carpentry, "liberated" scrap lumber and built bunk beds. Some even hung beds from the walls.[239]

Administrative and MP barracks seemed palatial compared to evacuee apartments. Administrative apartment buildings were slightly smaller than evacuee barracks (twenty-four by one hundred feet) but were built of higher-quality construction materials. Each administrative apartment building had wooden subflooring covered with tar paper and fir tongue-and-grove flooring. Subdivided into four apartments and one multipurpose utility room, each apartment included four to five rooms, closets, and individual restrooms.

MP barracks were equally well equipped. Smaller than evacuee barracks (twenty by one hundred feet), each MP barrack building consisted of a ten-by-twenty-foot living room, three to nine bedrooms, closets, a kitchen, and bath and laundry facilities. Compared to the spaces allotted to evacuees, the living quarters of staff and military members more closely resembled apartments found outside the center.[240]

The differences between evacuee living quarters and those of the WRA and military staff were dramatic. One Caucasian teacher recalls some of the luxuries of the staff apartments. "The building had running water, mind you," wrote this teacher in later years. "It had a bathtub for all the teachers to use, and a tub for soaking if no one else was needing it."[241] However, she goes on to mention that in

---

[239] "Amache: Patriotism Amidst Prejudice," Iuruma taped interview.
[240] Records of the War Assets Administration, Real Property Case Files 1940–1946, Federal Archives and Records Administration, Lakewood, Colo., Record Group 270-NN-372-195.
[241] Enola Kjeldgaard, "Impressions of a Japanese Relocation Center," 2, Granada Archives.

all fairness, the living conditions were extremely cramped. All single staff members, especially teachers, were required to share the apartments with several other people per apartment. One of the many things the Granada center never had enough of was living space.

Granada's relocation project had an equal number (720) of each size of evacuee apartments. Initially, the WRA had hoped to house two or three evacuees in the 16-by-20-twenty-foot apartments, four or five in the 20-by-20-foot apartments, and six or seven in a 24-by-20-foot apartments. However, the housing superintendent, Paul H. Freier, soon found the WRA's original design was not realistic. "It is an apparent fact," Freier wrote in a December 1942 housing report, "that normal sized beds to accommodate seven or eight people in a room 24' X 20' will take all of that room, leaving no room for toilet and other living purposes. This can by no means be desirable from a health and sanitation angle. It is not becoming of a democracy, where there are vast areas of living space."[242]

Even smaller 16-by-20-foot apartments designed to house a married couple and a child were crowded simply because infants or toddlers often required more space. Freier noted in his report that at least sixty couples were living in small apartments that had living spaces reduced to 8 by 10 feet after a child's crib or other paraphernalia had been added.

Freier further suggested that evacuee living space was diminished by the coal stove placed within each apartment. An area of fourteen square feet around the coal stove in each room was deemed unusable because of heat and fire concerns. Freier also added that with an additional twelve square feet taken for use as storage space in each room, evacuees were often left without adequate living space. "Give any persons, or family," Freier remarked, "a normal amount of minimum living equipment and clothing, and they shall find themselves cramped and crowded under our conditions. It is our frank opinion that to crowd resident individuals anymore here than they are now crowded will upset the morale and general welfare of the project."[243]

---

[242] Freier, "Housing Report."
[243] Freier, "Housing Report."

Freier continued his report by stating, "Each person's daily attitude is determined by his home adjustments. If a member becomes ill a whole group must adjust itself toward the ill person. To operate this project at maximum efficiency we must look toward each individual's home environment, determined especially by whether he is 'crowded' or not."[244]

Overcrowded barracks conditions left most evacuees little choice but to find refuge elsewhere when not sleeping. "It was crowded in my family's room," recalls George Hirano. "We had seven people so we got the end unit. Of course, there wasn't enough room for seven beds in the room, so we had to share beds. My mother and two younger brothers slept in a double bed we made and the three older boys slept in another double bed. My father got a single bed to himself."[245]

The property around the Granada center often added to the dismal environment. Lawns around evacuee barracks were nearly nonexistent. No sidewalks were built between barracks or blocks. No pavement covered the center's roadways. Lumber was much too scarce to construct covered walkways between buildings. And by the time evacuees began arriving in the Granada center, the Army Corps of Engineers had cleared out the majority of native brush from the center's site, leaving little more than dirt and sand.

In fact, sand and dirt were everywhere. In winter and spring months—after the infrequent snow and rainstorms had come—dirt roads and pathways turned to pasty seas of mud. In summer months, windstorms blew sand and dirt into living quarters and mess halls and onto clothing and beds.[246]

Outside evacuee barracks, clotheslines dotted the landscape. Small vegetable gardens growing crops like Chinese cabbage, daikon (a Japanese winter radish), and tomatoes could also be found against barracks.

Barracks were situated in rows on the east and west edges of each block. In between these rows, each block had a recreation cen-

---

[244] Freier, "Housing Report."
[245] Hirano, G., interview.
[246] Shigekuni, interview.

ter, a mess hall, and a laundry room / restroom building. Recreation center buildings were slightly smaller than evacuee barracks and were intended as spots where evacuees could meet, relax, and hold social activities. However, because incoming evacuees often required an immediate need for space, many recreation halls were used for other purposes. Block 6F's recreation center was converted into a Red Cross station, while block 6E's center was used to house the silk screen shop. Other blocks' recreation centers housed churches, offices, youth organizations, and stores. Some were even used as temporary evacuee living quarters.[247]

The center's mess halls were forty-by-one-hundred-foot buildings located at the front of each block. These buildings were constructed of wallboards on wooden frames and were covered with granular siding—material similar to those used in the evacuee barracks. Most of these mess halls had ceilings hung from the roof. All mess halls had concrete flooring.

Each mess hall had a kitchen that housed three coal-heated ranges, a small number of refrigerators, and large two-compartment galvanized sinks. A serving counter separated the kitchen from the dining portion of the mess hall. At the outside rear of most mess hall buildings stood a lean-to-type structure for storage purposes.[248]

The interior of the mess hall resembled standard army mess halls. The dining portion of the building was a large open room divided only by central support pillars jutting up from the floor. The expanse of the large open dining room was broken by a number of long wooden picnic-style benches on which roughly 250 evacuees could be served at a time. Besides the bare bulbs that hung from the ceilings, sliding windows placed around the circumference of the building supplied additional light to the often dark and drab interior. Evacuees enlivened this darkness by hanging curtains over windows and by decorating the interior for occasional dances and holiday parties.[249]

---

[247] Lindley, "Quarterly Report," 19; Lindley, "Final Report," appendix VI.
[248] Yorimoto, A., interview; Records of the War Assets Administration.
[249] Yorimoto, A., interview.

Within each mess hall, specific rules were expected to be followed. No smoking was allowed within the mess halls, nor were evacuees allowed to congregate without special permission from WRA staff members. All headwear was also forbidden while in mess halls at mealtime. Finally, evacuees were asked to leave immediately after each meal to provide continuity between shifts.[250]

Besides the mess halls, an H-shaped building that housed evacuee bathrooms, showers, and laundry facilities was also located at the center of each block. On one side of this building lay a twenty-by-eighty-two-foot laundry room that housed eighteen two-compartment laundry tables, a small area for ironing boards, and an array of washboards and laundry utensils. Some laundry rooms also housed a small eighteen-by-twenty-foot information office where evacuees could contact block managers or ask questions if necessary. In the cross section of this building lay a five-by-twenty-foot corridor that allowed access between the laundry room and the women's toilets. Within this passage lay a room with two coal-fired boilers that heated the water for shower and laundry room use.

On the other side of this H-shaped building stood the men's and women's toilets, communal showers, bathtubs, and lockers. The women's toilet facilities consisted of bare unfinished walls and usually housed fourteen commodes, fourteen porcelain lavatories, a porcelain sink, a drinking fountain, eight showerheads, and four bathtubs. The men's toilets included similar fixtures with the exception of urinals and the exclusion of bathtubs.[251]

These communal facilities were embarrassing to evacuees—most of whom had come from homes with private bathrooms. Shigeko Hirano remembers a young girl living in the same barracks who had a severe spinal disfiguration. "Because of that," recalls Hirano, "she was much shorter and disabled. The poor thing, she would go late, late at night when no one was there. I felt so sorry for her. No privacy

---

[250] The War Relocation Center, Granada, Colo., "Notice from the Police Department," 301:0053 L5.04, Japanese American evacuation and resettlement records, BANC MSS 67/14c, the Bancroft Library, University of California, Berkeley.
[251] Records of the War Assets Administration.

at all. She had to go at inconvenient times so that no one would see her. It was very sad."[252]

Of the 2,160 apartments located at the Granada's relocation center 92 apartments were used for purposes other than evacuee living quarters. The largest portion of these apartments (72) was taken up as classrooms in the educational block. All the barracks in block 8H, and later in block 10G, were set aside as a campus for the relocation center's school system. Eight other apartments were utilized as baby food stations where mothers could acquire formula and strained foods for their babies.[253]

The center's business district was also located in the housing area and included the evacuee police headquarters, the relocation information bureau, and a co-op building housing numerous evacuee-owned stores. The center's co-op, begun in January 1943, was one of the largest of its kind in the state. The shops included such businesses as a barbershop and beauty salon, variety and clothing stores, shoe and shoe repair shops, and a small number of repair shops.

"My husband," Fumiye Nishizaki recalls, "and another man, Mr. Koda, were at the co-op from the start. They had all kinds of items, not everything, but things like shoes—most people didn't buy shoes there—but there were shoes, and knick-knacks, a little bit of clothing, but not too much."[254]

Most evacuees made their own clothes or ordered them through catalog services. Nishizaki notes, "What I had, I sewed or knitted. Like my husband's sweaters, I knitted for him. You could buy through catalogs. Most of us spent money through the catalog. We didn't want that much… There was Granada, a tiny town—they didn't have anything there. We had to go as far as Lamar, which you [had] to have a car."[255]

The U-shaped co-op building was built by the WRA and included few amenities aside from eighteen rooms and electric and water hookups. A three-room co-op warehouse sat outside the main

---

[252] Hirano, S., interview.
[253] Freier, "Housing Report"; Lindley, "Final Report," appendix VI.
[254] Nishizaki, interview.
[255] Nishizaki, interview.

building. A small ten-by-eight-by-seven-foot concrete vault with a steel safe door was also attached outside the office of the warehouse to house valuable merchandise and cash.[256]

Mr. W. Ray Johnson, Amache's chief of community management, originally started the co-op. His initial investment of twenty-five dollars for candies, cigarettes, and soda eventually turned into a business venture bringing in over four hundred thousand dollars a year and included over three thousand members. The co-op building was built by the WRA at a cost of thirty-five thousand dollars.

This was the physical setup of the Granada relocation center. Brick flooring, lined walls, and an entrance hall for each pair of apartments distinguished Amache from other camps like Gila, Poston, and Manzanar. Here, evacuees would be housed throughout the remaining period of evacuation. The center was made of concrete and wood, bricks and wallboards—all formed into tiny enclosures designed to isolate an innocent people.

But the importance of the Granada relocation center lay not in its structures or its design, but in the lives of the people interned there. The real story of Granada's center resides in its tenants' resounding determination to survive under such adversity. Within these stories can be found true historical worth. And within these stories are found the true faces of evacuation.

---

[256] Records of the War Assets Administration.

CHAPTER 5

COLORADO'S NEWEST CITY

For the first time in months, President Roosevelt's demeanor appeared to be upbeat. In his October 13, 1942, fireside chat, Roosevelt eluded to great progress in the war. The American people, according to Roosevelt, were "united as never before."

Through the fall and winter of 1942, sacrifice was the call. Scrap drives continued around the nation—one such drive in early September brought in over 2,753,675 tons of scrap metal. Railroad lines asked citizens to refrain from traveling by train so troops stationed around the country could return home for the holidays. Phone companies around the country asked that calls be kept to a minimum so that government and military personnel could have better access. Even chocolate Santas and other holiday confectionery items were banned during the Christmas season of 1942 in an effort to save sugar.[257]

Roosevelt praised the country for "getting ahead of our enemies in the battle of production." In late 1942, the War Production Board converted the production of whiskey and gin at 128 distilleries nationwide to the production of 476 million gallons of alcohol for use in synthetic rubber and smokeless powder. Chevrolet had

---

[257] *Rocky Mountain News*, 20 December 1942, 5, 8; 6 December 1942, 10.

converted its Leeds assembly line to the production of ammunition shells. Tanks, ships, food, clothes, and weapons—the United States astounded the world with its amazing output of these products.[258]

In fact, the very swiftness of the conversion to wartime production was what really astounded the world. Steven Ambrose notes, "When President Franklin Roosevelt called for the production of 4,000 planes per month, people thought he was crazy. But in 1942, the United States was producing 4,000 a month and by the end of 1943, 8,000 per month… And all this took place while the United States put a major effort into the greatest industrial feat of that time, the production of atomic weapons."[259]

As Americans struggled to keep up with the demands overseas and the labor shortage at home, they paid little attention to those people placed "safely" under guard. A war was on. The united aim of victory overshadowed all else. Only occasionally would Americans hear of life within their county's concentration centers.

But those interned could not forget. Every morning, when an Issei or Nisei opened his or her eyes to see the shabby, dark interior of their cramped one-room dwelling, they felt the thrust of intolerance. Every glance at the cold barbed wire and the guards sitting high above were vivid reminders of how their fellow citizens truly viewed them.

It was hoped by one Nisei writer that "all loyal individuals will again be accepted into the American society and permitted to share the freedom and liberties [of] an American citizen."[260] But until then, residents of Colorado's newest city were forced to transition into their newest role as innocent captives under guard.

Many of those confined within Amache were American citizens. The WRA knew it. The American government was constantly reminded of it. And even though these citizens had had most of their rights taken away from them through the evacuation process, they still deserved the same rights other citizens of the United States were afforded. So to deal with the issues of constitutional rights, the WRA

---

[258] *Rocky Mountain News*, 1 September 1942, 1, 3.
[259] Stephen Ambrose, *D-Day June 6, 1944: The Climactic Battle of World War II* (New York: Touchstone, 1994), 57.
[260] "Amache," 31.

half-heartedly allowed evacuees to create a representational body within the camps. Certainly, the WRA would still insist on the final say in all matters concerning camp operations. But with the creation of self-government—a self-government consisting of a community council and a block managers' assembly—evacuees were given a small voice within the camps.

According to one source, the evacuee governments, known as community councils, were originally designed for "the prescription of ordinances, regulations, and laws governing community life within the center." But in reality, community councils were never afforded these powers. The WRA dictated what rules and laws would be enforced. In truth, community councils at Amache served not as a camp legislative body, but as a mouthpiece to go between the evacuee population and project director, James Lindley.[261]

The roots of the community council at Amache started on August 31, 1942, when five men—three of whom were Issei—were brought to the surface as a mouthpiece for evacuees already in camp. By Thanksgiving, the small group of five had been replaced by twenty-nine Nisei men chosen by the evacuee population.

The WRA had hoped outsiders would see community councils as effective governmental rule by fellow citizens. With this in mind, Issei were not given representation on these councils until the summer of 1943. Nisei representatives to this council were elected—one from each of the twenty-nine blocks—by popular vote. To be considered as a candidate, all nominees had to be male, Nisei, and eighteen years of age or older.[262]

Most relocation centers excluded Issei from service on community councils. But Fumiye Nishizaki notes that because the number of available Nisei was diminishing due to seasonal and indefinite leaves, the Amache staff allowed Issei to become a part of the center's community council.[263]

---

[261] "Amache," 6.

[262] Lindley, "Quarterly Report," 9; author unknown, "Project History," Ernest Tigges Collection, Box 1, Folder 1, Auraria Library Archives and Special Collections, Denver, 1946.

[263] Nishizaki, interview.

AMACHE

The creation of a "government" behind the barbed wire of Amache led to a great deal of interest outside the center. In a November 27, 1942, *Rocky Mountain News* article, it was reported that Nisei were busily formulating a charter based on the Mayflower Compact and various New England town council charters. "Just now council members are discussing a proposal for a unicameral legislative system," the reporter remarked. "I attended one meeting of the subcommittee in one of the small recreation halls. The debate over the question of one or two legislative houses followed the lines of the original Constitutional Convention in Philadelphia."[264]

Although the Nisei had attempted to create a self-led governing body, no constitution would be effectively created or followed. Evacuees laboring over these legislative plans were simply wasting their time. The WRA had already determined the true purpose of the councils. Relocation centers were not designed to become independent cities with long-term governmental rule. Relocation centers were, in the minds of the WRA, simply rest stops in the process of relocating evacuees to interior states.

What the WRA really wanted from community councils was a group of evacuees who would serve as liaisons, advisors, and governmental enforcers of rules. Simply stated, evacuee self-government would be neither practical nor useful to the true goals of relocation. Michi Nishiura Weglyn, in her book *Years of Infamy: The Untold Story of America's Concentration Camps*, notes that the community council was often "ridiculed as 'a baby's plaything,' as something 'to make the kids feel good.'" According to Weglyn, "In neo-colonial fashion, the Project Director held the reins of power tightly, maintaining the absolute power of veto over his youthful Council members… Project directors everywhere assumed the role of judge, jury, and prosecutor."[265]

In theory, at least, the community council was the organization with political clout in Amache. But in reality, the Issei-controlled block manager's assembly had more control over community matters

---

[264] *Rocky Mountain News*, 27 November 1942, 6.
[265] Weglyn, *Years of Infamy*, 121.

than did the Nisei-led community council. Block manager positions were primarily filled by Issei or Kibei who were supposedly charged with the mundane tasks of "handling the requests on housing, heating and household supplies, assisting the family in case of death in making all needed arrangements, relaying announcements and instructions from administrative sources and also to advise the personnel director on employment." Each manager also recorded weekly statistics necessary for housing, employment, food distribution, and leave clearances.[266]

As a block manager, Fumiye Nishizaki's husband, Torno, met with the evacuees on his block daily. "Every morning they had a meeting, and he [heard] the problem and tried to fix that, whatever is the problem. Later on, see my husband became what they called the coordinator between the administration and the evacuees. He would go to the administration—Mr. Lindley or Mr. Thompson—he would report if there's a message from the office, he would then report back to the block manager and settle whatever problem there is."[267]

However, underlying the block manager's role as coordinator was a subdued source of power. This power came not from any direct affirmation by the WRA. Instead, Issei and Kibei block managers gained their political sway from the respect traditionally given to such people. Often these men were held in high regard in local communities before evacuation from the West Coast. The cultural honor afforded to Issei and Kibei before the evacuation merely followed these men into the camps. Those who were household heads and those who had endured the disciplined education of Japanese universities were allowed both political and social respect within the confines of camp as well.

Ironically, block managers also gained their power from past connections with Japan. The Japanese government had become incensed in what they saw as the American government's attempt to disperse and eradicate Japanese centers of power on the West Coast.

---

[266] "Amache," 10–11.
[267] Nishizaki, interview.

Attempting to thwart this action, the Japanese imperial government made use of the Spanish embassy as a protectorate power in the interests of Japanese nationals in America. Issei could lodge protests and grievances to the Spanish embassy through a specially appointed consul. This presence of a neutral party and go-between provided leverage and power for Issei and Kibei leadership within the confines of Amache. No WRA official wanted to wind up as a source of enmity between the two countries. So when block managers wanted something, they would use the underlying threat of complaining to Spanish embassy officials in their periodic visits.

Sporadic inspections by Spanish consuls were, to say the least, uneasy moments for WRA officials. Any information gained by the Spanish consul often became important news for the Japanese Empire's propaganda machine. Likewise, any issues found at the centers such as low wages, poor living conditions, or the lack of proper nutrition for elderly and children residents could potentially be used as fodder by the Japanese to gain international support.

At Amache, the first official visit of the Spanish consul came on January 23, 1943, when a representative of the US Department of State accompanied the Spanish vice-consul. Other visits followed in December 1943, July 1944, and February 1945. Project Director Lindley noted that during these visits, the representative of the Spanish consul usually met with Issei residents and "listened to opinions and complaints and usually read a prepared statement from the Japanese government." Lindley further remarked that these visits were "brief and perfunctory" and that they "probably served their purpose."[268]

Although Lindley may have felt the visits as "perfunctory," Issei and Kibei at Amache—like those of other camps—found a new and vital ability to influence the very nature and quality of their captivity through these visits.

From the start, Amache's size dictated that adequate, well-staffed emergency services were put into force. There was no way that surrounding communities could effectively extinguish fires,

---

[268] Lindley, "Final Report," 4.

supply police protection, or furnish medical services. Distance and time factors were too great. Besides, all the communities surrounding Amache had only the barest of emergency services available. The closest community—that of Granada—had little police protection and even fewer medical services. According to resident Bruce Newman, by 1942, the city of Granada was still using a hose spun on a spindle on wheels to put out fires.

WRA officials had never entertained the notion of using the emergency services of surrounding communities. Having placed relocation centers primarily in out-of-the-way farming communities, officials realized resources would be limited or, most likely, nonexistent. They also understood that a certain amount of animosity toward the centers would exist if local taxpayer dollars were used for the protection of such federal projects. With these factors in mind, all relocation centers had their own emergency services.

Amache's fire department had its inception as a small makeshift crew of evacuees in early September 1942. At first, no buildings were provided to house fire equipment or personnel. But by the end of 1942, a one-story T-shaped building had been erected that could house up to four pieces of fire equipment as well as the small steady crew of ten evacuees.

Initially Amache's fire equipment consisted of a pickup truck laden with various firefighting apparatus, a 1,000-gallon water tank, an old International truck with a power-driven pump. But by December 1, 1942, the station had added two Ford 500-gallon-per-minute triple pumper trucks each carrying 150 gallons of water. These two trucks—previously used by the army—could throw 500 gallons of water per minute. They would become the center's primary fighting apparatus and would even be used to fight fires outside the center.[269]

Evacuees serving in the fire department were under a personnel infrastructure much like fire departments in cities of similar size. At

---

[269] Lindley, "Quarterly Report," 14, 15; "Fire Inspection of Granada Relocation Project," 10 December 1942, 309:0150 L6.95, Japanese American evacuation and resettlement records, BANC MSS 67/14c, the Bancroft Library, University of California, Berkeley.

the top of the structure were an associate fire protection officer and an assistant fire protection officer—both of whom were Caucasian. The men in these positions were paid an annual salary of $3,200 and $2,300, respectively. The rest of the department consisted of an evacuee, pyramidal-like command structure with a fire chief at the top, three assistant chiefs below, and six captains below them. At the bottom sat three platoons of fifteen firemen who, like in most chains of command, did much of the work.

Each platoon worked in twenty-four-hour shifts and was responsible for emergency duties, base inspections every two hours, and the general cleaning and conditioning of firefighting equipment. Volunteer and auxiliary firemen were also selected from each block and were trained to aid designated firefighters if needed.[270]

All firefighting positions—excluding those Caucasian positions of associate and assistant fire protection officers—were paid less-than-generous wages. Evacuee firemen were paid the standard WRA wage of $16 to $19 a month.

Throughout its existence, Amache had very little damage caused by fires. This was due, in part, to the preparedness of the WRA for such emergencies. Fire prevention talks and an annual Fire Prevention Week helped residents become more aware of possible community danger spots. Lindley used these annual drives to remove any sagebrush or rubble from the center that posed potential fire hazards. Likewise, Boy Scouts canvassed the camp in an attempt to spot additional safety hazards.[271]

To help extinguish fires quickly, fire hydrants were placed at strategic locations on each block of the project. Fire phones were also attached to red-and-white-striped telephone poles stationed at the hospital, the warehouse area, and on each evacuee block. Amber lights affixed to the top of these fire poles served to easily identify their location at night. To round out the list of equipment, each

---

[270] "Amache," 12, 13; "Fire Inspection."
[271] Vern Campbell, "Monthly Fire Report," September 1943, 309:0080 L6.92, Japanese American evacuation and resettlement records, BANC MSS 67/ 14c, the Bancroft Library, University of California, Berkeley.

block also was given a supply of two-and-a-half-gallon water and foam extinguishers.[272]

Such equipment was critical due to the nature of the construction materials used at the center. Hundreds of coal-burning stoves amid a sea of wood-framed buildings would send chills down the spines of today's fire safety managers. In addition, terra-cotta-style chimneys had become the primary source of extracting fumes from coal-burning stoves at all barracks buildings, including those used as the center's schools and mess halls. The design of these chimneys had inherent flaws. The clay material that made up the vent would sometimes overheat or simply crack, allowing heat to pass through to flammable materials. The design and material had been noted as the cause of many other fires in the relocation centers of Minidoka and Topaz. This faulty design was also responsible for the Amache's first fire on September 4, 1942.[273]

Amazingly, however, most fires came not from coal-burning stoves or their terra-cotta chimneys but from high winds that blew sparks from ashpits around the center, and from improperly installed electrical wires. Fire reports also routinely make mention of fires started by children playing with matches and people carelessly throwing cigarettes onto flammable material. Many reports speak of calls to the XY Ranch to extinguish out-of-control rubbish fires. One of the most destructive fires at Amache would come on February 22, 1944, when a night fire at the 7K mess hall destroyed more than $1,700 in property. Most fires, however, often left little damage—thanks to the quick response of evacuee firemen.[274]

Another aspect of the emergency services at Amache was the center's police force. The WRA had expected some resistance to relocation. They were also quite aware that the concentration of such a large number of people in one area would bring about a certain

---

[272] Vern Campbell, "Weekly Fire Report," 12 November 1944, 309:0150 L6.95, Japanese American evacuation and resettlement records, BANC MSS 67/ 14c, the Bancroft Library, University of California, Berkeley; Campbell, "Monthly Fire Report," April 1945.
[273] "Fire Inspection."
[274] Campbell, "Monthly Fire Report," May and September 1943.

amount of crime and violence. Anticipating these situations, Project Director Lindley established Amache's police force upon the first arrival of evacuees into the center. This police force, known in WRA records as Internal Security (IS), was created by Lindley as an attempt to control all internal policing of the camp. Consisting of Japanese American evacuees, the IS force was the WRA's method of cutting down on the number of MPs needed to secure the center.

IS would not, however, be responsible for guarding Amache. This responsibility went to the center's military police force. MPs at Amache averaged about 130 men in number. These men were housed at the northeastern portion of the center in a self-contained and isolated area. The major responsibilities of Amache MPs were to man the six guard towers surrounding the camp, check all incoming and outgoing evacuee and non-evacuee passes, and inspect packages for contraband.[275]

All other police duties went to the IS. Amache's initial IS force consisted of one Caucasian officer—Harlow M. Tomlinson, a former member of the Wichita, Kansas, police department—and a handful of untrained evacuees. But by the middle of November 1942, the number of evacuee officers had swollen to nearly ninety men. This number was eventually reduced over time to no more than thirty-five evacuee officers and a Caucasian staff of three.[276]

Amache's police force resembled other police departments around Colorado. At the head of the force was the chief of IS. Under him were three Caucasian IS officers. And at the heart of the force lay an evacuee staff consisting of one chief of police (appointed by the chief of IS), three captains, two desk sergeants, two field sergeants, three detectives, one release sergeant, one transportation sergeant, and a number of patrolmen.[277]

---

[275] Lindley, "Final Report," appendix II.
[276] *Denver Post*, 14 February 1943, 1; Forrest G. Foxster, "Granada Internal Security Final Report," 301:0053 L5.04, Japanese American evacuation and resettlement records, BANC MSS 67114c, the Bancroft Library, University of California, Berkeley.
[277] Foxster, "Granada Internal Security"; "Amache," 22.

Despite a lack of law enforcement training, Amache's IS force was relatively effective in controlling crime and violence. Housed initially in three separate buildings scattered around the camp, the IS department was finally located in an old sixty-by-twenty-foot Work Project Administration building erected in block 9F in the first few months of 1943. Within this building, the police set up their main headquarters office. The office chief of IS, however, was still located in the administration area.[278]

For the WRA, fears of uprising overrode any trust placed in IS employees. No evacuee police officer was ever allowed to carry a gun, knife, nightstick, or any other weapon that might be used in a mass uprising. In fact, few weapons at all were ever placed in the possession of Caucasian IS officers. Only a 45-caliber revolver and a tear gas gun were issued to the department—and these were to remain under lock and key and were to be used only in case of serious emergencies.[279]

Weapons didn't matter, though. Crimes at Amache were relatively minor in nature compared to those found in cities of a similar size. Crimes usually consisted of misdemeanor offenses such as burglary, larceny, drunkenness, or assault. Occasional gambling parties were broken up. Traffic and motor vehicle offenses were likewise minor.

The primary responsibility of an IS officer was to "preserve the peace, protect life and property, apprehend criminals, prevent crime, recover lost and stolen property, and enforce the ordinance of the city of Amache." Officers were also responsible for nonpolice activities such as serving as interpreters, Boy Scout masters, liaisons to selective services and relocation divisions, and acting as message couriers. The only duties the evacuees were not responsible for were those

---

[278] WRA, Granada, Colorado, "Internal Security Quarterly Report," January–March 1943, 301:0053 L5.04, Japanese American evacuation and resettlement records, BANC MSS 67/14c, the Bancroft Library, University of California, Berkeley.

[279] Joseph Dewitt, "Interviews on Status of Internal Security at Granada Relocation Center," 25 October 1944, 301:0053 L5.04, Japanese American evacuation and resettlement records, BANC MSS 67/14c, the Bancroft Library, University of California, Berkeley.

of patrolling the projects warehouse district and guarding the front gate. These tasks went to the MPs assigned to the base.[280]

Certain periods during 1943 and 1944 saw what Amache's staff considered juvenile "crime waves." Although these crime waves were, by most standards, fairly small, the center's administration did feel the need to take action.

In the fall of 1944—during the worst of these juvenile crime waves—James Lindley and other head administrators carried out a survey of the camp's internal security, with a special emphasis on the problem of juvenile delinquency. In their report, the rise of juvenile crime and vandalism was blamed on the lack of available recreation halls, limited numbers of available men for youth leadership roles, and the interim absence of a manager of community activities. Internment was never mentioned as a cause; nor were the societal causes surrounding such events.

The most serious cases of juvenile crime usually involved theft or violence. One case in 1943 involved three young men who had stolen a pair of shoes from a store clerk and, after finding out the young Caucasian clerk had called the police, returned to beat up the informant. Sets Sumikawa even remembers her older brother and some friends breaking some chairs and tables at a Lamar restaurant because of a "No Japs Served" policy.[281]

Few crimes, however, reached such violence. Juvenile crimes primarily consisted of no more than the defacement of property, pranks, and petty thefts. One rather lively event in December 1944 found four young boys driving a farm truck through the northwest gate and nearly sideswiping a patrolman stationed there. By the time the police caught up with the boys, the youth had abandoned the

---

[280] WRA, "Rules and Regulations: Amache Police Department," 301:0053 L5.04, Japanese American evacuation and resettlement records, BANC MSS 67/ 14c, the Bancroft Library, University of California, Berkeley; Foxster, "Granada Internal Security."

[281] M. Tomlinson, "Internal Security Quarterly Report," April–June 1943, 301:0011 L 5.02, Japanese American evacuation and resettlement records, BANC MSS 67/14c, the Bancroft Library, University of California, Berkeley; Dewitt, "Interviews on Status of Internal Security."

truck near an irrigation ditch on the XY Ranch. One of the boys was apprehended at the scene but later escaped from the police car on arrival back at the camp.[282]

Most infractions by young evacuees seemed to come from minor rebellious acts. Henry Okubo remembers such acts of rebellion were much easier after the number of MPs were reduced. "We used to go to the west end of camp and crawl between the barbed wire fence," recalls Henry Okubo. "When we got through the fence, we would cross the farmer's field and go to Hideaway Lake. We would swim and fish for catfish most the day and then come back late in the evening. I remember on the way back, we would stop by the farmer's watermelon patch and break open a watermelon. The heart of the melons always tasted so cold and sweet in that cool night air."[283] Okubo and his friends stopped their journeys only when local officials condemned the lake.

If serious adult arrests were made, those apprehended were sent to the local jail in Lamar. No jail ever existed at Amache. This was due, in part, to the head of IS who felt the lack of a jail would cause "less comment, less commotion, and less unrest" among Amacheans. In contrast to adult arrests, juvenile offenders were usually brought before the chief of IS for an informal hearing. Since most of the center's juvenile cases were a result of pranks and petty crimes, the reaction of the IS was to treat such cases under the mentoring of an officer who handled and disposed of each case as a "big brother" would.[284]

All told, only 208 cases were reported and investigated by the IS throughout the life of the center. Of these cases, only one—a felony charge—resulted in an imprisonment in the state penitentiary. Thirty-four IS cases stemmed from evacuees who were convicted for violation of the selective service draft. Remaining offenses consisted

---

[282] WRA, Granada, Colorado, "Internal Security Monthly Report," December 1944 and January 1945, 301:0011 L5.02, Japanese American evacuation and resettlement records, BANC MSS 67/14c, the Bancroft Library, University of California, Berkeley.

[283] Okubo, interview.

[284] Dewitt, "Interviews on Status of Internal Security," 4.

of lesser crimes and accidents. Of these offenses, the juvenile crime rate—totaling only twenty-five cases in the center's history—was considerably less than that found in cities of similar size.[285]

As one looks back at the crime rate found at Amache, one must wonder how a gathering of so many could result in so few incidents of violence and misbehavior. Harlon M. Tomlinson, the chief of IS, reported that "as a general rule, the people in this center are law-abiding and do not want to commit any crimes that will get them into trouble or embarrassment with the law enforcement agency of the state or nation."[286]

Modern-day cities could only hope to have such success in managing crime.

Rounding out Amache's emergency services was the center's hospital. When Amache opened its gates in August 1942, the main portion of the hospital was not yet ready for patients. Evacuees needing immediate medical attention were assigned to a temporary clinic set up in a nearby converted barrack building.

Once completed, the hospital would become the center's largest complex with 17 buildings and 150 beds. Double doors graced most entrances and walkways and, for the most part, connected all wings. Heat for the hospital was provided by steam run through overhead pipes and stand-up floor radiators. The hospital's flooring consisted of poured concrete laid over a wooden subflooring. The building was also equipped with a sprinkling system in case of fire.[287]

"We had some of the best doctors on the West Coast," recalls Emory Namura:

> Some of the doctors were brought here from Stanford, UCLA, and White Memorial. We had a surgeon out of White Memorial and we had an internal-medicine guy out of Stanford. We had a lot of dentists also. In fact, we had better X-ray

---

[285] Foxster, "Granada Internal Security."
[286] WRA, "Internal Security Monthly Report," January 1945, 121.
[287] WRA, "Fire Inspection," 6–7.

> equipment than Lamar. Oh, they had one—but it was small. So after the camp closed we gave ours to the hospital in Lamar. We even had penicillin in the camp. Most people in the general population didn't even have that.[288]

The x-ray department at the hospital was only one of several medical divisions at the camp. Amache's hospital also included a surgery section, a children's ward, a morgue, and an isolation ward. Evacuees also had access to a pharmacy, dental clinic, and optometry clinic. An independent sanitary staff made up of evacuees worked out of the hospital complex and conducted periodic inspections of mess halls, latrines, schools, and other places where health issues might arise.

To staff these various departments, the center had a WRA medical doctor and eight WRA nurses as well as an evacuee staff of five medical doctors, seven dentists, and a large number of evacuee employees also served as nurses, aides, and medical technicians.[289]

"I used to work for the optometrist," recalls Helene Ioka. "I was the receptionist for him. The hospital was like other hospitals, but it was nothing like what you would have now. It was put together in camp. The doctors were mostly Japanese. The optometrist I worked for was a Hawaiian Nisei. I worked for him until I got married and moved. He was the only optometrist at the camp. It took months to get an appointment there because there were so many people. They were tough schedules to accommodate everyone."[290]

Doctors received pay for their work at Amache similar to that of other professional evacuees in the camp—nineteen dollars a month. Compared to current wages, or even the wages of contemporaries outside the camp, such wages were laughable. Evacuees realized the medical care they received came not from a well-paid individual, but from a caring person who sacrificed his time and energies on behalf of

---

[288] Namura, E., interview.
[289] Lindley, "Final Report," appendix IL.
[290] Helene Ioka, personal interview, 17 April 2000.

the community at Amache. The small number of doctors at Amache struggled to keep up with the demands of such a large population.

Realizing these factors, evacuees began an organization called the Ishi Koen Kwai that promoted the health and welfare of individual evacuees. The organization provided financial support to all members of the camp's medical team. It was hoped that the Ishi Koen Kwai would both entice doctors and dentists within the center to stay in the service of Amache instead of relocating. Evacuees, including those out on leave, were asked to give five cents per person to a monthly fund. The center's co-op was also asked to provide an additional five hundred dollars per month to supplement the remaining amount needed.[291]

Like the doctors at Amache, all emergency personnel provided necessary services to the camp at extremely low wages. None received more than nineteen dollars per month. Most worked hours well over that of a standard work week. Life in Amache had little to be desired. But those who served in emergency capacities were able to look back at their service to the center and be proud of the service they rendered.

The transition to life within the center had to be as effortless as possible. To operate the facilities at Amache, the WRA had appointed over 150 administrative employees. These Caucasian men and women who worked primarily in leadership or service positions were usually assisted by evacuee workers. Staffing was often difficult due to the sensitive nature of these administrative assignments. In his book *Uprooted Americans*, Myers hinted at the difficulty in finding caring, responsible employees who "not only had the necessary skills but were also tolerant and understanding in their dealings with the evacuees. In this latter respect we were not always successful in the early months, as some of the early staff members were not able to meet the problems and the emotional impact of the WRA program

---

[291] WRA, Granada, Colorado, "Weekly Report for 9/14 to 9/21 Inclusive," 22 September 1944, 304:0027 L5.70, Japanese American evacuation and resettlement records, BANC MSS 67/14c, the Bancroft Library, University of California, Berkeley.

adequately. Consequently, we had some separations or resignations before the program was well under way."[292]

WRA employees were predominately hired through the Civil Service Commission and were provided with salaries comparable to those found outside the camp. For those who wished to live on-site, small barrack apartments were also provided at a nominal charge of eight dollars per month. Most employees, however, chose to live outside the center in the neighboring communities of Lamar and Holly.

All administrative employees were expected to work an eight-hour day, Monday through Saturday, with overtime at time and a half. As a stipulation for employment, WRA employees were also asked to pledge 15 percent of their salary to the purchase of war bonds. Benefits included twenty-six days of annual leave as well as daily meals provided on-site at a cost of forty cents per meal. Because medical services were not available to the Amache staff on-site, staff members were expected to find medical services in outlying communities like Lamar.[293]

Education was Dillon Myer's passion. Myer saw schooling as a primary gear in the machine of Americanism. Enthusiastically, Myer and his WRA set about planning an instruction system for relocation centers around the country. The goal was simple—to provide an education while shaping youth into democratically responsible adults. In short, WRA schools served a role popular on many government-operated reservations for Native Americans. If WRA schools could provide education similar to that of schools outside the centers, while at the same time molding students into proper "Americans," their task would be complete.

To this end, in the summer of 1942, Lloyd A. Garrison was appointed as the superintendent of education for the Granada project. Well before the walls of the first barrack had even been erected, the school system of Amache was under preparation. Garrison began

---

[292] Myer, *Uprooted Americans*, 32–33.
[293] WRA, Granada, Colorado, "Summary Information Concerning the Granada Project of the War Relocation Authority," 288:0113 Ll.05, Japanese American evacuation and resettlement records, BANC MSS 67/14c, the Bancroft Library, University of California, Berkeley.

his initial duties by hiring a supervisory staff that would be sympathetic to the plight of the Japanese Americans at Amache. This staff included principals, assistant principals, and guidance counselors who were, in turn, responsible for the hiring of Caucasian teachers and evacuee assistant teachers.[294]

Although a number of Japanese Americans worked in administration and as teacher's aides, the makeup of Amache's school system was predominately Caucasian. The recruitment of instructors was done by Amache's educational staff along with the help of Denver's regional office of the US Civil Service Special Services, regional WRA offices, and various college placement bureaus around the state.

When first contacted about teaching in the relocation camp at Granada, Katherine Odum remembers that "I didn't know what they meant, I didn't know what they were talking about because I hadn't heard much about [the relocation center]." But she adds, "The pay was around $1,500 a year, which at that time was pretty good." Because the pay was right and the job assignment "sounded interesting," Odum agreed to the employment and began her trek to Granada.[295]

"It was no fun staying in Lamar and trying to get seventeen miles out to Amache," Odum recalls. "You had to thumb a ride from some government-licensed vehicle!... At four in the afternoon, the thing to do was to get down to the main administration area where the busses were waiting—there were always cars and trucks waiting to go into Lamar."[296]

The majority of the elementary and secondary Caucasian teachers lived in surrounding towns while employed at Amache. Carpooling was one source of travel as was riding on the back of army trucks. But in the winter, travel by truck could be a frigid experience. Tiring of this type of commute, Odum promptly began looking for rooms on base. When a coworker asked if she would consider

---

[294] Lindley, "Quarterly Report," 20.
[295] Katherine Odum, taped interview, Kathy Odum Collection, Box 1, Auraria Library Archives and Special Collections, Denver.
[296] Odum, interview.

staying as a roommate on base, Odum responded quickly. "Oh, was I the happiest person in the world." Odum laughs.[297]

Enola Kjeldgaard, an Amache fourth-grade teacher, notes that she and three other teachers at first moved into a small barracks apartment "surrounded by Japanese" until teachers' quarters were completed in the administration area. This initial apartment was situated within the evacuee housing area. With only four cots, three mattresses, fourteen quilts, one mirror, and two rough-hewn tables, Kjeldgaard's initial surroundings were just as primitive as those found in evacuee apartments. However, shortly after the administrative apartments were finished, Kjeldgaard moved into the comparably more luxurious surroundings given to staff members.[298]

The teacher population was fairly fluid in the beginning. Work was taxing, both physically and emotionally. Some worked only the first week or two before leaving. Others, like Katherine Odum and Enola Kjeldgaard, remained at the center the entire time. By the 1943 school year, most teachers had settled in for the remainder of the center's life. Eventually, over fifty Caucasian teachers would be employed. Not included in this number were the forty evacuees who faithfully served as assistant teachers and specialists for minimal evacuee wages.[299]

On December 2, 1942, the R. E. Rippe Construction Company of South Pasadena, California, arrived at Amache. Their mission was to begin the construction of three new schools. These new buildings, it was hoped, would provide a better learning environment for evacuee children than that found in cramped, stark barracks.

Nothing fancy was planned. Two of the buildings would include eighteen 32-by-21-foot classrooms and would be used to serve all elementary and middle school grades. The third building would include twenty-five 32-by-21-foot classrooms, and an auditorium/gym and would serve all high school grades. The cost? All three educational

---

[297] Odum, interview.
[298] Kjeldgaard, "Impressions," 2.
[299] "Amache," 17.

buildings were bid at a total of $308,498, with the cost of the high school building not to exceed $136,886.[300]

Each school building was to consist of simple designs and basic materials. Atop concrete foundations would stand walls built of cinder blocks to window level. Next, a wooden-framed construction covered with wallboard would be used. Inside the school, only the most rudimentary facilities would exist. Floors would consist of pine board, while each room was to have one window, as well as one electrical drop situated at the center of the room. Students were to build their own cupboards, shelves, bookcases, and nonessential furniture. Blackboards would consist of simple wallboard painted black—not the slate material most public schools used at the time.[301]

A primary emphasis was placed on completing the high school building first. To this end, construction on the high school proceeded at a rapid pace through December 1942 and into January 1943. Construction was progressing so well, it was decided to pour the concrete foundations of the two elementary building sites in the middle of January. It seemed crews might actually meet the April deadline for completion of the schools.[302]

But by the middle of January, press sources nationwide had spread the news that a relocation center was getting a permanent school. Suddenly, the WRA came under attack. The cost of such structures—which some viewed as being much more than the cost of similar structures outside the camp—were seen as a waste of crucial wartime tax dollars. If the camp was to be temporary, they asked, why was the expense being put forth? Colorado's Senator Johnson resurrected anti-Asian hostilities by describing the new construction as signs of "pampering" the enemy—this at a time when funding for new schools and teachers was nearly nonexistent in the state of Colorado. He also stated that his office had received numerous complaints from Granada area residents regarding such extravagant expenditures. Colorado's Rep. J. Edgar Chenoweth (R) joined the

---

[300] *Lamar Daily News*, 2 December 1942, 1; 5 December 1942, 1; 31 December 1942, 1.
[301] *Lamar Daily News*, 28 December 1942, 1; 31 December 1942, 1.
[302] *Lamar Daily News*, 18 January 1943, 1; 2 December 1942, 1.

fray when he noted that the building of new schools was unnecessary when vacant store buildings in Granada could be renovated for educational purposes.[303]

In response to Chenoweth's statements, the editor of the *Lamar Daily News* mused that "It is rather interesting to note that Representative Edgar Chenoweth who is actively opposing the school construction was pleased to announce…an additional million dollar appropriation for the alien concentration camp in Trinidad."[304]

Adding to the commotion, the Denver Building and Construction Trades Council voiced their unanimous support for Senator Johnson in his drive to stop construction at the camp. In a letter to Johnson, the business representative of the council stated that "while we as a building trades group earn our livelihood in the construction industry, and consequently seldom oppose any construction project, we feel that it is our patriotic duty to oppose that squandering of any money on such a thing as a school to educate Japs. If they were given an opportunity to show their true colors, I wonder how much their American citizenship would amount to?"[305]

The representative continued his berating by noting that "if there are any federal funds to be handed out for the construction of schools, let's build some additional space for our own children. I wonder if any American children who may be in Jap hands as prisoners are receiving even half civilized treatment."[306]

The construction of the school brought about a sea of debate in Colorado as well as across the country. Was it the responsibility of the United States to educate persons who were evacuated because of ancestral ties to a wartime enemy—two-thirds of whom were citizens of the United States? In the case of Amache residents, was the right to a quality educational environment consistent with that afforded to other citizens of Colorado? Or should primary and secondary schools be viewed as a luxury afforded only to those who were on the outside?

---

[303] *Rocky Mountain News*, 31 December 1942, 10; 16 January 1943, 4.
[304] *Lamar Daily News*, 16 January 1943, 1.
[305] *Rocky Mountain News*, 15 January 1943, 10.
[306] *Rocky Mountain News*, 31 December 1942, 10; 15 January 1943, 10.

Project Director James C. Lindley held that "these children cannot be brought up in idleness and ignorance. School, after a fashion, is now being conducted in barracks buildings, sorely needed for living quarters. Buildings for classes are needed badly."[307] Likewise, Superintendent of Schools Paul J. Terry responded:

> Democracy is a matter of environment, not heredity... It is a false loyalty for Americans to take a "poke" at these people of Japanese lineage. The hope for the assimilation of these people into the American system is to educate them in the American way... This is proven, in the fact those who have been attending American schools have taken up every American way and belief... They have left excellent schools on the Coast, and if we take away all education from them, we have a morale problem.[308]

But these opinions held little weight. By the end of January, Dillon Myer—fearing negative repercussion from public opinion—stopped construction of the elementary and middle schools. Only the concrete foundation of these two buildings would remain. Construction on the high school continued, however, when the R. E. Rippe Construction Company threatened to sue the WRA if not allowed to finish.[309]

Completion of the high school allowed secondary students to move out of barrack schoolrooms and into an adequate, more permanent learning environment. Although the school, compared to other high schools, was lacking in many ways, it did include, among other things, twenty-four classrooms approximately thirty-two by twenty-one feet in size, a fifty-by-ninety-foot auditorium, a library, vocational shops, and a number of staff offices. After its opening in

---

[307] *Lamar Daily News*, 28 December 1942, 1.
[308] *Lamar Daily News*, 22 January 1943, 1.
[309] *Rocky Mountain News*, 24 January 1943, 13.

the fall of 1944, the school would become a focal point for sports and community activities.[310]

After construction ended at the elementary and middle school building sites, the concrete foundations became a favorite play area for evacuee children. The concrete foundations, however, were not firmly entrenched in the claylike soil, and in April 1943, three boys who had been playing there became trapped in a cave-in. "One of my friends, Paul Takemura was one of the boys trapped in that cave-in," Tom Shigekuni recalls. "He and his brother were digging around one of the foundations when the earth just gave way." The accident trapped the two Takemura boys, as well as a friend who was with them. Two of the boys were able to dig their way out, but the fourteen-year-old Paul Takemura remained trapped. He died soon after rescue. "I went to his funeral," Shigekuni recalls. "It was a tragic accident—a sad situation."[311]

Class sizes averaged about thirty-five students in all of Amache's schools. At its peak, the project's nursery, kindergarten, and elementary schools would have an enrollment totaling more than a 1,000 students. The junior high and high schools would eventually enroll on average of 850 students and obtain the same full accreditation that other public schools received.[312]

"They were the most attentive and industrious pupils I ever had," remembered fourth-grade teacher Enola Kjeldgaard. "I learned not to give an assignment shortly before noon or I would find them in the room working when I came back from lunch. "[313]

Academics and school-related activities at every level were similar to those outside the project. The officially stated purpose of the WRA educational program was that of enabling "young citizens to make acceptable educational progress while temporarily withdrawn from normal American communities." However, WRA officials also hoped to "aid the individual pupils to overcome the shock of evacuation and to adjust to center living conditions." Underlying the

---

[310] *Lamar Daily News*, 31 December 1942, 1.
[311] Shigekuni, interview.
[312] "Amache," 17.
[313] Kjeldgaard, "Impressions," 2.

"acceptable educational progress" language used by WRA officials was the sentiment of guidance in traditional academic subjects as well as individual attitudes—strong, positive American attitudes. Great attention was given to the "maintaining and understanding of American ideals, institutions, and practices." To this end, WRA schools hoped to ready students of all ages for the "melting pot" of American society—to mold young and old alike into the American image desired by the government.[314]

For the young, a mix of general subjects was emphasized. Elementary-age students were taught a general mixture of reading, mathematics, history, and English. Junior high and high school students were taught subjects ranging from mathematics to physics, science to art, and physical education to civics. All students, no matter their age, were strongly encouraged to use English as their primary language both at school and at home. Through this discipline, it was hoped, students would, "develop self-control, initiative, appreciation and awareness for others, and a feeling of community responsibility."[315]

For older youth, training was seen as necessary. Myer's bent toward relocation provided ample reasoning to start a vocational program at Amache. Opportunities to apply these skills within the center were limited. Still, the program was open to all students in upper secondary grades. Those who took agriculture or shorthand classes could often apply their newly acquired education to jobs around the project in the last portion of their senior year. Those who took auto mechanics or advanced homemaking often had to wait until after graduation and eventual relocation. Summer employment was also offered to students who wanted to put their education to practice. Once their vocational education was complete, a few young men

---

[314] WRA, Education Program in War Relocation Centers, Lloyd Garrison Collection, Box 1, Folder 7, Auraria Library Archives and Special Collection, Denver, 2.

[315] Lloyd A. Garrison, "Information about Amache Secondary Schools," 26 March 1945, Lloyd Garrison Collection, Box 1, Folder 7, Auraria Library Archives and Special Collections, Denver, 1–2; WRA, Education Program, 12.

and women were assigned to an apprenticeship program within the confines of the center.[316]

For adults, "extracurricular" learning was essential. Vocational sewing was one of the more popular classes among the women in Amache. Flower-making and flower-arranging classes as well as English-language classes were also popular. Japanese-language classes were not offered until June 1943. Even then, lessons in the Japanese language were only available to women who could offer viable reasons for taking such a class. Other adult classes included such things as wood carving, cooking, shorthand, algebra, clothing design, piano, drafting, and art.[317]

The educational system of Amache is what many evacuees recall most vividly. "For myself," George Hirano recalls:

> I became very comfortable with [school] right away because I was surrounded by other Japanese American people. Immediately what you did was run for class office, you participated in everything socially, which I knew I could not do back in Sausalito—nobody told us, we just knew. Graduation dances, you just don't do those kind of things; but here, that barrier was all gone. So I enjoyed the school. I was really into studying, various activities, student council, and all of that kind of thing. School was really a God-send to me.[318]

Bonds formed through the shared experience of internment. And these bonds, say evacuees, have become the overwhelming bright spot of the entire evacuation process. "We've had friends—

---

[316] "Objective 4," 295:0022 L3.18, Japanese American evacuation and resettlement records, BANC MSS 67/14c, the Bancroft Library, University of California, Berkeley.

[317] WRA, "Quarterly Report," Adult Education Section, 30 June 1943 and 20 March 1943, 295:0035 L3.20, Japanese American evacuation and resettlement records, BANC MSS 67/14c, the Bancroft Library, University of California, Berkeley.

[318] Hirano, G., interview.

many, many friends—living throughout the United States that were started in the camp," remarks George Hirano. "Because of the commonalties of that experience—something about that [experience]—you bond with each other. You trust each other; it's a community kind of feeling that we still have."[319]

The sense of community and commonality would become the sinews of strength for young evacuees. For the children of Amache, new friendships would blossom and old ones would grow strong.

Education was an important aspect in camp life. But the activities that took place after school were the events that made imprisonment at Amache tolerable. Yoshi Tanita remembers the dances. "I met my first crush at one of those dances. I must have been, oh, no more than thirteen. Boy, I sure thought it was a big deal when he walked me home from the dance."[320]

Likewise, Grace Kimoto recalls, "We had dance bids so that you already knew who you danced with according to the sign-ups on our bids. Of course, the music was of the Big Band Era. You would save the last dance for that 'special boy.'"[321]

Some called it boogie-woogie and jitterbug music. Others called it swing. Most called it nothing more than a way to escape. Dances at Amache were usually sponsored by a school class or camp organization that would in turn invite another club to attend. The "bids" Kimoto spoke of were dance cards that were filled out at the beginning of the dance.[322]

George Hirano met his wife of fifty years at the sophomore dance. By the time this meeting had taken place, Hirano's notoriety as a band member was well-known around camp. Hirano recalls, "We had a bunch of guys on our block that were talented… They all came together to form a dance band called the Music Makers. It was a big swing band—we had a lot of fun with that. We used to go around to dances and play music for them. We used to go to the mess hall and take all the tables out, put corn meal on the cement floor and use it

---

[319] Hirano, G., interview.
[320] Tanita, interview.
[321] Kimoto, email; Hirano, S., interview.
[322] Hirano, G., interview.

as a dance floor." Hirano's band included a number of evacuees who played trombones, saxophones, trumpets, bass fiddle, piano, and drums. "We also had a piano player—I think we had a really good band. We made our own band stands out of scraps and painted them and added some glitter. We looked very professional."[323]

Evacuee youth could also participate in individual sports programs like Ping-Pong, badminton, and wrestling. "They had sumo wrestling tournaments in camp," notes Hirano. "I used to go down to watch them—they were really interesting to watch."[324]

But possibly the most popular program at Amache was the high school intramural sports program. An entire page in the *Pioneer* was devoted to it. Evacuees followed their teams with intensity. The Amache intramural program included basketball, football, and baseball teams.

And these teams were good. Playing other high school teams from Lamar, Denver, La Junta, and Las Animas, Amache squads always ended their seasons at or near the top. Playing teams from less-populated areas provided an edge for Amache's teams. An edge that rankled some. One incident in the fall of 1944 demonstrated clearly how Amache's competitiveness aggravated the racism of those in the surrounding community.

Throughout the 1944 football season, Wiley's high school football team had fought hard for an undefeated season. But Amache stood in its way. Although a loss to Amache would not keep Wiley from a playoff bid, it would certainly ruin a perfect season. Some said Wiley could outmatch Amache anytime. Many weren't so sure. After all, Amache was a much bigger community with a larger pool of talent. So by early November—with only Amache remaining as a serious threat—Wiley prepared to meet the camp's team in a classic matchup between the two powerhouse football teams.

Amache's team had anticipated the game for weeks. Players had spent hours of practice for this matchup, for the center's team had found itself with a near perfect season. A knock off Wiley might even

---

[323] Hirano, G., interview.
[324] Hirano, G., interview.

lead Amache to be declared the unofficial southeastern champs. To this end, coaches endlessly drilled players. Critical plays were honed to perfection. As game day approached, Amache players itched for the chance to show their stuff.

But only days before the two powerhouses were to meet, a handful of parents from Wiley's team filed formal protests. They refused to allow their boys to play against "Jap" boys at the Wiley football stadium. America was at war with Japan, they reasoned. Such activities would not be in standing with patriotism. The parents' protest brought an end to the game, and Wiley's football team would never face Amache in what remained of the 1944 season.

The effects of this cancellation were deep. In a letter to Superintendent of Schools Dr. Lloyd A. Garrison, one young player wrote:

> We really thought a lot about the game and practiced a pretty lot for it, but rather then feeling disappointed over the waste of our many practices I am rather more disappointed in the five boys' parents who would not permit their sons to play against us because we were Japanese Americans. I and many others, interested sports fans, who were eagerly waiting for that game, took this pretty hard and now hold a grudge against the parents of those boys, which I think is only natural.
>
> I remember last year I, with the varsity basketball team, went to Wiley to play and we enjoyed it very much. The hospitality and sportsmanship they showed us does not match the reason for Wiley's cancellation of the game. I think Wiley as a whole would like it very much to play us and haven't any hard feelings toward us because we are of Japanese parentage. It's a pity to think what a little bunch can do to disappoint over 1,000 spirited students because of race and color.

> Victory over Wiley would have put Amache in a pretty high place in the field of sports and we could have been recognized as the unofficial Southeastern Champs. I hope someday we or the next year squad can have better luck and chance.[325]

Because of the protest, Amache teams would be forced to play the remainder of the football season as well as the entirety of the basketball season—at home.

Did the parents of the five boys protest as a means to keep Wiley's team undefeated? No one can really be sure. But to the evacuees of Amache, the incident proved once again that their worth was based on ethnic background, not accomplishment. The incident also reminded evacuees just how tenuous their place in American society really was. Plans could be made, opportunities could be sought, but the ultimate decision to do anything still was influenced heavily by an Anglo-American public.

Regardless of how outside parties reacted to the evacuees of Amache, Issei and Nisei relocated to Colorado tried to live as near-normal lifestyles as possible. Youth clubs were everywhere. Boy Scouts and Cub Scouts, Camp Fire Girls and the FFA, YMCA and YWCA—all these groups offered Amache youth opportunities to be a part of a group. But these clubs also gave the youth of Amache opportunities to travel beyond the barbed wire fences of their environment. In a trip financed by the community council, fourteen members of the Future Farmers of America traveled to Denver in January 1945 to attend the annual stock show.[326]

Likewise, eighty members of Amache's Boy Scouts traveled to Mancos, Colorado, in August 1943. The purpose of the ten-day Boy Scout trip was to "help dismantle an old CCC camp thirty miles

---

[325] Ken Nakato, letter to Lloyd A. Garrison, Lloyd Garrison Collection, Box 1, Folder 2, Auraria Library Archives and Special Collections, Denver.

[326] WRA, Granada, Colorado, "Narrative Report," 31 January 1945, 302:0141 L5.32, Japanese American evacuation and resettlement records, BANC MSS 67/14c, the Bancroft Library, University of California, Berkeley.

west of Durango." Having recently acquired the old buildings at the CCC camp, the WRA hoped to transport each building's section to Amache. Lindley noted in a press release that "the boys are anxious to do their bit in supplying needed manpower, and we hope they also will find time for some relaxation in the mountain area near the camp. They have worked hard all year at the center and we know they will earn their leisure hours." After the Boy Scouts returned from the ten-day work/vacation program, thirty-six members of the FFA also made the trek west to continue where the Boy Scouts had left off.[327]

The various youth clubs of Amache held their meetings wherever they could find room. The FFA held some meetings in the auto mechanics room of the high school. Boy Scouts and other organizations often held their meetings in recreation halls around camp. Terry Hall, a large building located on the same block as the elementary and junior high schools, was also used for large activities.

Activities like intramural sports, dances, and youth clubs were merely a part of life for the youth of Amache. Leisure activities were provided by the evacuee population as a measure of normalcy in an abnormal situation. Tom Shigekuni suggested in later years that such activities often provide an appearance to moderns that the camp was in reality like that of a Club Med-type resort.[328]

Amache, with its barbed wire, dark and cramped living quarters, and oppressive atmosphere held no resemblance to a resort. If smiles were seen on the faces of children at Amache, they often hid the much deeper sentiments of fear, dread, hate, and sadness. Amache was not a Club Med. It was a military holding facility in which thousands spent their lives during World War II.

Children of Amache showed a wide range of tolerance for their plight as evacuees. Some children were vocal. Tom Shigekuni recounts a time when, as an eighth-grade student, he was brought

---

[327] Granada Relocation Center Reports Office, "Sample Press Release," 19 August 1943, 309:215 L6.99, Japanese American evacuation and resettlement records, BANC MSS 67/14c, the Bancroft Library, University of California, Berkeley.

[328] Thomas N. Shigekuni, "Amache and Granada, Colorado, 1942–1944," Southern California Subcommittee for the Amache Reunion, 1994, 3.

before the school's principal. "When they wanted to draft us in 1943," Shigekuni recalls:

> the war department sent some people down to find out how the people felt about being drafted. My eighth-grade teacher one day said "We want you to write an essay on the drafting of Japanese Americans from camp." Well, I thought it was just an exercise in English, so I wrote my true feelings about it.
>
> I really blasted the situation, saying that if they felt we weren't really Americans, they shouldn't be drafting us because if we were Americans we wouldn't be in this confounded place.[329]

The day after the writing assignment, Shigekuni was escorted to meet with the principal. Shigekuni thought he might be praised for some studious accomplishment. Or perhaps he had done something around the school of great worth. He had no idea that he was to be confronted about the letter he had written the day before.

"Finally," Shigekuni recalls,

> [the principal] gets my paper out and waves it at me from about ten feet away and says "Who made you write this? Who made you write this!" Oh, that infuriated me. I thought they were going to honor me and then he asked me that type of question. I really blasted him. I told him what I had written in the paper—and more—then he pointed to the door and told me to get out. Oh he heard me out—I blasted him for about two or three minutes, but then he told me to get out.[330]

---

[329] Shigekuni, interview.
[330] Shigekuni, interview.

Although no punishment was given, Shigekuni and his teacher did have an extensive discussion after school about the letter:

> We had a big argument about our condition—being prisoners. [My teacher] said, "You know Thomas, we are protecting you from the angry Americans." I told her that I lived right up by the guard tower off 12-G at the upper end of camp. I said, "Hey those machine guns are pointed in and those search lights are pointed in—how are they protecting us from the angry Americans." I still clearly remember what she told me. She said, "Thomas, you're nothing but a child. Someday you'll grow up and you'll understand what we're trying to do for you."[331]

Shigekuni holds that to this day, he is still trying to understand what relocation was doing for Japanese Americans.

In contrast to Shigekuni, many children at Amache chose to remain silent about their plight. One administration staff member remarked in a speech at a Pueblo YMCA conference:

> When I first came [to Amache], I was impressed by the number of smiling faces, and on two occasions made the mistake of asking whether they were happy. Their answers were no. I have since come to the conclusion that, as it would be the case for any group of children submitted to similar circumstances, those children have been hurt—many of them much more deeply hurt than they themselves may realize. And although with the passing of time the healing process has done its good work, the scar is still present and

---

[331] Shigekuni, interview.

unless we are very careful, it can very easily be opened again.[332]

The wounds were indeed deep. Self-hatred was one of the worst dangers to young Japanese Americans. One teacher recalled a young boy sitting against a barrack wall crying. With a play rifle in hand, the boy hung his head low as the woman approached. When the teacher asked the young boy why he was crying, the youth raised his head and explained that he had been playing war with a group of boys. It seemed that the boys pretending to be the American soldiers had chosen the young child to be the Japanese soldier in the game. "I'm tired of the being the damn Jap all the time," concluded the boy.[333]

This story of the young Japanese American boy spread rapidly around the camp's administration. Many administrators saw the story as a source of pride and assurance. To them, the incident merely proved the true loyalty found within the gates of Amache. They didn't see the incident as hatred of self. The leaders of Amache saw this as clear evidence they were doing their job of acclimating young minds to the "American way."

But no amount of loyalty could ever make their imprisonment disappear. Tom Shigekuni recalls playing baseball by the camp's fence on sunny days. "We would play ball at the edge of the camp, and sometimes the ball would go through the fence. If we looked like we were going to go after it, the guards would point loaded rifles at us and yell at us to get back. I really resented being cooped up and not having the freedom to even chase a ball."[334]

---

[332] Public Relations—The Pueblo-Amache Y.M.C.A Conference, 302:0285 L5.39, Japanese American evacuation and resettlement records, BANC MSS 67/ 14c, the Bancroft Library, University of California, Berkeley.
[333] Mildred Garrison, taped interview, Lloyd Garrison Collection, Box 1, Auraria Library Archives and Special Collections, Denver.
[334] Shigekuni, interview.

AMACHE

Michi Nishiura Weglyn cites a story describing the attitudes of MPs at relocation centers around the country. A 1942 WRA investigation revealed that

> the guards have been instructed to shoot anyone who attempts to leave the center without a permit, and who refuses to halt when ordered to do so. The guards are armed with guns that are effective at a range of up to 500 yards. I asked Lt. Buckner if a guard ordered a Japanese who was out of bounds to halt and the Jap did not do so, would the guard actually shoot him. Lt. Buckner's reply was that he only hoped the guard would bother to ask him to halt. He explained that the guards were finding guard service very monotonous, and that nothing would suit them better than to have a little excitement, such as shooting a Jap.[335]

Sets Sumikawa recalls just such an incident with an Amache guard. "One day," Sumikawa recalls,

> I was with a group of friends and we were playing in the snow. There was a man in the watch tower pointing a rifle at us. He said, "If you know what's good for you, you'll get the hell out of here—you're going to get shot." I guess we were playing too close to the barbed wire. Oh, when we heard that, we ran home. Each of us were so scared. I cried. We went home and told our parents about it. You know, Japanese people are so quiet about things like this. [My parents] really couldn't say much about it. What could they say—they would have to go against the govern-

---

[335] Weglyn, *Years of Infamy*, 91.

ment. That image left a very real impression on me even to this day.[336]

Myer's job wasn't to meet the emotional needs of an evacuated people. Myer's job was that of relocation. To meet this goal, education was established. Emergency services were put into place. In the end, Myer's relocation camps were in place and functioning as he had hoped.

The only problem remaining was that Myer's relocation center in Granada, Colorado, could never be the sort of temporary way station he had hoped for. This temporary place, this makeshift city called Amache was filled with too much pain and anxiety to be a place of peace.

Nonetheless, there it stood. Sitting on the plains of Colorado, Amache—with all the turmoil it represented—had become the newest city in the state.

---

[336] Sumikawa, S., interview.

CHAPTER 6

"THE STRANGE DRAMA"

This is Amache, Colorado. It is one of the most unusual cities in the State. It literally sprang up overnight on a desolate prairie where a short time ago only sagebrush, cactus and Russian thistles survived the winter snow and hot summer sun. Under this setting, we find the strange drama of the Japanese in a relocation center unfolding day by day. The teeming thousands who were literally uprooted from their native home and transplanted to this novel environment work, play, attend schools and carry on activities of everyday living not totally different from those of an average American community. People become married, give birth, and die just as they have been normally doing. (Amache brochure)[337]

It was indeed a strange site. This small, tightly compact community jutting up from the sand of southern Colorado had—nearly overnight—become the tenth largest city in the state. With an average

---

[337] "Amache," 5.

population of 6,500, Amache had need of emergency services such as fire and police departments. A hospital "employing" some of the best doctors in the country treated every kind of ailment and injury. Evacuee children attended the center's state accredited school system. An employment and welfare office, a post office with its own zip code, and a regularly published newspaper all made Amache seem much like any other normal American community. But the environment surrounding this temporary community was far different from that of a normal community.

Barbed wire surrounded this city. Armed military police walked among the residents of this village. In towers high above sat uniformed men—all of whom had rifles and searchlights pointed in. Although it may have been organized much like other Colorado cities, Amache was filled with inhabitants who neither chose to live there nor wished to remain. But within these confines they would—over the next few years—live, work, and play.

Jack Carberry's purpose was simple: make a fact-finding journey down to the town of Amache. The *Denver Post* wanted to inform its readers about the strange new city in southeastern Colorado. Naturally, the investigation was to be conducted "impartially, with open mind, with the investigator seeking the good as well as the bad, and telling the facts as they exist, permitting the facts to speak for themselves."[338] As the *Post*'s sports editor, the paper felt Carberry was the best candidate for the job.

Carberry arrived at the center on February 10, 1943. It was a cold and blustery day. The MP at the gate had reluctantly left his heated shack to approve Carberry's clearance. Once inside the center's gates, Carberry set about his work. He met with James Lindley who "extended every possible help and courtesy." Carberry remarked, "I was told I might go anywhere, interview anyone I wished, and spend as much time as I thought necessary on the job. I took full advantage of these opportunities so I might set down for *Post* readers the story Amache as I found it." Carberry investigated, interviewed, and wrote. He talked with local farmers. He questioned Amache's staff.

---

[338] *Denver Post*, 14 February 1943, 1.

He walked around the camp and the town of Granada, looking for items to make his story interesting. Within a few days, Carberry had enough information for a six-article series that he would present to the *Post* for print in mid-February.[339]

For many in Colorado, this was the first glimpse into the daily routines of the center. Carberry accurately listed the plain living conditions of barrack apartments—the potbellied stove, the small cots, the straw-stuffed mattresses, the bare light bulb hanging from each apartment ceiling. He described the winter climate as "cold" and "raw." He gave detailed descriptions of an everyday life at the center, even going as far as to describe the use of hot plates by some evacuees for cooking Japanese dishes "such as fish heads and various soups the contents of which (to the Caucasian) are almost beyond belief."[340]

But the Amache sketched within Carberry's series was not what the Amache evacuees were truly experiencing. The paper's editor had a deeper agenda in mind—that of selling newspapers. Next to Carberry's first article lay the headline "2,700 Workers among 7,006 Japs in Camp Amache." This article half-heartedly noted that of those unemployed, 2,000 were children and over 1,600 people were either stay-at-home mothers or elderly men and women too unwell to work. The photographer making the journey to the camp staged two photos that would accompany Carberry's article. The photos showed evacuees lounging in comfortably furnished apartments. One photo showed a young boy and his mother and sisters happily conversing in "one of the 20-by-30-foot apartments" (an exaggeration, since the largest evacuee apartment was only twenty by twenty-four feet). The other pictured an elderly man enjoying a pipe and a newspaper while resting on a well-built bunk—an industrious wife was seated next to him peacefully sewing.

Evacuees in both photos were pictured amid brightly painted walls decorated with wall hangings and shelves. Several lamps provided illumination. Both rooms appeared spacious. Tables, desks, and chairs added a certain refined coziness. These photos, the employ-

---

[339] *Denver Post*, 14 February 1943, 1.
[340] *Denver Post*, 14 February 1943, 3.

ment article, and Carberry's report provided the impression that although camp experience was somewhat limited in conveniences, it was in reality one of comfort and ease. By picturing Issei and Nisei in comfortable surroundings, the patriotic fodder found in the text was made even more effective. The Issei and Nisei Carberry recorded in his articles—the lazy, the pampered, the uncaring—were made out to be those things Americans despised.[341]

Carberry remarked that locals spoke of great ineptness on the part of evacuees. Locals, it was said, "roared with laughter" at the failure of the center's first radish crop failure caused by planting the crop too late in the year. Farmers also criticized the use of valuable irrigation water for the project's vegetable crops—water that many local farmers felt should be put toward already established beet, alfalfa, and grain crops in their own fields.[342]

Of the Issei, rumors claimed that those in Amache heavily favored Japan: "[The Issei] heart, it is true, lies in Japan. But his head tells him to do nothing, to say nothing that might hurt America. In this he is looking out for himself. He tells himself that no matter who wins this war, he, as an individual will be the victor." If Japan were to win, the Issei would, by his very citizenship, also win. If America triumphed, an "ever-forgiving Uncle Sam" would bestow upon the Issei fair treatment.[343]

Of their treatment, evacuees were coddled. One article of Carberry's series was entitled "Amache Relocation Camp Japs Get Good Food and Plenty of It." In the article, Carberry described average meals consisting of eggs, milk at every meal, and even a small variety of meats and vegetables—scarce items in the rest of America.[344]

The *Post* was not the first to level such pampering charges. In January 1943, the *Rocky Mountain News* printed headlines screaming "Jap Internees Feast as Yanks Fast." The text of the *News* article told of detention camps in western states receiving ample supplies of eggs, sugar, butter, coffee, and meat, while those outside the camp did not.

---

[341] *Denver Post*, 15 February 1943, 5.
[342] *Denver Post*, 16 February 1943, 4.
[343] *Denver Post*, 19 February 1943, 11.
[344] *Denver Post*, 19 February 1943, 11.

The *Post* may have not been the first with reports of this type, but it certainly was trying its best to influence its readers with blatantly untrue fodder.[345]

And of their work ethic, Carberry wrote of evacuees' laziness. This was one of Carberry's most destructive claims. Considered prisoners of war, evacuees were never forced to work. Jobs were filled by recruitment only. But Nisei, asserted Carberry, remained "a group in which a feeling of great self-pity dominates." The Nisei—local farmers claimed—could often be found in local pool halls playing a game of kelly as trucks loaded with coal sat outside awaiting transport to the relocation center. Many, Carberry claimed, would only work in jobs that provided opportunities to go into town—opportunities that led to the purchase of wine and other alcoholic beverages.

Carberry reported that farmers around Las Animas also complained that Japanese farm workers would "do no more than he has to when working for somebody else." Others claimed the Japanese refused to care for the soil on which they farmed—"mining" it of all nutrients until it no longer could produce. In American society, especially an American society in the throes of war, such actions were regarded as nothing short of a crime.[346]

Carberry's report was misleading. The majority of evacuees who could work did. They didn't have to—they were considered prisoners of war. Those who refused work often did so out of protest, not from laziness. Some believed that by refusing employment they were showing their resistance to the WRA's authority in a nonviolent manner. Evacuees were well aware that their internment was not for their own personal safety. If this were the case, why weren't Italian Americans and German Americans also evacuated from their homes? If the government was going to intern the Japanese Americans unjustly, evacuees reasoned, then it also had the responsibility to provide care for them. Tom Shigekuni recalls, "Some of the Issei—the noncitizens—felt that they were prisoners and why should they work. They refused to work. They didn't have to work; they were guests of the

---

[345] *Rocky Mountain News*, 10 January 1943, 14.
[346] *Denver Post*, 17 February 1943, 7.

U.S. government. Why should they work? You know, I think they had the right idea."³⁴⁷

This resistance was played out on many levels. On an individual level, some refused to work in particular jobs. An agricultural department report remarked that evacuees refused to stack hay under all circumstances, claiming, "Hay stacking no good, too dirty," or "Hay make me sick." The report noted that "consequently, it was not an unusual experience for staff people to help stack hay." At a group level, many would withhold help in harvesting center crops until absolutely necessary. Every fall, administrators at Amache were forced to send out pleas for enough manpower to harvest the center's crops. At an individual level, some evacuee farm laborers would even pace themselves by sitting "under the shade for two hours each day" during lunch hours.³⁴⁸

Joe Smart, regional director of the WRA, understood clearly these attitudes of resistance. In a letter to James Lindley, Smart noted that the use of mass suggestion should be used as a "powerful implement in time of war." To accomplish total center-wide employment, Smart frankly urged Lindley to "stimulate the evacuee leaders to inaugurate and maintain a vigorous campaign through the press, through clever posters, meetings, through interesting entertainment skits and in other ways, to recruit their total man-power to accomplish the work that needs doing."³⁴⁹

Smart was well aware of Lindley's past maneuverings and had full confidence in what had been done at Amache. But Smart strongly suspected that the desire to work was "still coming too much from our staff and not enough from the members of the community The effective mobilization of manpower is probably the most important one we have right now and justifies the best means and energies which we can devote to it." In Smart's opinion, Lindley needed to organize

---

³⁴⁷ Shigekuni, interview.
³⁴⁸ WRA, Granada Relocation Center, "Historical Report-Operations Division, Agricultural Section," Granada Archives, 5.
³⁴⁹ Joe H. Smart, letter to James Lindley, 3 November 1942, 305:011 L6.00, Japanese American evacuation and resettlement records, BANC MSS 67/14c, the Bancroft Library, University of California, Berkeley.

a manpower mobilization commission on the project made up of the best Caucasian, Issei, and Nisei people. He felt such an energetic and imaginative group might be able to "whip up a program which will not only solve our problems but be a credit and an example to the entire program and to the country."[350]

Although the majority of evacuees at Amache found consistent employment in one way or another, total camp employment would remain an issue throughout the life of the camp.

Those who did work in Amache were often misunderstood, mistreated, and underpaid. A 1943 relocation guidebook mandated that "the majority of evacuee residents who work on WRA-sponsored jobs or in consumer enterprises at the relocation centers will be paid at the rate of $16 a month. For apprentices and others who require close supervision, the rate will be $12 per month. For those with professional skills, unusually difficult duties, or supervisory responsibilities, it will be $19 a month."[351] The pay was for a standard workweek ranging from forty to forty-four hours per week.

Compared with the salaries of Caucasian employees at the camp (a Caucasian teacher was paid between $1,500 and $1,600 a year; a Caucasian electrician's helper, $1,500 a year), these salaries seem ludicrous. A small monthly clothing allowance was also given to those families whose household head worked for the center—$3.50 for all family members over the age of fifteen, slightly less for those under that age. But even this extended aid could not bring the evacuee's total compensation package in line with that of other Americans of the time. In essence, evacuees were expected to accept low salaries to build and maintain their own confinement—and to do so in a far better fashion than the average citizen.[352]

The vast majority of Amacheans overlooked the low wages, the blatant lack of constitutional rights, and the consistent paternalistic treatment. The major reason for this was simple patriotism. They worked not out of docility—one could not be docile and still hold

---

[350] Smart, letter to James Lindley.
[351] WRA, *The Relocation Program—A Guidebook for the Residents of Relocation Centers* (New York: AMS Press, 1975), 5–6.
[352] WRA, *The Relocation Program*, 5–6.

true to cultural ties. They worked not out of submission—one could not be weak and endure the hardships they had faced. Those who chose to work did so out of a patriotic desire to serve their chosen country.

Within the "novel environment" of Amache, work became as much a part of life as anywhere else in America. Adult evacuees could find employment in nearly all aspects of camp operations. Jobs within the camp were necessary to the very existence of the camp. From the center's newspaper to janitorial services, from maintenance to emergency services, from teaching to mess hall operations—Amache was a large operation, and it required many people to operate it effectively.

One of these individuals was Emory Namura. "It was just like any other city," Namura recalls. "I would take the mail to the office at each block and then a carrier would take it around to the barrack apartments—or bring [returning mail] back to the office. We had a lot of mail go through there."[353] The assistant postmaster of Lamar, Namura adds, supervised the entire Amache postal service.

The post office was opened in the administrative area of the camp shortly after the arrival of the evacuees. Although the office was a branch of the Lamar Post Office and was administered by five Caucasian employees of the US Post Office, it also included an evacuee postmaster as well as a number of evacuee clerks and postal deliverers.

Amache received its name by way of this postal service. Fearing the relocation project at Granada might become confused with the actual town of Granada, the camp was named after Amache Ochinee Prowers, the Cheyenne wife of Colorado cattle baron John Prowers. By some reports, the camp was called Amache by the assistant postmaster of Lamar, who strenuously wanted to make his job easier by delegating a portion of his duties to a new post office. By other reports, the name was suggested by the mayor of Lamar, R. L. Christy, who wished to honor Amache Ochinee's husband—the man who lent his name to Prowers County. Whatever the case, the

---

[353] Namura, E., interview.

name stuck, and Granada's relocation center would forever have the nickname of Amache.[354]

The department employing the most evacuees was the mess hall operations unit. Each mess hall was given its own staff of cooks, kitchen helpers, waitstaff, and supply stewards. To appreciate the total number of people in this division, one need only look at an evacuee employment census for the month of May 1943 that listed 1,486 evacuees working in the mess division alone. In comparison, the next closest division was the public works department with just over 470 employees.[355]

The public works department was responsible for the upkeep of the center. Caucasian engineers led this department, but like other departments, the bulk of its employees were Issei and Nisei.

The agriculture industry—although often employing less than 200 people—was considered the most important for Amache's existence. The agricultural industry not only helped the camp be self-sufficient, but also sent vast quantities of food to other evacuation camps.

The sheer volume and wide variety of food produced in the fields surrounding Amache astounded local farmers who, at first, scoffed at the new procedures brought by the evacuees. The effects of the evacuees on the area around Granada can still be seen today. "Our local agriculture has a lot to do with what they brought in," remarks John Hopper, Dean of Students at today's Granada School District. "I mean, you figure Rocky Ford where you have melons and everything else; then you get to Los Animas where it starts tapering off—west of Lamar there's nothing. Then all of a sudden, it picks up again. There has to be a reason. Before that time there were mainly sugar beets."[356]

---

[354] WRA, "Public Relations," 304:0067 L5.71, Japanese American evacuation and resettlement records, BANC MSS 67/14c, the Bancroft Library, University of California, Berkeley; "Amache," Introduction.

[355] Walter J. Knodel, "Quarterly Report—Employment and Relocation," 1 April–30 June 1943, 305:0011 L6.00, Japanese American evacuation and resettlement records, BANC MSS 67/14c, the Bancroft Library, University of California, Berkeley.

[356] Hopper, interview.

The variety of crops produced by evacuees was amazing. An October issue of the *Amache Bulletin* boasts that with the use of irrigation from the Lamar Canal and the Manvel Ditch, evacuee farmers were growing such crops as hay, alfalfa, barley, sorghum, pyrethrum (used for commercial fly spray), potatoes, lima beans, spinach, and sugar beets. Even celery—a crop never before produced in southeastern Colorado—was grown successfully by evacuees. An introductory guide to Amache notes that from Amache's commercial acreage, more than 3,838,600 pounds of vegetables would be harvested in 1943 alone.[357]

A wide variety of livestock was also raised. In 1944 alone, evacuees were responsible for raising over 700 head of cattle, over 3,600 chickens, and nearly 1,000 hogs. And when the time came for slaughter, much of the project-raised livestock was sent to the camp's own slaughterhouse, poultry plant, butcher shop, and food-processing plant.[358]

The self-sufficiency of Amache's agricultural section was a model of efficiency among internment camps. By growing crops on project land, raising livestock for camp consumption, and processing food within the camp, evacuees in Amache and other internment camps would eventually reduce the average food cost of a single evacuee to less than thirty-one cents a day.[359]

"We used to make posters for the navy and the army—'Come Join the Army'—signs like that," remembers Tae Namura. Namura worked in what was possibly the most well-known of all the Amache industries—the silk-screen unit. "I wasn't an artist, but I helped make the posters. The artists would draw something and [we would] cut the film and use the screens to make the print. I think it was about the first of its kind. It was very new at that time."[360] The products designed by the shop, which opened on block 6E on May 31, 1943, included such things as navy recruitment training posters, personal greeting cards, calendars, menus, and informational posters.

---

[357] "Amache," 27.
[358] "Amache," 27.
[359] "Issei, Nisei, Kibei," 74.
[360] Namura, T., interview.

Namura recalls, "We had all our friends working together, it was kind of fun. We used to make our own Christmas cards and things like that." Eventually, the print shop became so important to the center—and to the war effort—that it employed well over fifty evacuees as artists, apprentices, and laborers.[361]

Amache's newspapers employed only a small number of evacuees. But the work they produced is of great historical importance. The *Granada Bulletin* (October 14–24) and the *Granada Pioneer* (October 28, 1942–September 18, 1945) were semiweekly publications run entirely by evacuees.

Written in both English and Japanese, the papers—which were ultimately sponsored by the WRA—were subject to censorship. In return for the freedom to publish, it was understood that "the WRA will expect the paper to publish official announcements or releases and to check such stories (in the interest of accurate presentation) with the appropriate project official in advance of publication."[362]

The newspapers at Amache had a circulation of about 3,500. Very few articles mentioned confinement. Unrest within the camp was rarely written about. In reality, the *Pioneer* served primarily as a vehicle for internal communication. News of the latest high school matches, crop information, and WRA announcements were highlighted. The paper also included listings of upcoming events and adult education classes as well as camp vital statistics such as the latest births and deaths.

Through these news sources, Amache's staff hoped to paint a positive picture of the outside world. A report by the first editor of the *Pioneer*, Oski Taniwaki, noted that an officer from the Washington WRA suggested "residents" of the camp should be informed of the "type of country that is outside of these relocation centers, since there are now many people who are contemplating leaving the centers and relocating themselves in employment elsewhere in the country." The WRA did not want the *Pioneer* to provide negative connotations of what evacuees might expect. Only the basic information—"what

---

[361] Namura, T., interview.
[362] WRA, *The Relocation Program*, 10.

type of town is Kansas City, St. Louis, Chicago, and what are the major industries, etc."³⁶³

WRA center newspapers were meant to disseminate vital information to evacuees. Few controversial topics were to be addressed. In the same manner, all outside news sources such as magazines and national newspapers were subject to approval before being sold within the center.

Other publications were also produced in addition to the camp's newspapers. A monthly magazine called *Pulse* (featuring short stories, articles, and poems about life in Amache) was attempted in 1943. However, a lack of contributors made the first edition of the *Pulse* its last. Two issues of an illustrated booklet called *Amache* were also issued in the spring of 1943 and 1944. These booklets were primarily promotional in purpose and were given to visitors to the center as informational tools. Other camp publications included various high school and grade school papers as well as a Boy Scout publication entitled *Reveille*.³⁶⁴

Over the lifetime of the center, approximately twenty-five different departments employed evacuees within Amache. Mechanics and machinists kept the center running. Typists and secretaries worked in administrative steno pools. Old men cleaned the bathrooms. Young men kept the coal heaps full. It was the evacuees of Amache that made the camp come alive. It was their labor that made the unusual city breathe life. But when their work was done, they also made time for play.

"I was in charge of the recreation department," recalls Harry Shironaka. Harry Shironaka led the Amache's adult recreation division in the early years of the camp:

> We had hardball, but no organized football teams—they tried it, but it just didn't work out. We had some softball, but that was mainly for the

---

[363] Oski Taniwaki, "Weekly Report of Meeting," 3 February 1943, 293:0011 L2.01, Japanese American evacuation and resettlement records, BANC MSS 67/14c, the Bancroft Library, University of California, Berkeley.

[364] WRA, Granada Relocation Center, "Reports Office Final Report," 309:0215 L6.99, Japanese American evacuation and resettlement records, BANC MSS 67/14c, the Bancroft Library, University of California, Berkeley.

girls in the camp. We played outside the camp a couple of times.

When we did this, we picked all the good players and made a team out of them. We had, oh, about six or eight teams, I guess. We did the same for basketball. Los Animas had a Japanese American basketball team. They wanted to play us because they could come into the camp and play our team and visit. I got to know quite a few of those outside the camp that way.[365]

As time went on, more and more activities like those set up by Shironaka were established for times of leisure. For those who enjoyed sports, the center provided events in basketball, baseball, and unorganized games of football. For men who preferred less strenuous leisure, activities such as wood carving, shogi (a Japanese game similar to chess), goh, and mah-joneg were available. Women found enjoyment in classes and clubs for knitting, flower making, and weaving.

Old and young alike enjoyed movies. "We had the latest movies in the camp," Emory Namura notes. "We could only watch them in the mess halls though. It was like in the army, they would haul the film [projector] in a truck from mess hall to mess hall. I think they had two different showings every night in different blocks." Movies were rotated among the mess halls at Amache. Show times were scheduled to change twice a week. "I think it was a dime or fifteen cents to get in," adds Namura. "They had some sort of connection with someone important, because we even saw the latest musicals and detective films."[366] Bruce Newman recalls that as a boy living in the town of Granada, he would sometimes even venture into the camp to view the films shown there.[367]

Many evacuees also enjoyed working in the small victory gardens that dotted the landscape of Amache. A source of pride to those

---

[365] Shironaka, interview
[366] Namura, E., interview.
[367] Newman, interview.

who planted them, these victory gardens often amazed local farmers. Exotic plants such as Chinese cabbage, habucha (an Asian tea plant), mung beans (used for bean sprouts), and daikon were all introduced to the region through these victory gardens. These gardens also served a certain therapeutic value. To Japanese Americans who had lost a lot of control over their lives, victory gardens remained one area where control was maintained. Gardening was one of the simple freedoms evacuation did not take away.[368]

Besides gardening, bounties set on rattlesnakes and jackrabbits made hunting a very profitable hobby in the center. "The government put a ten-cent bounty on jack rabbits," Bruce Newman recalls. "There were millions of them running around Granada. Guys would go out and trap them by the dozens and skin them for sale to the army. I guess the army would use the fur for military gloves to use overseas. One guy in town got a contract to skin the rabbits and dug a pit in the backyard of his place to bury the bodies of those skinned rabbits. Boy did it stink, it made the whole town smell."[369]

On weekends, shopping passes for travel into Granada and Lamar were also popular. A few evacuee farmers would pass the time in the Granada restaurant owned by Bruce Newman's grandmother. Women of the camp also ventured into Granada to buy goods in the local drugstore owned by Newman's father. Newman suggests that his family's businesses improved greatly when the relocation center was opened—especially his father's drugstore. "Because of its size, my father's drugstore was limited on what it could sell," Newman recalls. "But we had imported huge wooden barrels of hard candy from Mexico (it wasn't very good candy) and a lot of pina nuts. My father also bought a popcorn machine. At night, the whole Newman family would package the pina nuts, popcorn, and candy in small paper parcels and stack them on the shelves in the store."[370]

Newman's store in Granada was not the only place in which evacuees could purchase supplies. The shops of Granada also included

---

[368] "Amache," 27.
[369] Newman, interview.
[370] Newman, interview.

a billiard parlor, a café, a gas station, and bank. An evacuee-owned fish market was also opened next door to the drugstore. "It really sold both fish and poultry," notes Newman. "People would send in their orders during the day. I would work in my father's drugstore after school for a couple of hours and then I would go over to the fish market and ride on the delivery truck that delivered wrapped packages of fish and poultry to the camp. The fish market also sold things like soy sauce and noodles—the sort of things you would find in a small Japanese market."[371]

"As the camp progressed," Newman continues, "some of the people there had devised a means—I'm not really sure how—of cooking these things without having to go to the mess hall. The camp had telephones, so when someone wanted to place an order, they would just phone it in. Any-way, after I would finish at my father's store, I would jump on the truck with a carpenter's apron filled with $50 in change and we would head to camp."[372]

Evacuee youth also traveled into surrounding communities to shop or to hang around. "We went into town every once in awhile on a shopping pass," recalls Henry Okubo. "But instead of shopping, we would usually go to the pool hall and hang around. We never had any money, but we went anyway—it was just something to do."[373]

Granada was the community nearest to Amache. "I always felt the people in Granada were fairly nice to us who were in the camp," recalls Kimi Shironaka.[374] Besides Granada, the city of Lamar was also used as a shopping destination, largely due to its size and number of businesses. Unlike businesses in Granada, those in surrounding communities welcomed the revenue brought in by evacuees—but not necessarily their presence.

At first, there were complaints by some local residents that the evacuees were depleting merchandise stocks at Lamar businesses. Some locals also distrusted evacuees who spoke English to town residents and Japanese to each other. But in October 1942, the Lamar

---

[371] Newman, interview.
[372] Newman, interview.
[373] Okubo, interview.
[374] Kimi Shironaka, personal interview, 15 July 2000.

Chamber of Commerce hosted a dinner in Lamar in an effort to overcome these hostilities between the townspeople and evacuees. The October 21 edition of the *Pioneer* reported that the Chamber of Commerce "had foremost in their minds the economic advantage to be gained through trade with thousands of evacuees and also through accessibility to a large supply of agricultural laborers." One merchant at the dinner was even heard stating, "Why there's thousands of dollars waiting to be dumped into your laps. The people up there [at the center] are just begging to hand over their money to you. Their money is just as good as anyone else's, isn't it?"[375]

Evacuees were well aware of their position within the community. In a letter to a non-Japanese American outside the camp, *Pioneer* editor Oski Taniwaki wrote, "Frankly, we would say that the money spent by the evacuees at this town is supporting the merchants of this 'would-be forsaken' village. There has been no discrimination nor incidents to mar the excellent reputation and relationship between the people of Granada and the evacuees."[376]

Taniwaki felt that most people and businesses in Granada and Lamar were accepting of their new neighbors. "The city of Lamar, which is located eighteen miles from this colony, has often made gestures to accommodate and welcome the shoppers from the relocation center. Bus lines have been even suggested but due to rationing, this project has been canceled." However, acceptance of evacuees often went no further than that of consumer and provider. Taniwaki remarked that "as the two mentioned cities are only of a financial relationship, very little social contacts have been made, and we may state that socially we are still strangers."[377]

"We had the privilege to go out once a month," recalled Itsako Kuruma. "Some stores, they didn't want us to buy anything. They asked, 'Are you Chinese or Japanese.' I would say Japanese, and they would say 'No!' They were in Lamar. It was sad—everyone would

---

[375] WRA, "Public Relations."
[376] Taniwaki, letter.
[377] Taniwaki, letter.

just look at us and say 'Are you Chinese or Japanese.' Later on we'd just tell them we were Chinese."[378]

According to Mildred Garrison, wife of Lloyd Garrison—the director of education for Amache—Lamar residents tried to have little contact with those living in Granada's relocation center. "At first, merchants would hide their valuable merchandise when evacuees arrived in town to shop," Garrison remembers. But as the locals began to become familiar with the evacuees, Garrison added, they began to trust them more. "I don't really recall many people from Lamar going into camp. [The center] had some plays performed by the Japanese, but they were mostly attended by the camp's staff and those within the camp." Evacuees did invite those from surrounding communities to other events like fairs, art shows, and various sporting events. However, the majority of those in outlying communities never ventured inside the gates of Amache.[379]

Some citizens in surrounding communities would not have associated with evacuees at any invitation. Harry Shironaka recalls, "There were some businesses in Lamar that would have 'No Japs Allowed' signs in their store-fronts. They all seemed to be at the north end of town for some reason. If you went into town for shopping purposes, you just knew to not go north of the tracks. I never understood why they would refuse our business. They could have made a lot of money off of us if they would have not treated us like that. "[380]

Likewise, Emory Namura recalls how even the local undertaker refused to accept business of families from Amache. "One said definitely no, but the other one [in town] said that, yeah, he would take the business. Then the other one began to raise hell. Some of the places wouldn't even let you in restaurants and the liquor store. But later on they knew where the money was flowing from."[381]

Even some who claimed to have higher callings had little trust for Japanese Americans. One pastor recalls an incident that began

---

[378] "Amache: Patriotism Amidst Prejudice," Kuruma, taped interview.
[379] Garrison, M., taped interview.
[380] Shironaka, H., interview.
[381] "Amache: Patriotism Amidst Prejudice," Namura, taped interview.

simply because evacuees attended a church service. "One of the trustees of a certain church called me on the telephone for a conference at his home. He told me a very discouraging story of the antagonistic attitude of the minister of his church toward the Japanese and how there had been an angry debate at the board meeting that week because of my having taken two girls to their worship service the Sunday before. Some of the members had suspected me of being a spy."[382]

It was true that on the outside much of Amache's existence seemed like other communities. Couples married. Babies were born. Teenagers fell in love. Monday mornings came. Weekends were spent having fun. Weeks and months passed. And evacuees lived lives that were, in many ways, similar to the day-to-day existence of other citizens. But beneath the surface of this apparently normal existence lay the dark shadows of physical hardships, economic loss, and sociological deterioration.

Evacuees remember the extreme climates found at Amache. When building the center, the WRA had bulldozed all vegetation into open pits, leaving only a flat plain of dirt on which barracks were to be placed. With nothing to break the reflective rays of the sun, summer temperatures reaching well over one hundred became nearly unbearable. Evacuees were unaccustomed to such extreme temperatures. Some Amacheans tried to deal with such temperatures by throwing water on the brick floors to keep barracks cool. Others planted trees for shade.[383]

"It was so hot and dry," George Hirano recalls. "Plus the dust storms came, I hated that. It would cover everything. We would close off all the windows and do everything to try to keep the dust out, but the fine particles of sand would just be over everything."[384]

---

[382] "The Minutes of the Meeting of Colorado Council of Churches on Relocation," Colorado Council of Churches, Western Historical Collections, University of Colorado, Box 1, 12 November 1943.
[383] Momii, interview.
[384] Hirano, G., interview.

Dust was everywhere. "We were used to a green and lush climate," recalls Chez Momii.

> The weather [at Amache] was terrible. As a matter of fact, we had a dress code back then. In the winter it would get windy and cold, and our legs were just raw, you know from the sand hitting them. So the principle came in after school had started, and said there would be no more dress code. We tried not to be out when there was a storm coming—and you could see them coming. I guess they looked like a tornado or something like that. They were so bad you couldn't even see the barracks across the way.[385]

"The dust storms of Amache were just awful," Shigeko Hirano recalls. "We had to put something over our heads. It would hurt us, the sand would blow into our faces—it would actually hurt us. You could hardly breath. I remember they gave us White King soap bars; ·it was laundry soap—very harsh soap. I remember going to the laundry and scrubbing these sheets on the washboard, with that White King soap. Then at the end, we would rinse them and then [my sister] would get on one end and I'd get on the other and we would twist those sheets to ring them out. Then we would go out and hang them on the line. In the wintertime, they'd freeze like boards—and in the summer time, that dust would get all over them. Oh golly, that was just terrible. I can laugh about it now."[386]

The heat and dust—magnified by a lack of vegetation and shade—made summer life in the camp nearly unbearable for evacuees used to milder climates. But winter extremes could be even worse.

The first snowfall of 1943 took place in mid-October and brought much delight to these transplanted Californians. After the first storm, however, the snow and cold soon lost their appeal. With

---

[385] Momii, interview.
[386] Hirano, S., interview.

little to block their path, strong gales drifted snow high against barracks walls and into the cracks of windows and doors. January temperatures in 1943 reached twenty-two below zero. Evacuees often found themselves neither physically nor emotionally equipped for their first winter at Amache.[387]

George Hirano recalls:

> You were on a ridge. Amache is sort of located slightly higher than the area where the Arkansas river is, so it was like a gradual incline. Boy, did that expose you to a northern wind. It used to really hit us there. We got a lot of snow, which we had never experienced before. We were given navy coats—the black ones with a big collar. Thank God for that, since we had no real means of buying clothes. Those coats pretty much became our standard winter uniforms.[388]

Those coats and the little coal stoves provided in each barrack were the items that kept evacuees from the frigid elements of southeastern Colorado. "I don't remember being so cold that we were freezing," recalls Chez Momii. "We had a potbellied stove in the corner and every night my brother and I would go to the coal pile by the laundry room and bring a bucket of coal back to keep us warm at night."[389]

Remembering the many evenings her family huddled in their room for warmth, Yoshi Tanita remarks that "I think the winters were worse than the summers at Amache. The little stove they gave to us never really kept the room warm enough when it got cold. If you wanted to stay warm, you had to stand close by the stove to feel the heat."[390]

---

[387] Lindley, "Final Report," appendix IV, 2.
[388] Hirano, G., interview.
[389] Momii, interview.
[390] Tanita, interview.

Another hardship evacuees faced was the substandard meals. Those with special nutritional needs received very little assistance at Amache. Yoshita Tanita's father acquired diabetes while in the camp and was placed on a special diet by the camp's hospital staff. "He had to walk to the hospital every day to get special meals. It was such a long way to walk every day, especially when it was cold in the winter. But he didn't have much choice." Outside the camp, Tanita's father probably would have had special meals prepared by his family. But there was no such luxury at Amache. Access to food not served by the mess hall was usually found only through the hospital's dietician.[391]

Children's diets were also limited in Amache. The nourishment requirements of infants and toddlers were much more restrictive than those found outside the camp. Formula stations were set up to provide various types of food for infants and toddlers. Babies who were not breastfed received evaporated milk until the age of ten months. At two months, babies were also given orange juice in gradually increased increments. At five months, the infants were then provided with strained foods and eggs.

Only between the ages of ten and eighteen months could children receive fresh pasteurized milk from the stations. Because the WRA had allotted the center only two hundred pints of fresh bottled cow's milk per day (this amount would be cut drastically as the war progressed and milk supplies became more and more scarce), every child above the age of eighteen months, without a prescription stating otherwise, would receive only powdered milk.[392]

Children at the camp who were old enough to eat solid foods were fed a diet high in starch and low in nutrients. Mildred Garrison, wife of the center's director of education, noted that the center usually had two "meatless" days a week.[393]

The quality of meals at the camp depended greatly on who was preparing the food. Some mess halls had average chefs; others had

---

[391] Tanita, interview.
[392] WRA, "Quarterly Report-Baby Food Section," 31 December 1942. 302:0100 L5.28, Japanese American evacuation and resettlement records, BANC MSS 67/14c, the Bancroft Library, University of California, Berkeley.
[393] Garrison, taped interview.

extraordinary ones. Fumiye Nishizaki claims that her block was fortunate to have the best cook in the center. "That's what they told us," Fumiye recalls. "We had the best cook in the camp. We always had rice. For breakfast, [we had] cereal, coffee, tea, whatever. Oh, I think it was ample—for me, it was ample. We had a hot cake on Saturday or Sunday—I think it was. I wasn't very particular about food anyway. Although if you are a gourmet cook, it was not the place to be."[394]

Highlighting the quality of food at Amache, a July 1943 edition of Denver's *Monitor* stated, "Occasionally the camp mess gets 'forced issues' of rather better rations. This causes a false impression of 'coddling the palates' of evacuees. Actually, the food is none too good. Sugar is served only during the morning meal. There are two meatless days, and on 'meat days,' one often has to carry out a thorough investigation to find the meat."[395]

Besides the quality of food served at mealtimes in Amache, other aspects made these times unpleasant. Mildred Garrison recalls that mealtime could be an embarrassing time for some. "Meals in the camp were often served on benches. Some of the grandmothers and older women had to crawl up on these benches to eat. This came as an embarrassment to some of them, because their legs would just hang there, not really touching the floor."[396]

Another hardship came from an unexpected enemy. In the fall of 1943, southeastern Colorado was hit by infantile paralysis. Polio had hit the entire Arkansas Valley especially hard. By September 16, 135 cases had been reported statewide. Within two weeks, the number would grow to nearly 170.[397]

It was hoped that as cooler weather approached, the disease would lesson in severity. But until such weather arrived, the quick spread of the epidemic mandated that those infected be quarantined. The typical response for physicians in normal communities was to quarantine infected individuals for a predetermined amount of time

---

[394] Nishizaki, interview.
[395] The *Monitor*, 16 July 1943, 1.
[396] Garrison, taped interview.
[397] The *Pioneer*, 22 September 1943, 1; 2 October 1943, 1.

to keep further exposure from occurring. But for the community of Amache—which, by its very location within the path of the epidemic, was also susceptible to the disease—exit to outside locations was simply denied.

When two cases of the disease were discovered in Amache in September 1943—both of whom were teenagers who had acquired the disease outside the camp while on short-term leaves—doctors recommended that the entire center go into isolation. A September 18 edition of the *Pioneer* stated that no shopping passes were to be distributed, no short-term leaves would be granted, and all public meetings, movies, and church services within the center were to be prohibited until threats of the epidemic were over. Even those outside the camp on leave or in military service were asked not to return to the center until further notice.[398]

At first, evacuees ignored these precautions. But Amache's WRA staff admonished evacuees in the September 25 edition of the *Pioneer* to take all polio warnings with great seriousness. "Residents are exposed to polio," so the warning claimed, "more than an outside community with buildings so close, and with the serious problem of sanitation in mess halls, laundries, and latrines."[399]

Throughout the end of September and the beginning of October, evacuees remained isolated from the outside world and—to a large degree—from one another. Each new polio case found at the center reminded Amacheans of the danger they were in. Within a month of its outbreak, the polio epidemic had claimed four lives at Amache and had left several others in various stages of debilitation. The ban was not lifted until October 25, at which time evacuees were allowed to resume contact with outsiders.[400]

Even as the polio epidemic was hammering the camp, evacuees were getting news from outside that made their plight even more dismal. On October 6, 1943, Amache evacuee Cecil Itano had left for Los Angeles, California. Escorted by evacuee property agent Mr. R.

---

[398] The *Pioneer*, 18 September 1943, 1.
[399] The *Pioneer*, 25 September 1943, 1.
[400] Lindley, "Final Report," appendix IV, 19.

W. Schmitt, Rev. Jitei Ishihara, and Rev. Chikyo Kurahashi, Itano's purpose was to verify the condition of property left behind by evacuees at the Nichiren Church. What Itano found was devastating:

> The catastrophe before my eyes was a hopeless mass of deliberate destruction. Everything was a conglomeration of unrecoverable damaged things. Nothing was untouched, sewing machines were ruined, furniture broken, mirrors smashed to smithereens, broken glass from breakable articles, household goods scattered helter-skelter, trunks broken beyond repair, albums, pictures precious only to the respective owners thrown to the four winds.
>
> While surveying the irremediable damage, I noticed that things of instrinic [sic] worth were what the plunderers were searching for and anything that could be converted into immediate cash were taken and residue was abandoned regardless of value and preciousness. Electric irons, sewing machines, refrigerators, washing machines, radios, Persian rugs, typewriters, were systematically filched—not one box went by unscathed. Could this unwarrantable plundering be averted if such vicious propaganda libelously slandering us—American citizen of Japanese descent—who have complied with every government phantasy [sic], forsaking our homes, giving up established business, farmlands which would be cultivated and producing food for the army and civilians at this time of man-power shortage, to be depicted as a despicable and undesirable human race and other unfound accusations necessary? After all California did gain much for our taxes, donations, our contributions to the community, our dogmatic loyalty to the state. Why this ostracism?

> Through days and nights of endless separating, dividing, segregating merchandise to the rightful owners—my only thought was how was I to face these unhappy people again and report their losses that money could never buy again. Things that we did gather up carefully were not so much of monetary value but for sentimental reasons dear to the owners' heart only—the other things were things needed to carry on the future necessities of life. How can I prevent the people from becoming too bitter? Will this unscrupulousness be accepted? Can I justify this pilfering? Will they be satisfied with only remnants of their belongings? Vandalism is indeed heart rending. In my heart I keep repeating dear God why did this happen and please show me how not to become too resentful.[401]

Evacuees had left their belongings behind, not by choice, but by mandate. They were simply not allowed to bring more than they could carry. Literally thousands of West Coast homes, businesses, and vacated churches like the Nichiren Church in Los Angeles were turned into temporary warehouses. From where evacuees stood, they knew not when—or if—they would return. In their haste to evacuate, West Coast Japanese Americans were forced to entrust everything to people they barely knew.

Considerable risks were involved. Some evacuees were aware of that fact. Government agencies had agreed to provide storage facilities, at "the sole risk of the owner," for such items as iceboxes, pianos, washing machines, and crated or boxed items. Within these government facilities, only one small, cramped storage unit was given to each head of household. But these facilities were often viewed with disdain or distrust. If the government could so easily dispose of a

---

[401] Cecil Itano, personal letter, 293:011 L2.01, Japanese American evacuation and resettlement records, BANC MSS 67/14c, the Bancroft Library, University of California, Berkeley.

person's constitutional rights—many reasoned—what would stop it from destroying that same person's personal property?

So instead of storing their property with government sources, many evacuees stored personal items with friends and neighbors. George Hirano's mother and father—immigrants who had worked as domestics in Sausalito, California—were able to store their few possessions with a faithful Caucasian friend.

Likewise, Tunney Shigekuni, who built racing engines, arranged to store a prized engine with a neighbor. "He did it as a hobby," recalls Tunney's brother Tom. "He was very prominent in the West Coast in racing right before the evacuation—with guys like Vick Edlebrock." Eventually, Tunney's friend Vick Edlebrock—fearing that the valve springs might lose their effectiveness if compressed too long—moved the engine to his house so the crankshaft could be turned on a regular basis.[402]

Torno Nishizaki was even able to store his car in California and get WRA officials to transport it to Colorado. Tome's wife, Fumiye, recalls that her husband had just bought a new Oldsmobile:

> He said, "I don't want to sell this, I don't want to part with this." So he had it in a garage there [in Winters, California]. One of the administration fellows, my husband's friend, was going to Sacramento, so he asked him to pick the car up in Winters. So when he went, all the tires were gone. So then he went to the WRA to get those four tires. He could do it. If it were my husband, he couldn't have done that. Anyhow, it was lucky that WRA man went. He got the four tires for us. It was really lucky. He brought it back to us. They used it sometimes, but it was stored, he had a friend who ran the farm. I think he kept it for him.[403]

---

[402] Hirano, G., interview; Shigekuni, interview.
[403] Nishizaki, interview.

AMACHE

For those who feared they would never return to their homes on the coast, the only choice was to sell or give away their belongings. Harry Shironaka recalls that he was forced to sell his new car (one he had just paid $1,000 for) for $250. Chez Momii remembers her family selling tables, chairs, fixtures, and equipment from their restaurant at greatly reduced prices. Grace Kimoto's family was forced to sell their trucks, tractors, and farm equipment for whatever buyers would offer.[404]

Sets Sumikawa's recounts, "When my family was forced to move, we had to leave all of the goods and fixtures in our store behind. We were fortunate in some ways because we knew someone who was willing to keep our furniture and piano for us until we returned." Even Yoshi Tanita remembers that, as a young child, she was forced to leave behind the only worldly possession she owned—the bicycle she had gotten for Christmas only months earlier.[405]

Having endured evacuation, the loss of all worldly possessions, and internment in assembly camps, evacuees were forced to live a rudimentary and often stark life within the gates of Amache. Surrounded by military and WRA personnel, evacuees adjusted to the emotional and societal impact of being incarcerated.

The overcrowded confinement of Amache brought about problems the army and WRA had not anticipated. By herding Japanese Americans from varying life experiences into the thickly packed boundaries of assembly, relocation, and internment camps, the WRA brought about a situation ripe with personal and ideological conflicts.

First came the initial clashes between the urban and rural populations of the camp. "There was a very definite clash between the farm folks and the city people," recalls Tom Shigekuni.

> Some of the younger guys from the city came into camp with zoot suits—which were big at the time—while the guys from the country wore a lot more simple stuff. You know, they were just from

---

[404] Shironaka, H.; Momii, interview; Kimoto, email.
[405] Sumikawa, S., interview; Tanita, interview.

such different backgrounds that it was hard for them to agree on things at times. I could never figure out why the government had put two different groups together. Unless maybe they felt it would break up the unified thinking that might take place in the camp.[406]

The "farm folk" Shigekuni speaks of came primarily from the Merced assembly center. In contrast to these Merced evacuees who had come from rural areas and small communities were those from the urban areas of Los Angeles transferring to Amache from the Santa Anita center. These evacuees were more accustomed to accommodations found within a city environment.

At first, these origins were irritating to many on both sides. A community analyst for Amache, John Rademaker, remarked:

> Assembly-center origin immediately became a significant factor in the new relocation center. It affected the day-to-day relationships between evacuees and between evacuees and appointed personnel, and influenced the nature of the development of the formal structure of the community... That most of the Mercedians arrived at Granada before the Santa Anitans gave the Mercedians an advantage, Santa Anitans believed, in regard to housing, jobs, and community government. The grievances reflected the existence of the feeling between in-groups and out-groups, and the sharing of the grievances increased the solidarity.[407]

---

[406] Shigekuni, interview.
[407] John Rademaker, "The Influence of the Assembly Center Bond in the Relocation Center," 304:0067 L5.71, Japanese American evacuation and resettlement records, BANC MSS 67/14c, the Bancroft Library, University of California, Berkeley.

Rademaker also noted that tensions existed because Santa Anitans felt Mercedians had arrived earlier, they were allowed to choose the housing closest to the center's hospitals and schools. He recalled:

> Blocks became predominantly or entirely either Mercedian or Santa Anitan. Despite later shifts and inductions from Jerome and Tule Lake Centers, this character persisted until the last days of the center… The selection of barracks and blocks was one of the most obvious, early manifestations of a spirit of solidarity and group feeling among the transfers from each assembly center. The Santa Anitans also felt that the Mercedians having arrived first had the advantage as to employment. They complained that the Mercedians had cornered the most desirable jobs open to evacuees and had left the hard, dirty, and undesirable jobs or no jobs at all for the Santa Anitans.[408]

Most incidents of conflict between these two groups occurred among adolescents. Gangs of boys seemed to form quickly with feuds focusing again on assembly center ties. Gang members hailing from Merced were called Skeebos, while those from Santa Anita were known as Seinens or West-Enders. The Seinens wore zoot suits, had long hair, and obtained "other sartorial attributes of zoot-suiters throughout wartime America." Both gangs followed a strict code that "required that a gang could not attack an 'enemy' en masse but must take turns in beating him up."[409] Each gang likewise had its own individual group of girlfriends that closely found their own identity through the gang they supported.

---

[408] Rademaker, "The Influence of the Assembly Center Bond," 2.
[409] Rademaker, "The Influence of the Assembly Center Bond," 3.

To illustrate the divisions found in Amache, one only has to look at one issue of the *Pioneer*. Rademaker recalled an illustration from the newspaper:

> The creator of the comic strip character, "L'il Neebo," brilliantly depicted the various groups at odds in the center. A Santa Anitan was portrayed wearing a Zoot suit, his long hair hanging over his coat collar, his cigarette dangling from one corner of his mouth, and remarking, "You know it." A Mercedian was shown in a "hick" costume, complete with a ragged straw hat on his head and a hay straw in his mouth, and remarking, "Lose fight"; a Nisei, a Joe College type, was exhibited as exclaiming, "Woo-woo." Also in the cartoon was an elderly, toil worn Issei. Precocious "L'il Neebo" is pictured as stating, "We're Granadans. And more than that a part of the people working for a common cause."[410]

Although tensions ran high at first, they would weaken over time. Soon, Nisei of all ages began to buy into a "Granada Spirit." Rademaker remarked that although some instances of assembly center rivalries might have occurred throughout the life of the center, such "negative aspects of tension, friction, and hostility were no longer sufficiently worrisome or troublesome for evacuee leaders or center administrative personnel."[411]

Another division between evacuees in Amache was brought about in part because of the differing experiences of Issei and Nisei. Issei had little or no constitutional rights in their adopted land. They had never become accustomed to the rights and economic influence citizens of the United States had. Nisei, on the other hand, were—by their very birth—given the same constitutional rights and finan-

---

[410] Rademaker, "The Influence of the Assembly Center Bond," 3.
[411] Rademaker, "The Influence of the Assembly Center Bond," 3.

cial opportunities as other native-born Americans. Oski Taniwaki addressed this issue in 1943 when he wrote:

> It may be interesting to know that the "reaction of the Japanese to the social and economic problems" is divided between the first and second generation Japanese. The second generation, being citizens of this country, are vastly different in their mental make-up compared to those of the first generation, which includes the parents, mothers, and older men and women who have no citizenship in this country.
>
> Socially and economically, the Issei has less hardship than the Nisei because the Issei has been confined in the homogeneous group similar to surroundings at home; whereas, the Nisei has been used to associating with the Caucasian society. The major complaints among this group is the fact that their association with Caucasian friends, teachers and acquaintances has been limited and they are about to lose all contact with them.
>
> Furthermore, the Nisei, being of a rather independent nature, do not feel that his evacuation and confined life is doing their initiative and talents any justice. It is the desire of the majority of this group to relocate themselves in various parts of the state as soon as permission can be granted and reasonable assurance of a livelihood can be secured.
>
> Many of the Nisei are experiencing novel problems for they have not been accustomed to associating with purely Japanese society. Their speech, manners, and associations with the older groups in general make them feel rather out of place. Their place, definitely, is with the democratic American society.[412]

---

[412] Taniwaki, letter.

The issue of political freedom aside, possibly the most significant social problems experienced at Amache was the breakup of century-old traditional familial boundaries. For generations, the father had been seen as the head of the traditional Japanese family. All economic and welfare provisions came from him. If the father could no longer provide, such responsibilities became those of the oldest son. But with the onset of evacuation, these roles were torn away and given to the centralized authority of the WRA. Fathers no longer provided shelter. Fathers no longer were accountable for savings, businesses, and farms. Overnight, family wage earners became ineffective figureheads having little impact on their family's welfare.

Work was no longer seen as a means of providing a family with food, shelter, and financial stability. Instead, work became a means of providing for the camp's general population. Men set out to build room dividers and bunk beds, tables and benches. They painted barrack interiors and repaired damaged walls and windows when needed. And they worked in jobs within the Amache compound—no longer to provide for their families, but merely to stay busy and help their fellow evacuees survive.

Women's roles were also unstable within the camp environment. For centuries, Japanese women were seen as the nurturers of the family. They had been trained from generation to generation to be efficient mothers and loving wives. These traditional roles were challenged by internment. What had always been seen as the responsibility of women in Japanese society—in particular, the preparation of meals—became the responsibility of the WRA. Women now were freed from the daily task of cooking and baking. They were freed from the routine of grocery shopping.

Work for women evacuees, instead, became the protection of their families against the realities of internment. Stark and cramped barrack apartments were decorated. Clothes were mended. Drapes were sewn for barracks and mess hall windows. Decorations and wall hangings were created to liven drab surroundings. In essence, they attempted to deaden the sting of internment.

Mothers fought to thwart the conditions that were driving their families apart. For most youth at Amache, the camp represented newfound social freedoms. As in the assembly centers, Japanese American youth often ate with friends instead of family at designated mealtimes. They challenged parental authority, and they watched as parents became powerless to control surrounding circumstances.

With the advent of relocation, parents no longer represented the authority figures found in traditional Japanese or Japanese American communities. In interviewing the evacuees, Jack Carberry found that "many of the older persons object bitterly to community mess. They argue family control has its very foundations in the family meal, and the community mess hall has all but robbed them of the authority of their children."[413]

Although traditional limits were tested within Amache, many families kept bonds tight and traditional hierarchies in order. In fact, parents often served as a stabilizing factor amid a difficult time. They were not defenseless against the tide of internment—nor against the anti-Asian propaganda directed at them from the outside.

---

[413] *Denver Post*, 14 February 1943, 3.

Amache Historical Site Archives—Kameoka Collection

The Boy Scouts at Amache were given leave to dismantle an old CCC camp near Mancos in the Southwestern corner of the state. While on leave, they were allowed to visit Mesa Verde National Park.

Amache Historical Site Archives—Ochikubo Collection

Evacuees creating posters for the war effort.

AMACHE

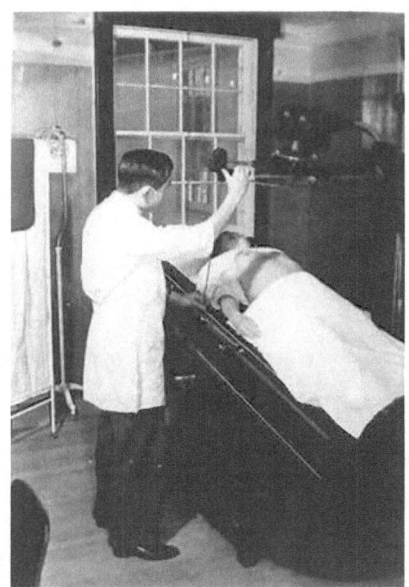

Amache Historical Site Archives—Kameoka Collection

Amache's hospital was the first in Southeastern Colorado to have an X-ray machine.

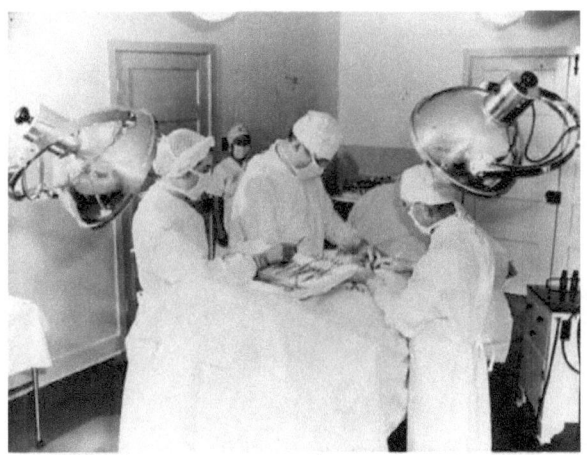

Auraria Library Archives—Joseph McClelland Collection

Amache medical staff performs an emergency procedure.

Auraria Library Archives—Joseph McClelland Collection

Issei and Nisei helped support the war effort and the center's need for food through farming and ranching around the center.

Auraria Library Archives—Joseph McClelland Collection

AMACHE

Amache Historical Site Archives—Kameoka Collection

Employment was found by many in meal preparation and service.

Amache Historical Site Archives—Ochikubo Collection

Amache Historical Site Archives—Turck Collection

Caucasian military police training off-site.

Amache Historical Site Archives—Ochikubo Collection

The screen-printing shop at Amache was a point of pride for the WRA. Dillon S. Myer, the director of the War Relocation Authority, tours the camp's screen-printing operations with other camp staff.

Amache Historical Site Archives—Fujita Collection

Guard towers stood vacant toward the end of the center's existence.

Amache Historical Site Archives—Lindley Collection

Strays were the only remaining tenants in the aftermath of Amache

CHAPTER 7

"BECAUSE WE ARE OF DIFFERENT COLOR AND RACE"

America in the 1940s was far from racially tolerant. A democracy that was intended to shine on the path to freedom was too often dimmed by those who could not—or would not—understand the plight of those different from themselves.

The news of the lynchings of three African Americans in Mississippi in 1942 sent a clear message around the world that America's constitutional democracy was still stained with racist inequality.[414]

"Zoot suit" incidents—clashes between Los Angeles police and rebellious young Mexican American men wearing oversize ostentatious zoot suit clothing—brought new strife to the West Coast.

Even the government authorized racial hatred when—in an effort to prepare the American public for the brutal battles taking place in the Pacific theater—it lifted its information ban on Japan's treatment of US war prisoners. Anti-Japanese propaganda blazed through the country—and with it came inflammatory remarks about Issei and Nisei living within America.[415]

---

[414] *Rocky Mountain News*, 13 October 1942, 3; 18 October 1942, 17.
[415] Murrin et al., *Liberty, Equality, Power*, 852.

The flood of anti-Japanese propaganda, as well as the arrival of Japanese Americans at relocation centers through the fall of 1942, showed the world that America's freedom was intended only for those of particular heritages.

This lack of freedom was clear to young Akiko Nakano. While in Amache, Nakano wrote, "I know there are many people who don't know anything about us. These are the ones who discriminate against us. Still, there are many who discriminate because we are of different color and race… I hope that this country will soon realize what it would mean to all of us, when there would be no kind of discrimination against the people who are of different race and color, since we are all Americans." Nakano's dream of a color-blind country depended greatly on an empathetic America. An America willing to shove aside all previous notions of race. An America that desired an end to stereotypes and bigotry. An America willing to begin anew.[416]

Few Americans in the 1940s truly understood what Japanese Americans were dealing with. Life inside relocation centers was a mystery to them. News about evacuation and relocation and life within WRA camps came primarily from sources with racial agendas. The terms "Japs" and "pampered" and "lazy" were all too often used to describe evacuees in both the press and individual discourse. This was how America saw evacuees who had had their lives torn apart by racism. This is how America justified concentrating both alien and American citizen within relocation centers.

Addressing this point, the editor of Amache's newspaper the *Pioneer*—Oski Taniwaki—noted:

> The main difficulty, standing as barriers to better understanding of the Japanese problem, has been definitely established that due to the lack of information of these evacuees, all facilities at hand to better acquaint the American public will

---

[416] Akiko Nakano, letter to Lloyd Garrison, 16 November 1944, Lloyd Garrison Collection, Box 1, Folder 2, Auraria Library Archives and Special Collections, Denver.

> be used in the future to do away with misunderstanding as much as possible. Those who have come to know of their complete Americanization have immediately thrown away any prejudices caused by the spreading of propaganda through newspapers and uninformed sources.[417]

But tossing aside preconceived prejudices would not be easy. News sources around the country had ingrained a certain image of Japanese Americans on the minds of Americans. To their readers, the nation's newspapers had portrayed those of Japanese ancestry as many things.

The Japanese were inherently vicious. Proof, or so it was claimed, could be found in the unannounced attack of Pearl Harbor and the ongoing accounts of Japanese war crimes in the Pacific theater. Such incidents were given credibility by stories like that of George Honda, a Japanese American who had stabbed and killed his wife in a hotel lobby in downtown Denver. The *Rocky Mountain News* headlines screamed, "Denver Jap Butchers Wife in Hotel Lobby." Despite the fact that other murders involving non-Japanese parties had happened in recent months, Honda's conviction both overshadowed all else and cemented in the minds of many that the Japanese were vicious killers.[418]

The Japanese were dangerous. In 1940s America, martial arts were still heavily linked to the Japanese culture and were shrouded in a great cloud of mysterious danger. An August 1943 edition of the *Rocky Mountain News* reported that the Denver Civilian Defense Corps—a volunteer organization of police officers designed to protect the city if attacked—had begun training in the art of yawara. Yawara—a martial art said to be more potent than judo—was taught to the wartime defense officers by F. A. Matsuyama, whose family had studied it for over 1,400 years. Matsuyama noted that an important factor in a victory over Japanese warriors was the knowledge of how

---

[417] Taniwaki, letter.
[418] *Rocky Mountain News*, 4 May 1942, 1.

to fight them. "To defeat the Japanese, you've got to know how to fight the way he does," Matsuyama remarked.[419] American national defense, it was deemed, needed to become as deadly as the enemy it would fight.

The Japanese were untrustworthy and unwanted. Racial prejudice ran high in America throughout the war. In the spring of 1943, Congressman J. Parnell Thomas of California strongly condemned the removal of Issei and Nisei from evacuation centers back to the West Coast. Likewise, other members of the state's legislator remarked that the people of California would not accept evacuees back to their state under any circumstances. Even California's state attorney general Earl Warren—the future Supreme Court judge who adamantly backed civil rights legislation in the 1960s—pushed for legislation supporting anti-alien land laws. In a press release, Warren stated, "It seems to me there has been a studied effort to have no fifth-column activity in California until a designated 'zero hour.' We can prevent landholding by alien enemies-and I believe every Japanese alien should be regarded as a possible fifth columnist."[420]

And possibly more than anything else, they were coddled. Virtually all relocation centers were accused of coddling evacuees. Early in 1943, Sen. Robert R. Reynolds accused the WRA of allowing evacuees to live in extreme comfort while the rest of the nation sacrificed for the war effort. Likewise, in April of the same year, a disgruntled former steward came forward with charges that the WRA was coddling evacuees by allowing mass quantities of food to spoil by hoarding supplies and, in general, by allowing a fair amount of "high living" among the evacuees.[421]

Wyoming's Heart Mountain relocation center especially received a barrage of coddling accusations. In August 1943, Rep. John J. Meintyre of Wyoming brought charges against Heart Mountain's staff members who, he claimed, were receiving greater salaries than those of similar occupations outside the camp. McIntyre specifically

---

[419] *Rocky Mountain News*, 17 August 1943, 8.
[420] *Rocky Mountain News*, 14 May 1943, 11; *Denver Post*, 3 February 1942, 3.
[421] *Rocky Mountain News*, 16 January 1943, 4; 27 April 1943

attacked Caucasian teacher salaries, claiming the wages paid to the camp's teachers—ranging between $1,620 and $2,000 a year—were well above the norm given to teachers outside the center.[422]

But evacuees and WRA officials were quick in their responses to these accusations. In reference to an earlier coddling statement by Sen. Robert R. Reynolds, Bill Hosokawa, the twenty-eight-year-old editor of the *Heart Mountain Sentinel*, extended an invitation to the senator to experience the "luxuries" of camp life. In a January 25 issue of the *Sentinel*, Hosokawa declared, "We should be pleased to share our one-room apartments and the rationed mess hall fare with him and perhaps walk through the snow with him to our 'fine bathroom' when the temperature is 30 degrees below zero."[423]

Regarding "high living" accusations, Malcolm Pitts—the field assistant director for the WRA—responded that the hoarded supplies and food spoilage was no greater than could be expected for such a large population. Pitts remarked that with an average food cost of well below fifteen cents a meal for each evacuee, it would be hard to "pamper anyone on that amount."[424]

As regional director of the WRA, Joseph H. Smart likewise stressed that teachers' salaries should be seen as covering the twelve-month period WRA teachers were employed, as opposed to the standard nine-month period found outside the camp. "Similar jobs at Laramie," Smart noted, "pay high school teachers with a [BA] degree and three years of teaching a top salary of $1,920. They teach but nine months each year. If they were paid at the same rate for twelve months of teaching, they would receive $2,556 a year."[425]

In defense of WRA schools, Smart continued, "We do not expect to give the Japanese children at the camp better education than other Wyoming pupils but we do want to inculcate in them the finest ideals and standards of Americanism. This cannot be done with inferior teachers, for it will be a difficult job."[426]

---

[422] *Rocky Mountain News*, 8 August 1943, 14.
[423] *Rocky Mountain News*, 24 January 1943, 10.
[424] *Rocky Mountain News*, 27 April 1943, 5.
[425] *Rocky Mountain News*, 8 August 1943, 14.
[426] *Rocky Mountain News*, 8 August 1943, 14.

Even Mrs. Eleanor Roosevelt was asked to visit the relocation center at Gila, Arizona, to investigate coddling charges. But she found no coddling on touring the facilities at Gila. Mrs. Roosevelt's findings showed that "they are not being pampered, though they are not being mistreated... However, I would not choose their situation as a way to live." After adding that the long hours of work seen at Gila were typical of other centers, Mrs. Roosevelt said she would not need to visit other camps.[427]

The authoritative voice of Mrs. Roosevelt may have calmed the rhetoric of politicians and the press. But if it soothed inflammatory remarks, it did so only temporarily. Threats to democracy and world unity, a blatantly unchecked freedom of the press, and decades of racial tensions all combined to become explosive ingredients in the powder keg of hostility. And citizens of Colorado could not escape from the wake this explosion was creating within their state.

Colorado in the 1940s, like the rest of the country, was also far from racial tolerance. Citizens of Colorado, too, were entrenched in rising war demands. Citizens of Colorado, too, were united in the fight to overcome Axis powers. They, too, were constantly subjected to inflammatory stories of irresponsible newspapers. And around southeastern Colorado, evacuees were often treated as the enemy.

From the beginning, there was little trust of these strange newcomers. The *Lamar Register* reported that it was rumored Amache was to have ten new blocks added to the camp. In blunt language, the paper reported:

> Rumors are rife about this community concerning the supposed enlargement of the local relocation center. Gossip flies thick and fast and, of course, many claims are greatly exaggerated. As has been customary ever since the first government inspector arrived in this vicinity a little less than a year ago, every move that is being made is shrouded behind a thick veil of mystery.

---

[427] *Rocky Mountain News*, 27 April 1943, 5.

> Just why such great secrecy has been or is now necessary has never been explainable, either by personnel, soldier, or layman. It has always been know that the Japanese were being located here for their protection. Much unfair criticism could have been avoided if an open program had been announced.[428]

At other times, evacuees were accused directly of sabotage. Bruce Newman recalls a railroad trestle that caught fire and burned for nearly two days just outside the town of Granada. Evacuees at Amache were automatically suspected, and the FBI was dispatched to Granada. "The FBI was sent into town to find out how it was started. It caused quite an uproar around my school, because these FBI agents interviewed some of the students. I guess they must have suspected sabotage from someone within the center." After several interviews, however, the FBI found little evidence of any foul play. Newman continued, "I don't think they really ever found anything. But it was exciting for the students in my school."[429]

Surrounding communities also found it necessary to accuse evacuees at Amache of new coddling charges in the summer of 1943. This time, it was rumored that a new swimming pool was being planned for the evacuees of the camp. Although no such venture had ever been discussed by WRA officials, a *Rocky Mountain News* article claimed that Amache officials had asked for $50,000 to finance the project.[430]

To some, the rumor was laughable. A July issue of Denver's *Monitor* remarked, "The answer to the swimming pool rumor is simple. The Japanese evacuees at Granada have no pool; they do have three sewage disposal tanks, but they can't swim in a cesspool."[431]

---

[428] *Lamar Register*, 18 November 1942, 1.
[429] Newman, interview.
[430] *Rocky Mountain News*, 29 May 1943, 5, 11.
[431] The *Monitor*, 16 July 1943, 1.

But to evacuees of Amache, as well as Japanese Americans in Colorado, the rumor was regarded with the utmost seriousness. Tom Shigekuni recalls:

> That was the same cesspool that Congressman Martin Dies said that the government was coddling the Japs with swimming pools while our boys are fighting and dying in the Pacific against these very same people. He never retracted that. He was the chairman of the House Un-American Activities Committee and he was the most un-American thing about the whole committee.[432]

Likewise, the same edition of the *Rocky Mountain News* that spoke of the pool also included an article quoting the national commander of the Foreign Legion as saying that if allowed to remain in the United States, those of Japanese ancestry would eventually overrun the country's current Anglo population by the millions. He attempted to prove his point by adding that a "handful of Negro slaves" had grown to be more than fourteen million. In the press, it seemed that those in Amache had become easy targets for hate.[433]

These accusations again reminded Amacheans that their standing as American citizens with equal rights was tenuous at best.

Outside Amache, Japanese Americans were having a similar fate. Colorado native Alley Watada recalls that as a boy living in Platteville, Colorado, classmates often harassed him. "Before the war," says Watada, "my family felt like part of the community. My father would try to introduce various aspect of Japan to the classrooms in the schools in town. He would also, bring toys to the children at school and things like that."[434]

---

[432] Shigekuni, interview.
[433] *Rocky Mountain News*, 29 May 1943, 5, 11.
[434] Alley Watada, personal interview, 28 February 2000.

But with the advent of war, life in Platteville changed. Children who Watada thought were his friends "stepped back" from any and all contact with him. "Two boys," Watada remarks,

> especially tried to agitate me all the time by calling me a "Jap." They also tried to get the other boys at school to attack me physically. I did have some Caucasian friends who supported me, but they really couldn't do much to help the situation. That whole period was really an emotional time for me. People who I thought were my friends no longer were my friends. I think, though, that most of the boys who did attack me were doing so because they were coaxed on by those other two boys.[435]

Albert Watada, Alley's older brother, recalls his experiences as a child were somewhat different from those of his brother. "I didn't have much problem while I was in school during the war," recalls the eldest Watada:

> Most of my classmates supported me. I do remember a basketball game I played in where the opposing team was a little rough on me. But my team-mates all backed me up and protected me. I also remember a time when my family and I had company visiting and we went to LaSalle to buy fresh trout. We were told by the storeowner that we weren't welcome there and that we would be asked—or rather told—to leave. Another time we had a creamery refuse to sell us ice cream. We experienced a few things like that during the war. My father just really ignored this treatment—he had to.[436]

---

[435] Watada, interview, 28 February 2000.
[436] Albert Watada, personal interview, 23 March 2000.

Likewise, Albert Watada remembers his father as being under the same restrictions as Issei on the West Coast. Only allowed to travel a limited amount of miles from home, Watada's father had to get special permission if he wished to travel any farther than twenty-five miles outside his own property.[437]

Most citizens of Colorado were not guilty of direct racial or economic oppression. Most would never have dreamed of asking a Japanese American to leave a store. Most would never have refused to sell goods to someone because they had the same racial makeup as an enemy of war. Most, in fact, would have opted to just mind their own business instead of dealing with the complex issues brought by evacuation. But this in itself became part of the problem evacuees faced in Colorado—and the rest of America. When people did nothing but mind their own business, they took away a much-needed voice of support.

Sensational press sources and politicians with economic and racial agendas were slamming evacuees continually. On top of this, evacuees were being asked to relocate into states where such attacks were taking place. For evacuees to relocate into an area they had never seen before was overwhelming. But relocating into an area filled with great hostility and little support was terrifying. If those who had decided to mind their own business had instead shown their support, the state of Colorado would not have appeared so vicious, and the state's overzealous patriots would have lost ground to reason.

Nevertheless, evacuees from Amache were expected to move out into the world as it existed—pretty or not. Most opted to stay in the camp and ignore the relocation desires of the WRA. But for those who attempted to brave the world outside, relocation would hold a myriad of experiences and emotions.

In 1943, Dillon Myer suggested the WRA "should keep in mind at all times that we would rather have the evacuees on the outside than on the inside if they can pass the leave regulations or are willing to accept employment on the outside." This was the entire reason—in Myer's mind at least—for the existence of the WRA. Although

---

[437] Watada, interview, 23 March 2000.

Myer hoped to make life in his relocation centers comfortable for the evacuees housed there, his primary aim was to work himself out of a job.[438]

To Myer, the goal of relocation of evacuees to interior states was of utmost importance. In later years, Myer talked of this relocation process as necessitated more by those outside the camps than distrust for those on the inside. "Those of us who were closely associated with the evacuees soon learned about the complex pattern and the wide diversity of interests represented. We soon became convinced that few, if any, of these people were dangerous to the interests of the United States. However, because the general public was not as convinced of this as we were, it became necessary to establish a rather elaborate leave procedure. Furthermore, this policy was essential for the protection of evacuees, because they had all been tarred with the same brush by the evacuation and establishment of centers."[439]

In Myer's view, relocation was established to protect the evacuee, not to protect America. Evacuees saw things differently, though—especially as they were surrounded by barbed wire and armed MPs with weapons and spotlights facing in. But the WRA's major task was—on the surface—to serve the evacuee, and relocation went ahead as planned. To accomplish the task of relocation, the WRA created three different types of leaves—short-term, seasonal, and indefinite leaves.

The WRA never intended the first type of leave—the short-term leave—as a pathway toward employment. Rather, short-term leaves were simply granted for "brief periods to permit visits to medical specialists, negotiation of property arrangements, or transaction of other similar personal business which cannot be handled at the center. It provides for travel only to specific destinations and may be granted by the project director without referral to the Washington office." Short-term leaves were to be used sparingly by the evacuees of

---

[438] Dillon Myer, letter to James Lindley, 3 November 1943, 305:011 L6.00, Japanese American evacuation and resettlement records, BANC MSS 67/14c, the Bancroft Library, University of California, Berkeley.

[439] Myer, *Uprooted Americans*, 293.

Amache—wartime rationing, lack of financial provisions, and strict requirements curtailed extensive use of this type of leave.[440]

Although short-term leaves were seen as necessary in the life of evacuees at Amache, they could also be painful. Amache evacuees Harry and Kimi Shironaka were granted a short-term pass to visit relatives in Arkansas. Their experiences during this leave demonstrate why many evacuees chose not to use such passes. "Boy, that was a tough ride," Harry Shironaka recalls. "They allowed us to go, but that was about it. We were sent by train, but they made us stay in the areas where the trains connected. We went to Kansas City the first night and looked around for a place to stay overnight near the train station. But we weren't too welcome around there." After walking around the city for several hours, the Shironakas finally gave up. "We finally went back to the station and slept there until our train left the next day. I guess it could have been worse."[441]

Evacuees of Amache used the second type of leave—the seasonal leave—more often. Established as early as May 1942, the seasonal leave was intended to serve as an avenue for brief periods of employment outside the camp. These leaves were temporary and had very definite geographical and time restraints. Those who used seasonal leaves eventually found themselves back in the camps when the duration of their work was complete.[442]

Seasonal leaves were especially popular for those internees who went into mountain and midwestern states to assist in harvesting crops. Many high school students also took this type of employment as a means of gaining vocational training or as a source of adding to a family's income during the summer months. Evacuees also found that seasonal leaves were a legal means of getting out from behind Amache's barbed wire enclosures for a short time.[443]

---

[440] WRA, *The Relocation Program*, 1.
[441] Shironaka, H., interview.
[442] WRA, *The Relocation Program*, 2.
[443] WRA, *The Relocation Program*, 5.

Art Yorimoto was one of those who wasted little time getting out. "I didn't want to stay there very long," Yorimoto notes. Using a seasonal pass, Yorimoto found a farmer in Colorado to work for.

> I think it was sometime in March. We had a friend that was married to a girl from La Jara, near Alamosa. Anyway his brother-in-law was farming down there—on a pretty large scale. This friend of mine was married to this farmer's sister and this guy says "who wants to go out for a job." Everyone wanted to get out. So he asked me to round up about five guys. We all jumped on it. So we went down to Alamosa to farm. My wife stayed in camp all this time, when I went out, because everything was so uncertain.[444]

Life on a seasonal pass could be adventuresome for an evacuee. Yorimoto recalls:

> On the farm we planted lettuce, peas, cauliflower, and cabbage. It was hard work, but we had fun. That's where I learned how to trout fish. On Sundays, the boss went out when it wasn't busy. You know, after planting—between planting and harvesting there was some slack time. So he used to take us up to the headwaters of the Conejos River. It was good fishing—a lot of good eating size fish. Anyway, we had fun. That's where I got my fishing bug.[445]

For some locals, the seasonal leave was a questionable undertaking. The *Holly Chieftain* reported that if labor could not be obtained from ordinary sources, "the Employment Service will then be forced

---

[444] Yorimoto, A., interview.
[445] Yorimoto, A., interview.

to offer employment to the regional WRA office for consideration and submission to evacuees at the Granada or Cody centers."[446]

But from a farmer's point of view, evacuees like Yorimoto were "God-sends." Sugar beet districts in Colorado particularly benefited from the presence of this new workforce. In the regions of Denver, Pueblo, and the southeastern part of the state surrounding Amache, Japanese Americans employed as laborers greatly enhanced the working conditions and housing facilities of the farms.

One WRA memo recounts the story of a Nebraska farmer who had hired a group of fifty Japanese American youth to work his sugar beet and potato fields. Working alongside these Japanese Americans were a couple of Caucasian employees who, for one reason or another, had come to despise the company in which they were employed. When the Caucasian workers become abusive toward their coworkers, the farmer took drastic action toward the two Caucasians—he fired them. After the dismissal, the farmer firmly demanded that if the other whites under his employment didn't treat the Japanese Americans with respect, he would promptly take similar actions. "I'll fire anyone who don't treat you as human beings," threatened the farmer.[447]

A number of those who employed evacuees were themselves of Japanese ancestry. Harry Shironaka recalls that "there were a lot of people in Ordway who had moved here—before the evacuation—on their own. There were also quite a few Japanese living in Rocky Ford only a few miles away. There really wasn't much animosity toward me when I got to Ordway—I think they were pretty used to the Japanese by that time."[448]

Alley Watada also notes that his father employed evacuees from Amache. "My father had a friend from Napa Valley, California, that had come to be placed in Amache. So my father brought this friend

---

[446] *Holly Chieftain*, 3 September 1942, 1.
[447] WRA, Granada Relocation Center, "Outside Employment Treatment and Reaction," 12 May 1943, 293:0157 L2.55, Japanese American evacuation and resettlement records, BANC MSS 67/14c, the Bancroft Library, University of California, Berkeley.
[448] Shironaka, H., interview.

and several others from camp to help with the sugar beet and potato harvests. At that time, sugar beet harvest was all done by hand."[449]

The labor-intensive crops of Colorado demanded an ample supply of workers, and the seasonal leave system of the WRA fit this demand well.

The final type of leave—an indefinite leave—was designed as a permanent method of relocating evacuees into career or educational opportunities outside the camps. Art Yorimoto remembers that while on seasonal leave in La Jara in the summer of 1943, he was offered employment as a mechanic with his brother in Denver. "I told him," Yorimoto recalls, "'Gee, that sounds pretty good.' So I told my farmer friend the situation. He said it sounded like a good chance, so I went back to the camp and packed up my things and came out to Denver and started up a garage at 24th and Larimer. I think that was in September of 1943." After getting situated, Yorimoto found a home to rent and moved his family from Amache to Denver.[450]

Established in July 1942, the indefinite leave process was seen as the primary source of evacuee relocation into long-term employment or education in midwestern and eastern cities. Evacuees granted indefinite leaves were allowed to move freely about the country. However, they were still required to periodically report their location and employment status to WRA officials.[451]

WRA relocation offices were set up around the country in cities like Denver, Salt Lake City, Chicago, Cleveland, and New York City. These offices relied heavily on volunteers outside evacuation centers who worked as sponsors and employment finders. These volunteers also served as positive liaisons in surrounding communities.

Field offices received and processed literally thousands of requests for varying types of labor. A letter from a seventy-year-old farm couple requested an entire family of evacuees to take over the operation of their farm. Construction companies requested laborers. Homeowners sought maids. Parents asked for childcare workers.

---

[449] Watada, Alley, interview.
[450] Yorimoto, A., interview.
[451] WRA, *The Relocation Program*, 2.

Requests flooding WRA offices were sent on to evacuation camps to be posted.[452]

Pay outside Amache was far better than that offered by the WRA. Domestic workers received $10.00 a week. Drill press operators received $1.50 an hour. And mechanical draftsmen hailed between $200.00 and $300.00 a month for their skills. Wages like these were far better than the top pay of $19.00 a month found in relocation centers.[453]

Amache relocation staff members found that most cities were unwilling to accept large numbers of evacuees. Due in part to an alleged danger of fifth column activities, most cities opted for smaller groups. "Apparently, the small group resettlement as a whole is more successful," one Amache memo noted. "Such reactions"—suggested the writer of the memo—were "to be expected despite the fact that investigations have been made by WRA previous to resettling the evacuees. It is simply a psychological reaction that is inevitable."[454]

Denver was a popular relocation site for Amache evacuees. Over 1,100 evacuees had relocated there. Most of them lived in areas around Larimer Street or around Denver's South High School. Yoshi Tanita recalls that her father went to Denver when he relocated. "My father's brother went back to Japan." As the oldest son of the family, Tanita's uncle was needed back in his home in Japan. "But my father," Tanita continues, "got a loan at the bank to buy a hotel in the Larimer section of downtown Denver. I don't know how he ever got that loan, because at the time Japanese Americans usually couldn't get money like that. He just met a man at the bank who was kind to him and was willing to take a risk. He bought this hotel with a friend

---

[452] Authors unknown, letters to Amache Relocation Staff, 293:0043 L2.50, Japanese American evacuation and resettlement records, BANC MSS 67/14c, the Bancroft Library, University of California, Berkeley.

[453] WRA, Granada Relocation Center, "Outside Employment Offers for Month of March," March 1943, 293:0182 L2.56, Japanese American evacuation and resettlement records, BANC MSS 67/14c, the Bancroft Library, University of California, Berkeley.

[454] WRA, "Outside Employment Treatment and Reaction."

and moved to Denver while the rest of us stayed in the camp to finish out the school year."[455]

Any type of assistance like the type received by Tanita's father was certainly welcomed by evacuees—but it remained rather rare. For the most part, evacuees gained support only from the WRA. Myer felt one of the WRA's responsibilities was to aid evacuees in their relocations. Those wishing to relocate from Amache were to first to speak with a family counselor before going out of camp. This counseling was provided to mentally prepare evacuees for hardships they might encounter. Then, financial assistance was provided. In a 1943 relocation pamphlet, mention was made that those desiring indefinite leave could apply for travel and subsistence relief above and beyond what they could finance themselves.[456]

Finally, the WRA hoped to provide railroad coach fare for the applicant and each dependent making the trip, money for any meals en route (calculated at three dollars per day), and reimbursement for housing during the period of adjustment (ranging from fifty dollars for an applicant traveling without dependents to a hundred dollars for an applicant traveling with more than one dependent). Although these types of assistance were available on paper, few evacuees recall receiving such amounts. In fact, a meeting of community council members in the spring of 1945 notes that an average family choosing to relocate received only twenty-five dollars in "assistant grants."[457]

Reactions from outsiders to evacuees moving into their neighborhoods were not always positive ones. Often, owners of rental homes would turn prospective renters down because they were afraid of what neighbors would think or because the Japanese were seen as "too forceful; they didn't stay in their place." Neighbors sometimes

---

[455] Tanita, interview.
[456] Amache Community Council, "Meeting Minutes," 30 January 1945, 290:0066 Ll.40, Japanese American evacuation and resettlement records, BANC MSS 67/14c, the Bancroft Library, University of California, Berkeley.
[457] WRA, *The Relocation Program*, 3; Amache Community Council, "Meeting Minutes," 2 February 1945, 290:0066 Ll.40, Japanese American evacuation and resettlement records, BANC MSS 67/14c, the Bancroft Library, University of California, Berkeley.

complained that these newcomers should "speak English if they are such good Americans," or that they were simply too "arrogant" to live next to.[458]

"It was frightening," Yoshi Tanita recalls of her move to Denver. Leaving the protection of Amache on indefinite leave was hard. "People would stare at us or call us 'Jap.' Having been in a situation with nothing but Japanese and then moving into this big city was terrible. We just never knew how we would be accepted by the people outside."[459]

Chez Momii likewise had trouble adjusting to life outside. "After I moved to Denver, I went to a public junior high school. It was really loud, you know, compared to Amache. The students were so wild and loud, I just wanted to transfer to another class—they were just too immature. Oh, it was a difficult time for me. I lost a lot of weight. It was hard."[460]

After bringing his family to Denver, Art Yorimoto describes the reaction of his infant daughter to life outside Amache: "We stayed in a motel until we could move into our house. My daughter—who was about one and a half at the time—could not remember anything other than Amache. While we were staying in the motel, she got tired of it and one night started to cry and said 'I want to go home.' She wanted to go back to Amache. It was kind of pathetic."[461]

For some evacuees, life outside the camp would prove to be uncertain at best. Soon after relocating to Denver in the spring of 1943, an evacuee known only as M wrote, "Everyday so far I've been scouting around for a job. I've had no luck and if this keeps up I'll have to go back to camp next week. I did go to a couple of places, none of them appealed to me for the hard work and low wages. It's really not worth it. The cost of living is terrific and it's really tough here in Denver if you're not sure of a job. X and Y seem downhearted

---

[458] Donald Irish, "Reactions of Residents of Boulder, Colorado to the Introduction of Japanese into the Community," master thesis, 1950. University of Colorado, Boulder.
[459] Tanita, interview.
[460] Momii, interview.
[461] Yorimoto, A., interview.

after being turned down at so many cleaners. Probably we'll start as a dishwasher or busboy if nothing else is available, can't loaf around much longer."[462]

Chez Momii's parents had a different experience. "I don't think my mother and father had a hard time relocating, they were very hard workers and real close with each other. They wanted to relocate—they wanted to get on with their life. They still weren't allowed to go back to the West Coast, but when he saw the opportunity, he took it."[463]

As part of a creative financial alternative available to some evacuees, Momii's father started a factory that produced sheets of seaweed for use in sushi.

> When he started the business, nobody had money, so there was a group of men who got together to form a group called Tano Moshi. Each person put in $100 and then a person who wanted to start a business would bid on the interest rate… That's how they got the money to start the seaweed business. These members of the group had so much confidence in each other; they were all kind of business partners. So that's how a lot of them got started in their enterprises. You know they couldn't borrow from a bank; no one was going to lend them money. So this is the way they did it. I think it was really resourceful.[464]

Initially, Amache staff officials were pleased with the relocation process of evacuees into areas outside the center. Through September and August 1942, 527 evacuees took employment opportunities out-

---

[462] Various authors, "Excerpts from Letters of Evacuees outside the Granada Relocation Center," 22 and 24 March 1943, 295:0011 L3.18, Japanese American evacuation and resettlement records, BANC MSS 67/14c, the Bancroft Library, University of California, Berkeley.

[463] Momii, interview.

[464] Momii, interview.

side the center. Another 15 evacuees were granted indefinite leaves to attend colleges and universities around Colorado and the Midwest.[465]

But by the spring of 1943, staff members began to notice a marked decline in relocation applications. Some in Amache's employment office saw little cause for worry. In a May 1943 report, one employment officer described the resettlement program as "progressing satisfactorily." The writer of the report seemed to suggest the interest shown by the evacuees revealed "their earnest desire to reestablish themselves in the various sections of the country." Evacuees were "taking advantage of the employment offers. Hence, the center employment office is crowded everyday with applicants. It has been the author's experience to observe some who consistently visit the office (twice a day) to see whether or not any work adapted to their own skill have been posted on the bulletin board."[466]

However, some saw the rate of relocations as a sign of resistance. In the summer of 1943, Caucasian staff members conducted a survey to find out why some evacuees were not relocating. Their published findings rang with anger toward the evacuees at Amache.

> As the survey and tabulation progressed, it became increasingly evident that a small percentage of the population wanted to go any place to do anything. Many reasons for this apathy, or resistance to relocation were advanced.
>
> You will note that we have 801 employable male citizens in the employable age range of 18 to 44 and 1,030 female citizens in the same group. It is probable that most of the reasons advanced by this group as to why they are not interested in relocation only covers a reason they are ashamed to admit. Most of them are nursing a grudge—admittedly with reason. But it is difficult to see how the Director or the Project Director can

---

[465] Lindley, "Quarterly Report," 4.
[466] WRA, "Outside Employment Treatment and Reaction."

continue to attempt to convince the general public that these people are good American Citizens when many hundreds of them sit idly marking time. The director has stated that not one of the sixteen hundred evacuees on indefinite leave has been suspected of disloyalty or subversive activity. It might be equally true that sixteen hundred employable, idle evacuees in a relocation center are guilty of subversive inactivity.[467]

Attempting to eradicate the 1943 employment situation, one of Amache's community analysts, Dr. John A. Rademaker, published a four-part series in the *Pioneer*. In his series, Rademaker concluded the ease "to center one's attention upon one's self and one's problems" should be set aside by evacuees. Instead, Rademaker suggested that all persons in Amache should "keep our eyes on the larger situation" and "base our decisions and our acts upon its principles and its needs rather than upon the small part of the picture which affects us most directly."[468]

The ploy worked. By 1944, the number of relocation applications at Amache had grown to about 300 a week. Still, the overall percentage of WRA evacuees who chose to relocate remained small. By April 1945, only 4,000 of the 10,331 evacuees had asked for indefinite leaves.[469]

In this regard, Amache was much like other relocation centers. By January 2, 1945, the day the War Department rescinded the evacuation order, over 75,000 Issei and Nisei remained interned. Only a quarter of the total evacuee population had been relocated through WRA programs.[470]

---

[467] WRA, Memorandum to James Lindley from Granada Leave Office, Summer 1943, 293:170 L 2.55, Japanese American evacuation and resettlement records, BANC MSS 67/14c, the Bancroft Library, University of California, Berkeley.
[468] The *Pioneer*, 13 October 1943, 6.
[469] Lindley, "Final Report," appendix IV, 38.
[470] WRA, *People in Motion: The Postwar Adjustment of the Evacuated Japanese Americans* (New York: AMS Press, 1947), 10.

The relocation process was not an easy one. Inside Amache, it was mired by paperwork and screening hurdles. And if allowed outside, evacuees were faced with the uncertainties of employment and racial prejudice. Throughout, relocation was not an attractive process to evacuees.

Those applying for indefinite leaves were carefully screened to prevent Issei with pro-Japan allegiance from entering society. Access to indefinite leaves were granted only if an evacuee could prove that "he has a place to go and means of supporting himself; a check of records of the FBI and other intelligence agencies, plus the applicants record of behavior in the relocation center indicates that he would not endanger national security; there is evidence that his presence in the community in which he proposes to go is not likely to cause a public disturbance; and he agrees to keep the War Relocation Authority informed of his address at all times."[471]

Issei who had records with the FBI—and most had been followed closely by the FBI, not out of guilt, but out of unwarranted suspicion—were not allowed out due to the WRA's desire to promote Caucasian confidence in the relocation process. Nisei had to complete a myriad of background checks and application paperwork in triplicate to be authorized leave from Amache. And if all these factors met the satisfaction of all involved, the evacuee could only find employment in an area of the country that racial concerns would not cause "a public disturbance." Crossing all the hurdles of the relocation process was overwhelming.

But if evacuees were able to meet these stringent demands and were allowed to relocate, they met with discouragement outside, for they often discovered they were fair game to prejudice. Some citizens of Colorado clamored that Japanese Americans were purchasing all the good land. In the northern part of the state, the American Legion of Colorado, headed by the then mayor of Brighton, attempted to have an amendment added to the state's constitution that would prevent Japanese aliens from owning property in the state. With WRA

---

[471] WRA; "Japanese Americans in Relocation Centers"; Joseph McClelland Collection; Box 1; Folder 9; Washington, DC., March 1943; 4.

statistics showing over 2,500 Japanese Americans in Colorado, various action groups hoped to keep the Japanese American minority from profiting in the area of agriculture.[472]

Still others claimed the Japanese could not be trusted to relocate into unprotected areas. In the mind of many Colorado citizens, the WRA was responsible for housing evacuees until the war's end, not for moving them into the general public. Malcolm E. Pitts, field assistant director of the WRA, highlighted the sentiments of Colorado citizens when he commented:

> We have uprooted these people from their homes, placed them in new situations, given them work at salaries which never exceed $19 a month-and that only to skilled technicians
>
> Our job of placing these people back into private industry has been enormously complicated by inflammatory charges of disloyalty. Many employers have cancelled jobs for these people either because they distrusted Japanese or were afraid of public resentment if they should hire them.[473]

Relocation was difficult. The process consisted of moving an oppressed group of people into a burdensome environment filled with another group of people who never wanted the first group to begin with. Dillon Myer had to develop some method to give assurance to all parties involved. Somehow, he had to prove to the United States that evacuees were loyal Americans filled with the best of intentions. In the spring of 1943—thanks in part to the United States Army—Myer stumbled on his answer.

The answer had actually been under Myer's nose all along. Throughout their history in America, Japanese Americans had served their country in both times of war and in times of peace. But during

---

[472] *Lamar Daily News*, 29 May 1944, 1.
[473] *Rocky Mountain News*, 27 April 1943, 26.

the initial stages of the relocation process, the right to serve in a military capacity had been taken away. Only those who had served before December 7—fewer than five thousand in number—were allowed to remain in support-based, noncombat military service.

But by the spring of 1943, the tide of exclusion began to change.

One force affecting this tide, ironically, was the Empire of Japan. Throughout the war, Japan had introduced propaganda campaigns against America. The main focus of this propaganda was aimed at the internment of Issei and Nisei in relocation and internment centers around the nation. True believers of democracy, the empire declared, would have never imprisoned citizens and aliens on the basis of race. Such campaigns sent chills down the spines of both military and political leaders. The image of a government fighting for democracy while oppressing its own citizens was not the image most in the United States wished to portray.

A second force changing the tide of exclusion came from within the detention camps themselves. Since Pearl Harbor, Nisei had clamored for an opportunity to fight in Allied forces both in Europe and the Pacific. It was their democratic right to do so, they demanded. It was also the best method of showing that they—like the rest of Americans—held duty and obligation in high regard.

A final force that chipped away at military exclusion came from sheer necessity. The demand for troops on the European front and the Pacific theater was extremely high. A large portion of military-age men had either volunteered or had been drafted. The amount of workers left at home struggled to keep production at needed levels. Men and women were desperately needed both at home and abroad. In this time of need, a ready, willing, and extremely able supply of Issei and Nisei being housed in detention camps seemed like a powder keg waiting to be tapped.

Some Americans, however, cringed at the thought of placing Japanese Americans amid the overseas fighting force. Mississippi representative John E. Rankin (D) noted that he was "shocked beyond expression" to learn that such actions were being taken. He urged Congress to stop the action, noting that "while our boys are being butchered by these brutal apes in the Pacific, and while these savages are now on our soil in the Aleutian Islands, I submit it is no time to continue that maudlin policy toward them that resulted in, if it did not invite, the Pearl Harbor disaster."[474]

Necessity won. On January 28, Secretary of War Stimson released a plan for the formation of an all-Nisei battalion unit. In a February 1 letter to Stimson, President Roosevelt responded:

> The proposal of the war department to organize a combat team consisting of loyal American citizens of Japanese descent has my full approval. The new combat team will add to the nearly five thousand loyal Americans of Japanese ancestry who are already serving in the armed forces of our country.
>
> This is a natural and logical step toward the reinstitution of the selective service procedures that were temporarily disrupted by the evacuation from the west coast.
>
> No loyal citizen of the United States should be denied the democratic right to exercise the responsibilities of his citizenship, regardless of ancestry. The principle on which this country was founded and by which it has always been governed is that Americanism is a matter of the mind and heart.
>
> Americanism is not, and never was, a matter of race or ancestry. A good American is one who is loyal to this country and to our creed of liberty and democracy. Every loyal American citizen should be given the opportunity to serve this country wherever his skills will make the greatest contribution—whether it be in the ranks of our armed forces, war production, agriculture, gov-

---

[474] *Rocky Mountain News*, 4 February 1943, 14.

ernment service, or other work essential to the war effort.

I am glad to observe that the war department, the navy department, the war manpower commission, the department of justice, and the war relocation authority are collaborating in a program which will assure the opportunity for all loyal Americans, including Americans of Japanese ancestry to serve their country at a time when the fullest and wisest use of our manpower is all-important to the war effort.[475]

An approval of the commander in chief—the very same individual who had authorized evacuation proceedings and the very same individual who had "denied the democratic right to exercise the responsibilities of his citizenship" in the first place—was all the military needed to end exclusion. Although Japanese Americans would only be allowed to serve in segregated squads, they would now, at least, be allowed the right to serve their country in a time of war.

But how could military leaders be certain of the loyalty of Nisei men? Could some Nisei indeed be loyal to the country of their father's birth? These were the same questions that haunted Dillon Myer in his attempt to relocate evacuees.

The solution devised by military leaders was simple. Pass out a twenty-eight-question form to be filled out by all male evacuees of military age. The bulk of the questions on the form would be designed to determine the gifts and talents of the applicant. The final two questions, however, would be designed to determine the willingness to serve and the allegiance of the applicant. In the opinion of the military, a method to determine Nisei loyalty was finally created.

And Dillon Myer believed that he could mimic the process by using his own set of questions. By asking the army to conduct a mass WRA registration paralleling their own, Myer could finally disassemble the blurred issues plaguing relocation into two very distinct and

---

[475] *Lamar Daily News*, 8 February 1943, 1.

concrete divisions—those evacuees who were loyal and those who were not.

On February 6, 1943, army personnel arrived at Amache to administer the questionnaires. Evacuees had already been advised by camp personnel that whoever was of military age and chose not to fight would be considered for war industry work outside the camp—no exceptions. By informing Nisei evacuees that they would be expected to participate in the war effort in one way or another, the leadership at Amache was hoping to send a strong message that military service was expected.[476]

Nisei of military age filling out the army questionnaire were given a document entitled "Statement of United States Citizens of Japanese Ancestry." All other evacuees filled out a WRA questionnaire entitled "Application for Leave Clearance." Although the WRA form was its own creation, the questions were borrowed heavily from the one administered by the military.[477]

This registration process turned out to be a comedy of errors. In the haste to distribute the forms among the centers, the questionnaires included misleading titles and faulty questions that confused evacuees.

One point of confusion was question 27 of the WRA form. The WRA failed to change the wording that originally read, "If the opportunity presents itself and you are found qualified, would you be willing to volunteer for the Army Nurse Corps or the WAAC [Women's Army Auxiliary Corp]?" All men and women not qualified for military service were expected to fill out the WRA questionnaire. Issei men especially found the question rather confusing. Were they truly being asked to join female branches of the army?

More confusion came from question 28. This asked, "Will you swear unqualified allegiance to the United States of America and foreswear any form of allegiance or obedience to the Japanese emperor, or any other foreign government, power, or organization." If Issei answered "Yes" to question 28, were they really expected to swear

---

[476] Lindley, "Final Report," appendix IV, 6.
[477] "Issei, Nisei, Kibei," 84.

allegiance to a country that had never allowed them any rights in the first place? Also, a response of "Yes" would surely force their dual citizenships to be canceled, and then Issei who had loved ones still in Japan would quite possibly never be allowed to see them again. On the other hand, a "No" response would mean deportation back to Japan for themselves and their families.

For Nisei of military age, the army questionnaire presented its own problems. Question 27 on this form asked if the registrant would be "willing to serve in the armed forces of the United States on combat duty, whenever ordered." The thought of the US government asking for military service rankled many. Was this not the very same government that had evacuated and interned its own citizens? Was this not the same government that had only recently stripped all Nisei and their families of their constitutional rights and earthly possessions?

Like the WRA form, question 28 on the army form also asked the registrant to foreswear all allegiance to "the Japanese emperor, or any other foreign government, power, or organization." Most Nisei found it ironic that they, American citizens, should be asked to foreswear allegiance to a country they had never seen and an emperor they had little knowledge of.[478]

For some evacuees, the registration process became a means in which to formally protest the entire act of evacuation.

The most popular form of protest manifested itself by simply answering "No" to questions 27 and 28. Most Nisei and Issei who replied in this manner did so not from lack of loyalty, but because of various personal convictions and external pressures. Lindley noted that of those who answered "No" to question 28, most were the average age of a junior in high school. These young men, so Lindley noted, were extremely susceptible to peer pressures as well as pressures associated with "a very strong parental influence." Lindley also felt that such a large response could be, in part, due to the Buddhist faith (73 percent of those answering question 28 in the negative attached themselves to this faith) and its tie with the emperor of Japan.

---

[478] "Issei, Nisei, Kibei," 84; Weglyn, *Years of Infamy*, 37.

WRA project leaders were disturbed with these protests. Originally, 106 military-age male evacuees answered "No" on question 28—a response that, if taken far enough, would eventually lead the protesting evacuees to not show up for reinduction physical examinations at the Atchinson, Topeka and Sante Fe Railway depot in Lamar. Such an action was considered in violation of the Selective Training and Service Act and was thus tried by the Federal District Court in Denver.[479]

After much "discussion" among Lindley's staff and evacuee leaders of the community council, it was decided to hold a series of meetings in which staff members could explain the issue surrounding questions 27 and 28 to male evacuees between the ages of seventeen and thirty-eight. Three such meetings were held in mid-February.[480]

Angered by what he felt was a large number of "No" responses, Lindley spoke to the evacuees in order to "clarify" responses. His stated purpose was not to change opinions, but to instruct. But his implied goal was, in reality, to end all notions of protest.

> Since its inception, the War Relocation Authority has worked for the relocation of the Japanese and Japanese-Americans, to change their status from evacuees to normal Americans. It has worked for months to get recognition for the Nisei youth to be treated as other American citizens. The first public recognition is the about-face of the Army in opening its ranks to enlistment. This offer has to be taken in the spirit in which it is given. There is no time to go back and reclassify-your classification means nothing-your registration, everything.
>
> The Army does not need you; 7,400 [Nisei volunteers] from Hawaii alone would more than

---

[479] James Lindley, letter to Dillon S. Myer, 2 March 1943, 304:0152 LS.74 Japanese American evacuation and resettlement records, BANC MSS 67/14c, the Bancroft Library, University of California, Berkeley.
[480] Lindley, letter to Myer.

fill the combat team. The U.S. Army wants to be able to say that the youth of the Nisei have shown their loyalty by their action in enlisting from the relocation centers—there can be no carping criticism that this action will not answer.

Now, as to question No. 28. That is a clear and straightforward question. "Will you swear allegiance to the United States and forswear allegiance to Japan?" There can be no qualified answer. The answer is "Yes" or "No."

We are at war! War with Japan. There can be no evasion or quibbling; if you are not for us, you are against us. If you are against us in this war for survival, then you are an enemy and for our own protection you will not be allowed the comparative freedom of a relocation center; you will not be allowed freedom of the community, by passes at the front gate; you will not be considered for outside employment—for you are not fit to be turned loose in the country of your citizenship. You are headed for internment and probable return to Japan. I hope you have given some thought to your reception and probable future life in the Japanese Empire.[481]

Reactions to Lindley's speech were mixed. Seventy-six of the original 106 who had answered "No" to question 28 changed their answers to "Yes." Those who kept a "No" response to both or one of the loyalty questions became known as no-no boys and were segregated to the camp at Tule Lake.

---

[481] James Lindley, "General Comments by Project Director., 20 March 1943, 288:018 Ll.15, Japanese American evacuation and resettlement records, BANC MSS 67/14c, the Bancroft Library, University of California, Berkeley.

Likewise, those who asked for expatriation were also sent to Tule Lake. Throughout the remainder of the war, Tule Lake would become home to those who made such choices.[482]

Still others turned to violence—destruction of property seemed the most visible method of gaining attention for the cause. Sets Sumikawa recalls her brother's reactions:

> My brother would not go into the service. He went with four or five guys to Lamar to take the test—the physical—and on the way home they stopped at a restaurant that had a sign that said, "We don't accept Japs." My brother and the other guys got really upset and really tore up the place and gave the owner a piece of their minds. At that time I was kind of ashamed and I thought what they did was really wrong. He would not serve his country because he said, "Look what you guys have done to us." He felt like we were in concentration camps for these feelings, the government took his citizenship and put him in jail.[483]

Resistance to the draft would come again in the spring of 1944 when a new call to duty was administered. This time, attempting to explain the reasons behind the negative responses, John A. Rademaker remarked:

> Experience has shown that segregation leads to the opposite of equality, and whether in the case of differential treatment or units, whether for Issei or Nisei, the first and strongest reaction to even a hint of segregation is "We feel that that is not just, and we protest against it." A more emotionalized type of reaction (fortunately not

---

[482] Weglyn, *Years of Infamy*, 37.
[483] Sumikawa, S., interview.

very frequent) is of the nature: "What's wrong with the Army anyhow? First they say we can't be trusted on the west coast because we'd be sure to sabotage it. Now they turn around and ask us to save the country through our patriotic self-sacrifice by acting as cannon fodder. We think we're entitled to an apology from the Army or from General Dewitt and the super patriots who kicked us out of California." The reaction to the civil rights matter is also normal. If they're asked to take the burdens of citizenship, they are certainly entitled to the advantages of citizenship. From the standpoint of the evacuees, therefore, we have again the egocentric thinking which characterizes many of their attitudes both before and after evacuation, but it is based upon realistic conceptions of cause and effect so far as their feelings are concerned, and as far as their experience with west coast politicians goes.[484]

But the "egocentric" attitudes Rademaker spoke of were not limited to the evacuees. The community analyst went on to note:

It is equally difficult for the ordinary non-evacuee to understand the evacuee's point of view as it is for the evacuee to understand the effect his demands and requests are likely to have upon non-evacuees... Allegations that the Nisei have refused to serve in the army, without explanation of why not, will unquestionably be published in the Hearst press, and friends and foes alike will feel that the protestations of loyalty and patrio-

---

[484] James A. Rademaker, letter to Dr. Edward H. Spicer, 16 February 1944, 304:0067 L5.71, Japanese American evacuation and resettlement records, BANC MSS 67114c, the Bancroft Library, University of California, Berkeley.

tism which the Nisei have so often made are just so much propaganda and hog-wash. It would hardly be realistic to expect the true story to be given in the press, and even if it were it would be hard to get the average non-evacuee with sons overseas to accept the argument that the Nisei will serve in the army only if and when their civil rights and equalitarian treatment are restored.[485]

The debate over the draft brought strife between family member, friends, and neighbors alike. One evacuee wrote:

My brother wrote to me and said that he just enlisted for the paratrooper [sic]. Was I happy, but my mother sure didn't like him to do it because the neighbors or the whole block would talk about it. Most of them had a different idea from our family; it was bad for a few weeks until recently. They found out because of a soldier who came on a furlough said that my brother joined and only brave soles [sic] joined. They all laugh about it later. In the block I live there are few persons who have the same idea as I do but they are called watch dogs, spy, and anything else you can think.[486]

Such disagreements would linger throughout the war. Those who would eventually serve in American military units did so in an effort to fight the battles found both at home and abroad. And the battles they waged would help change not only physical struggles in the European and Pacific theaters, but also the physiological and emotional struggles in Colorado and the rest of America.

---
[485] Rademaker, letter to Dr. Spicer.
[486] Author unknown, "Office Memorandum," 304:0067 LS.71, Japanese American evacuation and resettlement records, BANC MSS 67/14c, the Bancroft Library, University of California, Berkeley.

CHAPTER 8

WINNING THE WAR

Tule Lake was not the typical "way station" Myer had envisioned. Its beginnings may have been similar to those of other WRA relocation centers, but by the summer of 1943, the atmosphere of Tule Lake was more like a highly secured prison than a relocation center.

Myer never wanted Tule Lake as an internment camp similar to those run by the Department of Justice. It was not meant for those dangerous to the American war effort. In the mind of Dillon Myer, Tule Lake was simply a place to confine those "who had applied for repatriation to Japan and who had not withdrawn their application by July 1, 1943, and all those who had answered 'No' to the loyalty question during registration." For the WRA, Tule Lake was to be a holding place where those endangering the overarching plan of mass relocation could be kept.[487]

Tule Lake was chosen as the site for segregation for a number of reasons. First, with a capacity of over fifteen thousand people, it could house a large number of dissenters. Next, the farm at Tule Lake was well-developed and could sustain a large population. Finally, as a relocation center, Tule Lake had the largest number of residents who were designated for segregation. Leaving such a large number

---

[487] Myer, *Uprooted Americans*, 76.

of dissenters where they were would prove more cost-effective than segregation elsewhere.[488]

Myer and the WRA had hoped segregation of "disloyal" evacuees into a single center would limit discrimination against Issei and Nisei in other centers who expressed loyalty. Segregation would decrease the disunity found within the camps. Segregation would soften the racial tensions of Anglo-Americans on the outside. According to Myer, the program was not intended as a means of punishment to those who had expressed dissent. Rather, it was a program designed to recognize "the integrity of those persons of Japanese ancestry who frankly have declared their sympathy for Japan or their lack of allegiance to the United States."[489]

No longer could inflammatory sources question the true loyalty of those in WRA camps. Those left behind in relocation centers would finally have proof of their loyalty and would, it was hoped, find easy access into outside communities. Segregation of those deemed disloyal to Tule Lake would take care of loyalty questions once and for all in one neat, clean swoop.

But in truth, Tule Lake became much more than a holding center for those deemed disloyal. It became a hotbed for protest and unrest. Here amid the darkened air of mistrust and suspicion sat evacuees who were mostly just biding their time. Riots and clashes swelled its population. Armed guards were put on constant riot alert. A stockade even had to be erected to house the "dangerous elements" of the camp.

In his work *Keeper of Concentration Camps*, Richard Drinnon notes the heart-wrenching atmosphere of Tule Lake and the stockade there. Recounting the impressions of one WRA official—Field Secretary Thomas R. Bodine—Drinnon highlights the particularly sorrowful sight of

> mothers and children pressing against the barbed wire of the camp—peering across the parking lot

---

[488] Myer, *Uprooted Americans*, 76; *Lamar Daily News*, 13 August 1943, 1.

[489] Dillon S. Myer, "Statement of Policy Regarding Segregation," 304:0174 LS. 75, Japanese American evacuation and resettlement records, BANC MSS 67/ 14c, the Bancroft Library, University of California, Berkeley.

to the stockade where the husbands and fathers lean on the barbed wire there. Waving, trying to shout across. The children jumping up and down and waving their arms to show that they're okay and in good health. And, then, to soldiers stopping them, on the grounds that they are signaling secret and subversive messages. And, then, the children and mothers standing still just looking. And the husbands and fathers just looking back.[490]

Also within Tule Lake's gates sat a majority who never sought repatriation and expatriation. The camp's population included family members of those who were segregated as well as nearly six thousand evacuees who merely chose to remain at Tule Lake instead of enduring yet another move. One 1944 issue of *Fortune* magazine even told of children—some young and some beyond high school—who were there because they could not resist the overwhelming tide of familial pressure.[491]

This was the atmosphere in which evacuees from Amache who were considered a risk were sent. In the summer of 1943, the Tule Lake way-station-turned-prison began its conversion. Those in Tule Lake who donned the title of loyal were moved to other relocation centers. Those from Amache, who for one reason or another had refused the title, were transferred to the new "segregation center" at Tule Lake. And in the summer of 1943, Amache would begin the process of trying to determine who could be considered loyal and who could be considered disloyal.

The week Amache received confirmation that segregation was to take place—the week of July 14, 1943—had been filled with both the unusual and mundane. A sudden intense rainstorm had brought severe flooding to the center's school, mess halls, barracks, and co-op

---

[490] Richard Drinnon, *Keeper of the Concentration Camps* (Berkeley: University of California Press, 1987), 114.
[491] "Issei, Nisei, Kibei," 84.

building just under construction. The Spanish consul—Francisco De Amat—had visited the center along with James E. Henderson of the United States State Department to verify that all POW standards were being upheld at the center. And a three-day celebration and carnival had been staged to promote the sale of war stamps and war bonds.[492]

But no event could overshadow the news of a pending segregation. Dillon Myer arrived at the center on July 28, 1943, to explain the process. A crowd of over seven hundred attended the meeting held at the newly finished high school—a complex Myer described as "the most publicized and most famous high school in the United States."[493]

Myer's stance echoed the official stance of the WRA that held "the decision as to who will be segregated will be made in a spirit of fairness and justice." In his speech, Myer also mentioned, "While it is recognized that the segregation process will put too much trouble those persons who must move, I have no question but that the national interest and the long-range welfare of the thousands of loyal American citizens and law-abiding aliens justify the step to be taken." And, above all, in his speech, Myer encouraged evacuees of Amache to unite behind the process of segregations.[494]

So whether evacuees agreed with Myer's sentiments or not, through the months after his visit, the center prepared. The evacuee property section spent "much time" shipping over three hundred thousand pounds of freight and baggage—over eight freight cars and four baggage cars full of property. The carpentry shop also busily prepared crates to package evacuee goods for shipment.[495]

Pamphlets and news stories were also published to inform Amache evacuees of the segregation process. Lindley noted that more

---

[492] Lindley, "Final Report," appendix IV, 14.
[493] Lindley, "Final Report," appendix IV, 15.
[494] Myer, "Statement of Policy."
[495] WRA, Granada Relocation Center, "Quarterly Report," Evacuee Property Section, 30 September 1943, 306:0317 L6.31, Japanese American evacuation and resettlement records, BANC MSS 67/14c, the Bancroft Library, University of California, Berkeley.

than thirty news stories and editorials were printed in the *Pioneer* from the middle of July to the end of October. Even a diagram depicting the steps necessary to be taken in the process of segregation was published in the August 14 issue of the *Pioneer* as well as posted on bulletin boards around the camp.[496]

Some evacuees attempted to persuade those destined for segregation to change their stance. Fumiye Nishizaki recalls that as block manager, her husband, Torno, was one who openly discouraged repatriation to Japan:

> There were a lot of Issei who were very pro-Japan. But [Torno] really wanted to help the evacuee do it right. A lot of Japanese people wanted to go back to Japan. Because these poor people didn't have the money to go back to Japan before, they say they get a free ride this time—go back to Japan free. But my husband say, "Don't go back now. You can go back any time after. They are going to lose the war, you're going to go back to a land where they lost the war." They would say, "Well, they're not going to lose the war." But he told them Japan will lose. So he protected a lot of people. He saved all his friends from going back to Japan.[497]

While evacuees were discussing segregation, the project's attorney and the project's assistant director were busy conducting hearings. Segregation hearings began on July 10, 1943, in Amache. Lasting through July and August 1943, these hearings were designed to provide Amacheans who had answered "No" to loyalty questions with an opportunity to "clarify" their responses. Evacuees were also given opportunities to clear up any questions they might have had about the issues of segregation.

---

[496] Lindley, "Final Report," appendix V, 4.
[497] Nishizaki, interview.

The committee conducting these segregation hearings—known as the Committee of Project Investigation—was appointed by Project Director Lindley and consisted of a number of Amache staff members, including the two assistant project directors, the project attorney, the center's employment officer, and the chief of internal security. This committee was responsible for questioning evacuees about their families, connections with Japan, and their answers to questions 27 and 28 on the WRA questionnaire. In turn, evacuees could choose to answer the questions or remain silent on the grounds of self-incrimination.

According to Lindley, the segregation hearings were done in the most empathetic manner possible. "Before each hearing," recalled Lindley,

> the person interviewed was informed in detail as to the nature and purpose of the hearing, and care was taken to make sure that the person interviewed understood each question. All the hearings were conducted in an informal manner, and practically the same procedure was followed as [was] recommended for leave-clearance hearings. In other words, many more questions were asked than were required to be asked. This was done so that the board would have as much available information as was possible as to each interview.[498]

At the end of each investigation, the committee was responsible for sending all minutes of the hearings as well as their recommendations to Lindley who, in turn, was responsible for contacting Dillon Myer for approval.

Some hearings were cut-and-dried—the evacuees wanted the "free ride" to Japan that Fumiye Nishizaki had spoken of. Other hearings were not so easily determined. Most of Amache's segrega-

---

[498] Lindley, "Final Report," appendix V, 4.

tion hearings were filled with great emotional struggle and uncertainty. The following is an excerpt of one Amache hearing, showing an evacuee torn between two very distinct desires:

> Mr. Harbison: Q. Since you have indicated your interest in living in Japan it is quite reasonable for us to think you expect, and possibly hope, Japan will win this war. What are your views on this?
>
> A. I can't say that one, but I just wanted to go back and live.
>
> Q. Is it right to say that perhaps you don't care who wins the war?
>
> A. Yes. I could say this much: If the United States draft Japanese Americans, if they draft me I have a feeling I should protect this country. In case that happens I really put in all I have.
>
> Mr. Horn: Q. Do you want your answer to remain the same as it was originally?
>
> A. What do persons here think was right way to answer?
>
> Mr. Knodel: Q. When the war is over, from what you have said, I have been led to believe it is your father's and your intention to return to Japan for residence. In other words, you intend to live there with the balance of your family?
>
> A. Yes.
>
> Q. You have no desire to continue residence in this country?
>
> A. Yes.
>
> Mr. Harbison: Q. In answer to your question, the only answer we could give would be "yes" to number 28. We know this is a problem and we can appreciate the situation you are in. We can appreciate you knew something of Japan. Your mother, brothers, and sisters are there. Your father is here and he wants to go back. Frankly I

am not sure just what I would do in your situation. We have had some "neutral" answers.

Mr. Horn: Q. Do you want us to help you to try to return to Japan?

You mean right now?

Mr. Horn:

A. Yes.

A. I would like to stay here.

Mr. Horn: Q. Are you willing to join the United States Army and help shorten the war?

A. If I have to I will.

Q. If you are drafted you will?

A. In other words I think this matter over, and I feel if I am considered I have citizenship here and over there, which is making the trouble and feel if I get through high school in this country, if government gives order, I should take it and do it. Then I'll lose Japanese citizenship and fight for this country. Reason I said, "if I was drafted" is I don't want to go against my brothers and relatives.

Mr. Horn: Q. Do you agree not to do anything to impair the war effort in this country?

A. I don't have idea of doing things like that because right now I have taken the responsibility of children, taking care of little boys at Sunday School and I wouldn't want to show them the wrong thing first.

In this case, the subcommittee recommended the evacuee for segregation to Tule Lake.[499]

---

[499] WRA, "Hearing before Segregation Committee," 24 July 1943, 293:0217 L2.57, Japanese American evacuation and resettlement records, BANC MSS 67/14c, the Bancroft Library, University of California, Berkeley.

While segregation hearings were continuing, evacuees and staff members were busy preparing the camp for the arrival of Tule Lake evacuees who were deemed loyal. Initial figures had once indicated that between 150 and 200 Amacheans were to be exchanged for over 1,000 Tuleans. So bracing for this sudden influx of people, staff and evacuees alike worked night and day in preparing the camp. A housing freeze went into effect, stopping any internal moves. Residents from around the center began collecting lumber, cots, and bedding to supply the 280 housing units needed for the additional numbers. A reception committee was even organized to greet the incoming Tule Lake evacuees.

By late August, Amache seemed ready for the exchange. In an August press release sent out to all Colorado press sources, it was made known that "only 105 of the 6,700 evacuees at the Granada center will be sent to the Tule Lake segregation center on September 15." However, by September 16, 125 residents had been transferred from Amache to Tule Lake, while 35 had been expatriated and repatriated to Japan. Only one Amachean would be considered dangerous enough to be removed to Leupp Arizona's internment center.[500]

On the same day that Amacheans were heading for segregation, the first group of Tuleans—numbering 511—was arriving at the Granada train station. Within a week, 478 more evacuees would arrive at Amache, making it necessary to set up makeshift living quarters in fourteen of the mess halls. Project Director Lindley felt the addition of these evacuees from Tule Lake had an adverse reaction on the atmosphere of Amache. "The Tuleans," Lindley later remarked, "were about a year behind the other residents of the center in their thinking; they were still resentful and constantly harped on the wrongs of the evacuation, which most of the other residents had come to treat as water over the dam."[501]

---

[500] Granada Relocation Center Reports Office, "Sample Press Release," 21 August 1943, 309:215 L6.99, Japanese American evacuation and resettlement records, BANC MSS 67/14c, the Bancroft Library, University of California, Berkeley; Lindley, "Final Report," 3; Foxster, "Granada Internal Security."

[501] Lindley, "Final Report," 3.

From Lindley's position as director of the camp, the effect of such resentment was devastating to the established order and calm found in the residents of Amache. Lindley noted:

> Some leadership was developed among this Tule Lake crowd, most of it bad. Several of these leaders were elected to the Community Council and dominated that body, first through the existing chairman and later by election to the chair. A decided rift was created between the Administration and the Council. The Council began to act on the premise that the function of that body to oppose and frustrate the administration and that in so doing it was representing the people.[502]

In short, what the administration had fought so hard to establish began to be questioned with the influx of Tule Lake evacuees.[503]

In all, Amache would receive 1,050 evacuees from Tule Lake. In return, 160 Amacheans would become candidates for segregation and repatriation. These evacuees going to Tule Lake represent the fewest number of evacuees deemed "disloyal" of any WRA relocation center.[504]

The arrival of evacuees from Tule Lake came at a particularly dark time in Amache's history. Amache, like the rest of southwestern Colorado, was in the midst of a polio epidemic. Throughout September and into October, the entire camp of more than 6,000 people was quarantined from the rest of the world.

Passes to surrounding communities were no longer issued. All athletic events and center activities were frozen. And passes to outside visitors were no longer given.

---

[502] Lindley, "Final Report," 3, 4.
[503] Lindley, "Final Report," appendix IV, 17, 18.
[504] Lindley, "Final Report," 18–20.

In essence, the camp became entirely isolated. Even the final shipment of fifty-one Tuleans into Amache was postponed until the middle of November. By the end of October, the viral disease had taken at least four children's lives and had left countless others partially debilitated.

It was an absurd situation. Evacuees from Tule Lake had declared their loyalty to calm America's fears. In exchange for their vows, they were thrown into the very midst of a polio epidemic. It must have appeared to be a no-win situation for evacuees in the summer of 1943. It must have seemed that no amount of suffering would ever prove evacuee loyalty or accomplish Myer's dream of relocation.

Despite the hardships, Lindley declared the segregation program within his camp a success. Information about the program was disseminated efficiently. And discontentment was kept at a minimum. "Once the program was announced and detailed information provided," Lindley would later declare, "there seemed to be little, if any, misunderstanding anywhere in the center. In fact, the segregation program was accepted for what it was."[505]

In some ways, Myer's vision of a more tolerant America was taking shape. By the fall of 1943, the anti-Asian forces that had driven Issei and Nisei off the West Coast were becoming more and more silent. In many ways, they were losing ground to a more educated American public.

Since the movement to relocate had begun, anti-evacuation groups had attempted to point out the loyalty of Japanese Americans. The JACL had always fought to prove the loyalty of the Nisei in America. Fair play committees around the West Coast—and eventually in select relocation centers—were organized as a means to counteract the inflammatory remarks of anti-Asian forces.

A few Caucasian groups had likewise united in an attempt to inform the American public about the plight of Japanese Americans. One such organization—the Colorado Council of Churches (CCC)—had published a small booklet entitled "The Japanese in Our Midst" in 1942 that described the process of evacuation and

---

[505] Lindley, "Final Report," appendix V, 4.

relocation as well as the loyalties of evacuees. The booklet was again published in 1943, this time in an updated form that addressed the truths behind resettlement, coddling, and loyalty issues. The CCC approved of Dillon Myers's conclusion that "relocation centers are undesirable institutions and should be removed as soon as possible," but also hoped to educate the general public until such removal could take place.[506]

Besides the work of the CCC, newspapers also began to issue stories favoring the Japanese American—especially those efforts of evacuees aiding farm production around the country. S. J. Boyer of the Utah State Labor Commission remarked, "We can just as well face the facts, if it had not been for Japanese labor, much of the beet crop of Utah and Idaho (in 1942) would have been plowed up… These are industrious people who want work, and if they save our crops, they must be made to feel that they are wanted and must not be discriminated against… We are fighting a war to end slavery wherever it exists."[507]

Sugar beet crops around the west had been saved, in large part, due to the efforts of evacuees on temporary leaves. Western Farm Life, located in Denver, reported that in 1942 alone, "8,019 evacuees harvested approximately 915,000 tons of beets from 80,000 acres in western states—enough to produce 265,000 pounds of sugar." Likewise, in Pueblo, Colorado, an article appeared in the September 22, 1943, *Chieftain* that noted the "use of farm laborers of Japanese ancestry has been a contributing factor in avoiding a critical labor shortage in the Arkansas valley." The *Chieftain* article went on to add that H. R. Schmid, county extension agent, remarked that "some of the evacuees who are working here came out of evacuation camps last fall to work in the sugar beet harvest and have worked thru the entire year."[508] Many of these laborers were Amacheans out on seasonal or indefinite leave.

---

[506] Colorado Council of Churches, "The Japanese in Our Midst," 1943, Lloyd Garrison Collection, Box 1, Folder 8, Auraria Library Archives and Special Collections, Denver, 3.
[507] Colorado Council of Churches, "The Japanese in Our Midst," 8.
[508] Colorado Council of Churches, "The Japanese in Our Midst," 3, 15; *Pueblo Chieftain*, 22 September 1943, 1, Granada Archives.

Japanese Americans continually proved their patriotism and character through their work. Even President Roosevelt remarked to the Senate in a September 1943 statement,

> Americans of Japanese ancestry—like those of many other ancestries—have shown that they can and want to accept our institutions and work loyally with the rest of us, making their valuable contribution to the national wealth and well-being... In vindication of the very ideals for which we are fighting this war, it is important to us to maintain a high standard of fair, considerate and equal treatment of the people of this minority as of all other minorities.[509]

An issue of *Time* magazine illustrates this change in attitude toward Japanese Americans. On December 20, 1943, *Time* recounted an investigation into the actions of the Pacific Coast Committee on American Principles and Fair Play by Chester F. Gannon—a Republican member of the California State Senate. *Time* magazine turned on Hearst's sensationalism, calling the entire West Coast situation "the West's most violent racial hysteria since Yellow Peril pioneer days." *Time* also described those responsible for such turbulence as "professional patriots, demagogues and sensational newspapers," guilty of nothing short of stirring the "witches broth."[510]

The investigation had begun after the Fair Play Committee distributed to Foreign Legion chapters around the west a letter written by Marine Pfc. Robert E. Bocher. Bocher, who had served in the offensive against the Japanese on Guadalcanal, expressed his shock to find "that our American citizens, those of Japanese ancestry, are being persecuted, yes, persecuted as though Adolph Hitler himself were in charge."

---

[509] *Times-Herald*, 15 September 1943, 1, Granada Archives.
[510] *Time*, 20 December 1943, 18.

Bocher's letter struck a sore spot with the American Legion, especially when Bocher remarked:

> We find that the California American Legion is promoting a racial purge, I'm putting it mildly when I say it makes our blood boil. We should fight this injustice, intolerance, and un-Americanism at home! We will not break faith with those who died… We have fought the Japanese and are recuperating to fight again. We can endure the hell of battle, but we are resolved not to be sold out at home.[511]

Such accusations made for ripe discussions around the country. Tabloids like Hearst's *Examiner* claimed the distribution of Bocher's letter was an attack on the American people by anti-evacuation groups.

But even publications like the *Los Angeles Times* editorialized the ensuing investigation into the distribution of Bocher's letter as "no proper function of a legislative committee…to turn itself into a prosecutor of what may currently be unpopular… When they turn themselves into witch-burning agencies they go far afield."[512]

By the spring of 1944, periodicals around the country began to take note of the plight of Japanese Americans within WRA camps. A March issue of *Life* magazine detailed life at Tule Lake. Photojournalist Carl Mydan vividly captured the essence of life in the detention center. Mydan, who had himself been interned by the Japanese earlier in the war, wrote of the "troublemakers" and "18,000 considered disloyal to the U.S." living within the camp. He also hinted at the emotional side of the center by photographing the struggle Japanese Americans had with anger, desperation, and humiliation.[513]

---

[511] *Time*, 20 December 1943, 18.
[512] *Time*, 20 December 1943, 19.
[513] *Life*, 20 March 1944, 25.

One haunting photo entitled "What It Feels Like to Be a Prisoner" pictures a young Nisei boy holding a guitar and singing "Home on the Range." In the caption below it, Mydan wrote, "He sang it like an American. There was no Japanese accent. He looked at me the same way I guess I looked at a Japanese official when he came to check on me at Camp Santo Tomas in Manila. At the back of my mind was the thought, 'Come on, get it over and get out. Leave me alone.' This boy felt the same way. He was just waiting, killing time." Suddenly Mydan's article brought to the general public a horrific notion. Here sat an American citizen imprisoned much like the Japanese had imprisoned Mydan. The only real difference was that Americans were incarcerating this American, not the Japanese.[514]

Mydan's essay also compared WRA camps to Japanese POW camps. Mydan found that Nisei internment dealt more with "political and sociological conflicts" than the material needs of internees of the Japanese. Although Mydan never went out of his way to side with Japanese Americans incarcerated at Tule Lake, his photo essay marked the first time since the start of the evacuation process that a major periodical spoke honestly about life in a WRA center.[515]

Following on the heels of Mydan's *Life* photo essay came an even more striking article. An April 1944 issue of *Fortune* magazine entitled "Issei, Nisei, Kibei" focused on the racism behind evacuation and internment. Line drawings of Mine Okubo—an evacuee artist—illustrated the article. Overcrowding and poor living conditions were reported. Talk of the registration and segregation process was described as "almost as charged with emotion as that disturbing term evacuation." The periodical even lambasted states like Arizona for their role in "race hating" designed to "strangle prewar Japanese-American populations."[516]

Through this article, *Fortune* strongly reinforced the Americanism of evacuees. The report highlighted one Japanese American evacuee at Tule Lake who had "fought in the last war in

---

[514] *Life*, 20 March 1944, 31.
[515] *Life*, 20 March 1944, 25, 34.
[516] "Issei, Nisei, Kibei," 84, 106.

the U.S. Army, and is a member of the American Legion." The article continued that this man had "offered his services to the Army and to industry in California. He was turned down. Sent to a relocation center he became a troublemaker with the slogan, 'If you think you are an American, try walking out the gate.'" While in Tule Lake, the veteran had sent a check to Uncle Sam for the sum of $100. The check, it seemed, represented the evacuee's income tax for 1942 as "belated payment for his 1941 services as navigator on a Portuguese ship. He insisted on paying his tax, as usual." The article went on to add, "He has of course no wish to go to Japan. He, too, sits out the war, Tule Lake in protest against the failure of democracy."[517]

These scattered inclusions in the press began to slowly inform and educate the American public. Many began to apply a human face to evacuation and internment. Japanese Americans were now pictured as people of great integrity and drive who had been unjustly persecuted. In a small way, in very scattered instances, the press was now beginning to repair the damage it had caused.

But nothing made the American public stand up and take notice of Japanese Americans like the bravery of Nisei who served in the military. Japanese Americans were beginning to win the war at home as well as the one overseas. Through their battles at home and abroad, Issei and Nisei were proving they, too, were part of the American Spirit.

In its essence, it was integrity. By its nature, it was virtue. Frequently noble, often courageous, and always resolute, it was the shell encapsulating the beating heart of America's democracy. It was called the American Spirit.

The qualities of integrity and virtue found in the American Spirit had matured with each passing decade. Integrity had been nurtured through the blood lost at Valley Forge. Virtue had been fortified through the struggles of Fort Sumter and Gettysburg. And both were now being empowered through every new conflict of World War II.

---

[517] "Issei, Nisei, Kibei," 94.

As American citizens, Nisei were a part of this American Sprit. They, like other citizen soldiers, had become the very sinews of strength interwoven into an ever-evolving American tapestry. They were a part of what scholar Chuck Colson called the "product of creeds, family, and culture—a culture that placed higher value on duty and obligation than on self-fulfillment, self-expression, or self-esteem." Since the advent of war, Japanese Americans had clamored for opportunities to prove their own sense of "duty and obligation."[518]

But many in the 1940s had lost sight of the American Spirit. They refused to believe that Japanese Americans could be loyal in the fight against Axis powers. The subjective strands of self-righteousness were weakening the integrity and virtue of America. America's fight for decency and fairness abroad was slowly being undermined by the fear and condemnation at home. Nisei were US citizens by birth, but were refused the right to serve their country in a time of war. Issei and Nisei had become targets of outspoken rage.

Nisei youth had fought hard to gain entrance into military service during the war, but were turned down simply because of their heritage. An America at war found it difficult to distinguish between Japanese overseas choosing imperialism and Japanese Americans and aliens at home choosing democracy. At first, freedom to fight for democracy was denied.

But by 1943, many outside the center began asking why Japanese American youth were allowed to stay at home—and even go to college—while the rest of America's young were being sacrificed to military service. The placement of young healthy evacuees of military age in the confines of relocation centers was seen as a waste of manpower.

Sen. A. B. Chandler (D) of Kentucky, chairman of a military affairs subcommittee that investigated Japanese relocation center conditions, asserted in the spring of 1943 that his committee's findings supported these feelings. In a statement to the press, Chandler remarked that his committee supported the drafting of Japanese

---

[518] Charles Colson, "Flag of Our Fathers," Breakpoint broadcast, 12 December 2000.

American citizens, the internment of those found disloyal to the United States, and the placement of "able-bodied Japanese" in work positions "where they will be accepted and where the army considers it safe for them to be located."[519]

As the tide of war in Europe began to turn in 1943, Japanese Americans were finally allowed to prove their merit as citizens—and their value as part of the American Spirit.

Since Pearl Harbor, Americans had united to create one of the largest economic and industrial campaigns in the history of the world. By 1944, the American industrial war machine was effortlessly producing nearly $200 billion in goods and services—an impressive amount considering that only three years earlier, the nation had been suffering from a stagnant, depression-riddled economy.

Women and minorities, who, only a few years before, had been excluded from equal opportunities and pay, now made up a substantial number of America's industrial workforce. Record numbers of citizens visited blood banks to donate much-needed plasma. Buying war bonds became viewed as part patriotic duty, part necessity.

So as America toiled in preparation, the world waited anxiously for the moment Allied powers would make their move. For months, Allied troops had waited for the drive into Axis-controlled Europe. And for months, the tension over such an invasion hovered over the world like a thick fog.

Then in June 1944, the fog of uncertainty began to lift. On June 6, or D-Day, Allied troops sent wave after wave of troops into Axis-controlled France, heavily damaging German resistance. By August 1, over a million troops had landed in France, forcing a gaping hole—a hole through which even more Allied troops would later enter. Through the summer and fall of 1944, the domination of Europe by Axis powers was slowly and methodically being decreased as US, British, and Free French troops freed Paris and swept through France, Belgium, and Germany on their way to Berlin.

Likewise, in the Pacific theater, Allied powers were slowly winning battle after battle. Through 1944, military leaders like

---

[519] *Rocky Mountain News*, 9 April 1943, 8.

Gen. Douglas MacArthur, Gen. Curtis LeMay, and Adm. Chester Nimitz led Allied forces to numerous victories over Japanese forces. Victories at Eniwetok in January, Guam and Tinian in July, and the Philippines in October 1944 reenergized Americans in their efforts for total triumph.

Japanese Americans were a part of this triumph overseas. They were proving their worth as Americans on the battlefield. They were showing the world that they were of the same stock as any other American. And through their bravery and courage overseas, they were slowly demolishing the walls of racism at home.

Most Japanese Americans were grateful for the opportunity to prove themselves, but the road leading to the chance had been filled with uncertainty and discouragement. The opportunity to serve in a military capacity had been taken away when Delos C. Emmons—the commanding general of the army in Hawaii at the time—discharged all Nisei in military service and reclassified them as 4C, the same classification as enemy aliens. With a new status equal to that of a non-American, these reclassified veterans took whatever tasks they could in service to the military. They worked in carpentry shops.

They labored as groundskeepers around military compounds. They took employment in maintenance crews at military posts. And they waited until they could again serve their country in a military manner.

By May 1942, the behavior of these discharged veterans was so impressive that Gen. George C. Marshall issued orders to establish the Hawaiian Provisional Infantry Battalion. This battalion was primarily made up of those who had been in service before the advent of war. Once activated as the 100th Battalion, the segregation fighting force left for Camp McCoy, Wisconsin, where they were trained through the summer, fall, and winter months of 1942.[520]

The Military Intelligence Service Language School (MISLS) was also reestablished in June 1942 by the War Department. The MISLS academy was originally established in San Francisco as a

---

[520] WRA, Nisei in Uniform, "Nisei in the Army," Lloyd Garrison Collection, Box 1, Folder 11, Auraria Library Archives and Special Collections, Denver.

Japanese-language training school, but with the advent of war and the evacuation of the West Coast, the school was moved to Camp Savage and, later, Fort Snelling, Minnesota. Men and women trained in the MISLS would eventually go on to serve as interrogators and translators in the war. These Japanese Americans would prove to be crucial players in deciphering Japanese battle plans and enemy maps as well as interrogating prisoners of war.[521]

In January 1943, the 100th Infantry Battalion was transferred to Camp Shelby, Mississippi, where it underwent advanced unit training. It was during this period, while the 100th underwent its final preparations for combat, that Secretary of War Stimson released his plan for the formation of an all-Nisei battalion unit. On February 1, President Roosevelt issued the statement that activated the 442nd Regimental Combat Team including the 442nd infantry, the 522nd Artillery Battalion, and the 232nd Engineers Company.[522]

Nisei response to this call for military service was mixed. In Hawaii, although the initial War Department quota called for 1,500, nearly 10,000 Nisei volunteered. On the mainland, however—where they had been forced into internment camps—only 1,256 of the 23,606 Nisei of draft age volunteered to serve in the 442nd. Nisei from Amache responded in a manner similar to the other camps. The first volunteers signing up for the 442nd numbered a little more than 120 Amache Nisei. And over the next several weeks, few more would volunteer.

Lindley remarked that the lackluster reaction to military service came from the Buddhist Church and Tule Lake "influences" who were "openly averse to the call to the colors in this center." Lindley even went as far as to note that "the first volunteers and inductees to return in uniform to the center were treated by the residents almost as outcasts. One would see them wandering around the center, usually alone; almost never were their parents with them."[523]

---

[521] Namura, E., interview; WRA, *WRA: A Story of Human Conservation* (New York: AMS Press, 1975), 129.
[522] WRA, Nisei in Uniform, "442nd Combat Team," Lloyd Garrison Collection, Box 1, Folder 11, Auraria Library Archives and Special Collections, Denver.
[523] Lindley, "Final Report," 4.

As time wore on, however, Lindley noted that attitudes began to change within the camp. Internees began to swell with pride as news told of the bravery Nisei were demonstrating overseas. Lindley even remarked that "fathers would bring their visiting sons in uniform down to the project director and introduce them: 'This is my boy.'"[524]

By the end of the war, Amache's honor roll would show 953 names—the highest percentage of any other relocation camp. Included in this count were WACS and army nurses, volunteers, and draftees.

Robert Ichikawa—an evacuee from Amache—recalls, "I volunteered for the 442nd to show the people and the government that I was just as good of an American as them. I was also hoping that life would become better for my parents, brothers, and sisters… I trained with the 442nd in Camp Shelby, Mississippi."[525] Like Ichikawa, Nisei from Amache began arriving at Camp Shelby in late spring of 1943 to prepare for the 442nd Regimental Combat Team.

Basic training for the 442nd would last from May 1943 to March 1944. During this period, the 100th Battalion, also stationed at Camp Shelby, finished their training and were shipped to North Africa, where they regrouped for combat in Italy. Ichikawa recalls that by June 10, the 442nd would be joining the 100th near Rome. Like many young men going overseas, Ichikawa was awed by what he saw. "After training we were shipped to Italy in one of the largest convoys ever assembled, there were ships as far as you can see in all directions. Even a German sub captain upped his periscope and saw all of the ships and immediately surfaced his boat and surrendered." Together, the 100th and the 442nd would join the 34th "Red Bull" Division to fight in the European theater.[526]

---

[524] Lindley, "Final Report," 4.
[525] Ichikawa, letter; Granada Relocation Center Reports Office, "Sample Press Release," March 1943, 309:215 L6.99, Japanese American evacuation and resettlement records, BANC MSS 67/14c, the Bancroft Library, University of California, Berkeley.
[526] Granada Relocation Center Reports Office, "Sample Press Release."

AMACHE

Amache evacuees, like evacuees from other camps, would become proud of the Nisei who bravely fought in the war—and with good reason. The 100th Infantry Battalion fought intense battles throughout Italy before joining with the 442nd Regimental Combat Team. In the initial Normandy invasion by Allied troops in 1944, the 442nd and the 100th became part of a second front set up in southern France to divert enemy troops away from action in Normandy. After this, they were attached to the 36th Division, and on October 14, 1944, the 442nd arrived at a heavily wooded area near Paris called the Vosges Mountains. On October 16 and throughout the next three days, the 442nd and 100th struggled to take this area.

"We were treated very well by our own troops in general," remembers Ichikawa.

> Most of the time I worried about my family who were still in camp. The group I was with was E Company, 2nd Platoon, 3rd Squad. Generally we talked about home, the future, where to next, and when do we eat? I remember mostly seeing the dead and dying and the wounded and the risks we took every day. The first day of battle, we were barraged by enemy artillery, where our squad [Sergeant] Ayato Kiyomot was hit in the knee. Pfc. Tad Masaoda was also hit in the knee. We were immediately ordered out of the area because the Germans had the place zeroed in.[527]

On October 18, the 100th took Hill A, the key objective needed to occupy the small railway town of Bruyeres. Over the next several hours, the second battalion would take Hill B and enter Bruyeres. Less than ten days later, from October 27 to 30, the 442nd would be called to rescue an American battalion—the Texas Battalion—cut off by German troops. There were over 800 casualties in the 442nd for the rescue of 211 men in the Texas Battalion. Of the 2,943 men

---

[527] Ichikawa, letter.

in the 442nd to enter the Vosges Mountains, 161 died, 43 became missing, and 2,000 were wounded.[528]

John Tateishi, author of *And Justice for All*, points out that another battle—the battle of the Gothic Line—was also important in that it showed the determination of the 442nd. With only 4,000 men, the 442nd broke the German line of resistance in thirty-two minutes—a feat that two divisions of over 40,000 men had failed to do in the past five months of battle.[529]

The drive through Italy and France brought high praise to both the 442nd and the 100th. The 442nd, for instance, suffered the highest percentage of casualties for a team its size—a total of 9,486 by war's end—and became one of the most decorated combat teams of its size in American military history. During the 225 days the 442nd saw combat, over 700 were killed, and it has been reported that the wounded equaled three times the strength of the regiment. Likewise, members of the 522nd Field Artillery Battalion—a division of the 442nd—are thought by many historians to be instrumental in liberating the survivors at Dachau.[530]

Amache evacuees hoped the military advances by Japanese Americans would show the rest of America the true spirit of Issei and Nisei in America. One young Japanese American boy wrote in a letter to Amache's school superintendent, "The people in this community, as well as other communities, should know that there are many boys of Japanese descent fighting hard and dying for this country."[531]

Likewise, one young Nisei serviceman made his loyalty clear by stating,

> Some of us are abbreviated Americans. We aren't tall men. But damned if we're hyphenated. The term Japanese is used merely as a descriptive adjective, see? Look, you know our combat team motto? It's "Go for broke." In a crap game that

---

[528] Japanese American National Museum, *Japanese American History*, 61–63.
[529] Tateishi, *And Justice for All*, xxv.
[530] Japanese American National Museum, *Japanese American History*, 64–65.
[531] Nakano, letter.

means: shoot the works. Well, Bub, that's what we're doing. Because the showing we make in this man's war is going to help insure the privileges of our kids as Americans after the fight.[532]

It was attitudes like these that proved Japanese Americans as fierce in their loyalty to their country.

Those who fought alongside them duly observed this fierceness. One individual, Capt. George H. Grandstaff—a Caucasian officer who served with the 442nd—recalled the invasion of Cassino:

> I asked for volunteers for hazardous tasks, selected those to go and then saw men cry because they were refused permission to go with us. Yes, those were Japanese-Americans who cried—not because they had drawn hazardous duty but because they had not. One night in particular will always remain in my mind. Some forty enlisted men and I had picked a spot at which to meet at 2000. I was delayed by a persistent mortar barrage and arrived about three quarters of an hour late. Instead of forty men there was only one. Upon questioning him, I found that the balance were up in that barrage hunting for me because they knew that I was alone. There are many fancy definitions of "loyalty" but when those men straggled in at dawn after an all-night search for me, I needed no dictionary for my interpretation of the word.[533]

Many Caucasians who fought alongside the 442nd tried to erase racism found at home. One such serviceman—James M. Hanley,

---

[532] Capt. George H. Grandstaff, speech to Commonwealth Club of California, 27 July 1945, Lloyd Garrison Collection, Box 1, Folder 11, Auraria Library Archives and Special Collections, Denver.

[533] Grandstaff, speech.

commander of the 2nd Battalion—took exception to a comment by the editor of his hometown newspaper. The *Mandan Daily Pioneer* of Mandan, North Dakota, had stated, "A squib in a paper makes the statement that there are some good Jap-Americans in this country but it didn't say where they were buried."

To this remark, Hanley replied that he knew

> where there are some good Japanese-Americans—there are some 5,000 of them in this unit. They are American soldiers—and I know where some of them are buried. I wish I could show you some of them, Charlie.
>
> I remember one Japanese American. He was walking ahead of me in a forest in France. A German shell took the right side of his face off. I recall another boy—an 88 had been trying to get us for some time finally got him. When they carried him out on a stretcher the bloody meat from middle of the thighs hung down over the end of the stretcher and dragged in the dirt—the bone parts were gone. I recall a sergeant—a Japanese American, if you will—who had his back blown in two. What was he doing? Why he was only lying on top of a white officer who had been wounded, to protect him from shell fragments during a barrage. I recall one of my boys who stopped a German counterattack single-handed. He fired all his BAR ammunition, picked up a German rifle, emptied that, and used a German Luger pistol he had taken from a prisoner.
>
> I wish I could tell you the number of Japanese Americans who have died in this unit alone. I wish I could tell you the number of wounded we have had—the sightless eyes, the missing limbs, the broken minds. I wish I could tell you the decorations we have won. I wish the

boys in the "Lost Battalion" could tell you what they think of the Japanese Americans. I wish that all the troops we have fought beside could tell you what they know.

The marvel is Charlie, that these boys fight at all—they are good soldiers in spite of the type of racial prejudice shown in your paragraph. I know it makes a good joke—but it is the kind of joke that prejudice thrives upon. It shows a lack of faith in the American ideal. Our system is supposed to make good Americans out of anyone. It certainly has done it in the case of these boys. You, Hearst, and a few others make one wonder just what we are fighting for. I hope it isn't racial prejudice. Come on over here, Charlie. I'll show you where some good Jap-Americans are buried.[534]

Like Hanley, Commander Grandstaff was appalled at the response such men were receiving back home. Grandstaff recalled during the voyage to renewed action at the Anzio beachhead:

We managed to do a bit of reading and it was there that our men through the Stars and Stripes and local newspapers from home learned of many happenings on the Pacific Coast. They didn't say much about their families and friends in relocation centers nor did they rejoice over the fact that white men committed the only proven sabotage. The thing that really made my blood boil was to read of the mistreatment of our returning veterans. Had I been a Japanese-American, I believe that I would have become very embittered and doubts would have assailed my mind. But the

---

[534] *Oregonian*, 5 September 1943, 1, Granada Archives.

boys never relaxed and as the incidents increased so also did their determination to go on proving themselves Americans in spite of the un-American acts committed against them.[535]

On reaching Anzio Beach, Grandstaff recounted how two of these men—Captain Kim and Private Akahoshi—startled "all American units with their daylight capture of two German prisoners from behind enemy lines." According to Grandstaff, the two Nisei crawled on their bellies into an area occupied by a German platoon, then belly-crawled their prisoners back across enemy lines.[536]

Amache evacuees, like those in other relocation centers, were proud of the bravery their sons demonstrated overseas. But this pride came at a cost. By the war's end, thirty-one young men would lose their lives protecting the dream of democracy. One of these men, Pfc. Kiyoshi Muranaga—whose family was interned at Amache—gave his life as a member of the 442nd. In 2000, President Clinton awarded the Congressional Medal of Honor to Muranaga posthumously. Muranaga's willingness to fight off German troops single-handedly using only an 88-millimeter self-propelled gun allowed those fighting with him to escape, saving the lives of many.[537]

Muranaga's bravery was exceptional. And so was that of the others from Amache who died while in military service. They willingly went into service. They willingly gave their lives. And they did so despite the treatment they and their families had received at home.

While young Nisei from Amache were doing their part overseas, their parents, families, and friends were maintaining their existence at home.

There was the usual. Victory gardens of Swiss chard, Italian squash, and cucumbers were planted by elementary schoolchildren to help provide food for Amache's hospital and mess halls. Amache's silk screen shop

---

[535] Grandstaff, speech.
[536] Source unknown, "Officer Answers Slur against Nisei Loyalty," Lloyd Garrison Collection, Box 1, Folder 8, Auraria Library Archives and Special Collections, Denver.
[537] *Los Angeles Times*, 22 June 2000, A1, A14.

cranked out tens of thousands of posters for navy recruitment. Amache Boy Scouts, Girl Reserves, and FFA harvested crops both in the center's farms and in outside farms. A forty-four-hour week was established to keep up with work demands. And a canning plant, freezing plant, and various other buildings were erected on the center's grounds.[538]

There was the unusual. In May 1944, a small group of Amache evacuees out on a hike around the center found a gun with sixteen notches dated 1883. The center also experienced what was described as a "mysterious ball of fire" by residents of block 6F late in the evening on August 11, 1943. One evacuee commented, "For a moment, I stood fascinated, but when I felt my hair beginning to stand up, I ran into the shower room. My next destination was under the covers of my bed, which I reached in an amazingly short time."[539]

There was the ever-present shortage of workers. The center was missing so many of its young men by mid-1944 that filling employment within the center had become a job in itself.[540]

There was overcrowding. When the center at Jerome closed in the summer of 1944, the WRA decided to disperse those evacuees who remained to other WRA camps. Five hundred thirty of these evacuees were sent to Amache in June 1944. During July 1944, the housing department was busy dealing with overcrowding complaints. A report from that month states, "This office was also kept busy with the needs of the [Jerome residents]. Many of these came to the office for lumber, Celotex, benches, tables, and other requirements." Recreation halls were used to house members of the Jerome contingent. "Since the Granada Project took more than a 10 percent increase over its regular quota," officials claimed, "such emergency use could hardly be avoided."[541]

---

[538] Lindley, "Final Report," appendix IV, 10–18.
[539] Lindley, "Final Report," appendix IV, 16, 27; *Pioneer*, 11 August 1943.
[540] James Lindley, "Quarterly Report of Fire Department Activities," 3 April 1944, 309:0080 L6.92, Japanese American evacuation and resettlement records, BANC MSS 67/14c, the Bancroft Library, University of California, Berkeley.
[541] WRA, Granada Relocation Center, "Housing Office Report for July 1944," 301:0075 L5.12, Japanese American evacuation and resettlement records, BANC MSS 67/14c, the Bancroft Library, University of California, Berkeley.

And there was conflict. Although Amache was known as having one of the more submissive evacuee populations of WRA camps, it was not without conflict. After the initial registration period, most Nisei did not protest military participation until January 20, 1944—the date the draft came to Amache. But when Selective Service began at Amache, it was noted by IS that "immediately there became evident in the Granada center, as in all the relocation centers, a passive resistance to its provisions, embracing the theory of argument that, 'We, the Japanese Americans, have been denied our rights; first by forced evacuation, and second by forced existence in a relocation center.'"

The chief of IS addressed nearly 1,400 of those eligible for the draft attempting to dissuade any form of protest to the induction. He had a fair amount of success. In the end, only 34 of 1,012 accepted by the military for Selective Service refused to comply.[542]

As the war waged on overseas and evacuees weathered the storm out in internment centers at home, an end was drawing near to the relocation saga. Soon, evacuees would begin to filter out into the country that had locked them up. And most would be going home.

---

[542] Foxster, "Granada Internal Security."

CHAPTER 9

GOING HOME

The focus of the WRA had always been implicitly stated as the evacuation and resettlement of Japanese Americans and aliens from the West Coast to points inland. Dillon Myer never wanted a permanent reservation that would permanently care for people of Japanese ancestry. Amache, like the other relocation centers, was destined to one day become a ghost town. The $4.2 million spent in building the camp was meant to provide no more than a temporary fix to a sociological plague.

Understandably, evacuees never warmed to the idea of leaving their homes and relocating to inland states the way Myer had hoped. Evacuees often viewed seasonal and indefinite leaves as merely a means outside until evacuation orders were rescinded. Finally, at the end of 1944, those who had been torn from their homes on the West Coast got what they had for so long hoped for. The process of relocation was about to end and an evacuation in reverse was about to begin. Evacuees would be permitted—and for some, forced—to return to the West Coast.

Announcement of rescission came on December 17, 1944, with Public Proclamation No. 21. At that time, Dillon Myer also announced that all relocation centers would be closed by the end of 1945. Amache's *Pioneer* published a special edition informing evacuees about what the proclamation would mean to them. The lifting of the ban, so the *Pioneer* told evacuees of Amache, would take place on January 2, 1945. It was official; the relocation period was about to draw to a close.[543]

The task of preparing for this evacuation back to the West Coast began immediately. On December 18, an army team from the Western Defense Command arrived at Amache to help staff members with the details of relocating evacuees in a quick and timely manner. Likewise, a family counseling unit was set up on December 23 to advise and provide financial assistance to evacuees. This counseling unit was also responsible for interviewing evacuees leaving the center. The interview procedure was necessitated by Dillon Myer, who made it mandatory for all evacuees leaving relocation centers to have relocation plans approved by the WRA.[544]

Then, in early January 1945, James Lindley allowed five men to journey back to the West Coast. Fumiye Nishizaki recalls her husband, one of the five, was asked to check "the atmosphere of California." Nishizaki recalls how "five men went with our car—we had our car by then—they went with him, and found there was nothing they should be afraid of. That was the report they gave to Mr. Lindley. Then, as soon as they came back it started to open up."[545]

News from outside sources was encouraging to evacuees. The attorney general of California notified all law enforcement officers to provide full protection to evacuees returning to the state. The mayor of Los Angeles officially welcomed a group of Nisei who were returning to that city. And fishermen who had been displaced from their work were once again permitted to operate in West Coast waters.

Evacuees greeted Proclamation No. 21 with mixed feelings. Some Amacheans took the order with a welcome air and left camp immediately. Fumiye Nishizaki remembers, "I was happy to get out. I knew we had to leave, we just came out early. It was sad to leave, but we knew we'd see [our friends] again." Likewise, as early as December

---

[543] Lindley, "Final Report," appendix IV, 34.
[544] Lindley, "Final Report," 34, 35.
[545] Nishizaki, interview.

18, one family—Mr. and Mrs. Satera Doi—had eagerly signed up to be first to return to California since the exclusion order had been lifted. Four other families also applied for leaves at this time, but these families chose to go east instead, claiming they had no desire to return to California. By January 15, 1945, fourteen individuals, including the Doi family, had left Amache for the West Coast.[546]

But not all evacuees were anxious to leave Amache. One elderly Issei fearfully noted, "Now I have a lot to worry about. This is bad news."[547] Others felt great reservations about returning to the land they had been torn from. They had experienced racial discrimination before they had left. Most had had everything they owned either sold or stolen. One report noted that "there are still a great many who come in and say that they intend to stay at the center, and when they are informed that the centers are going to close, they are inclined to say, 'Well, I'll stay till the center closes and then I'll make up my mind what to do.' The general feeling was that there are at this time a good many people on the project that have taken that position."[548]

These mixed emotions surrounding Myer's announcement were underscored in Ralph McFarling's community analyst report for December. McFarling noted that the first reaction to the announcement was

> rather stunned surprise at the suddenness of the move. This was followed by an undercurrent of joy on the part of the younger people and children. The reaction of the older groups, who are never given to an out-ward expression of their feelings, may be more nearly expressed as a sense

---

[546] Nishizaki, interview; Lindley, "Final Report," appendix IV, 35.
[547] WRA, Granada Relocation Center. "Reactions to Center Closing Announcements" 288:0188 L1.115, Folder 4, Japanese American evacuation and resettlement records, BANC MSS 67/14c, the Bancroft Library, University of California, Berkeley.
[548] WRA, "Report of Visit to Granada Relocation Center," 16 January 1945, 293:0157, Japanese American evacuation and resettlement records, BANC MSS 67/14c, the Bancroft Library, University of California, Berkeley.

of relief. This is not so much relief at being able to return to their homes on the West Coast, but is rather relief of their civil rights, release from discrimination, release from the burden imposed by a sense of rejection, and relief that this is a tangible evidence of their acceptance by America.[549]

By acceptance, McFarling meant more than just a mere tolerance by the groups and individuals who had fought so hard to expel the Issei and Nisei from the West Coast. The acceptance McFarling was speaking of was a desire to be wanted and a need to be recognized for the sacrifices evacuees had made for their country. McFarling noted that "many, not all by a great deal, definitely would like to return to the West Coast. This reaction was stated negatively by many on the first day the ban was lifted when they said, 'If (the residents of the West Coast) don't want us, we don't want to go back.'"[550]

In short, Issei and Nisei wanted to begin again on a new footing. Evacuees wanted a true and lasting end to the racism they had experienced both before and after Pearl Harbor.[551]

But a fresh start would not come so easily. The pressing need to relocate was only made more frightening by the reactions of individuals outside the center. Residents of Shelton, Nebraska, protested the employment of relocating evacuees to area farms in April 1945. News came in May that two evacuee families had been fired on in Merced, California. And a statement by a California state senate committee detailed at great length that California—despite the earlier remarks made by the attorney general of the state and the mayor of Los Angeles—was still opposed to evacuees returning before the war's end.[552]

News from those who had already relocated was likewise discouraging. One of the harshest stories came from the first family

---

[549] Ralph J. McFarling, "First Reactions to Lifting the Ban on the West Coast," 304:0027 L5.70, Japanese American evacuation and resettlement records, BANC MSS 67/14c, the Bancroft Library, University of California, Berkeley.
[550] McFarling, "First Reactions to Lifting the Ban on the West Coast."
[551] McFarling, "First Reactions to Lifting the Ban on the West Coast."
[552] Lindley, "Final Report," appendix IV, 39.

to relocate to the West Coast from Amache—the Doi family. On January 8, the Doi family awoke in the middle of the night to find their ranch near Auburn, California, ablaze. Hoodlums had soaked the packing shed with gasoline and set it afire in an attempt to scare the family out of the area. Undeterred by the incident, the Dois extinguished the blaze. The following day, however, the family's home was sprayed with gunfire by a number of individuals to keep the family inside as still others attempted to place dynamite around the unburned portions of the shed. The plot was foiled when local police arrived and the attackers sped away.[553]

The Doi family was not the only one to experience this treatment. Thirty other such incidents involving Japanese Americans returning to the West Coast would occur between January and June 1945. Various writers denounced all attacks—both verbal and physical—on Japanese Americans and aliens. Even Secretary of Interior Ickes called such actions "planned terrorism by hoodlums."[554]

Such language held little weight, considering most of those who attacked returning evacuees received little or no punishment. A rancher found guilty of firing into a home of evacuees who had returned to Fresno, California, was given a probationary term of six months. A woman found guilty of harassing evacuees returning to the Walnut Grove area was given a ninety-day sentence. Even those charged with attacking the Doi family in January were eventually acquitted of all charges.[555]

The knowledge of such news was not the only deterrent to reverse relocation. The evacuee property section reported that the evacuees also had little confidence in the US government in "its ability or inclination to take care of their property or personal effects." Past experience had shown evacuees that the government had spent little or no effort protecting their property. Many evacuees returning to the West Coast had found their property either sold or destroyed. Some were even forced to use the services of Amache's legal division

---

[553] *Lamar Daily News*, 22 January 1945, 1.
[554] *Lamar Daily News*, 22 January 1945, 1.
[555] Lindley, "Final Report," appendix IV, 39, 40, 42.

because of—as one Amache legal report notes—an "apparent lack of interest on the part of law enforcement authorities in California, who apparently made little or no effort either to recover the property or to arrest those who had stolen it."[556]

Concerns about property protection and governmental responsibility were proven justified. In September 1945, a mysterious fire broke out on a freight car near Canyon Diablo, Arizona. The freight car housing evacuee personal property was en route to the West Coast when a fire ignited from inside the car. The proximity of the blaze's ignition brought suspicions of arson. However, the WRA investigated the blaze and did not reach any conclusion as to its cause. Thirteen families from Amache had property damaged in this fire.[557]

This was the environment into which evacuees were to return. Those in Amache had until the middle of October 1945 to leave the center.

By January, officials at Amache noted an increase in those who wanted to postpone making any relocation decisions until the bitter end. One official remarked:

> There are a good many that feel rather stunned and at a loss to know what to do. The great majority are going to wait for a while and be very cautious before moving in any direction. Even many of those who have property on the West Coast are in no hurry to go back there. Some of them, including two principal members of the Relocation Information Advisory Board, are contemplating resettling in the East for a while and watching what happens on the West Coast with the possibility of returning there at some later date.[558]

---

[556] Herbert J. Vatcher, "Granada Final Report, Evacuee Property Section," 306:0317 L6.32, Japanese American evacuation and resettlement records, BANC MSS 67/14c, the Bancroft Library, University of California, Berkeley.
[557] Vatcher, "Granada Final Report, Evacuee Property Section."
[558] WRA, "Report of Visit."

Regardless of their initial responses, evacuees were heavily pressed by the Amache staff to relocate. In the end, most families would take advantage of the summer months to move out. Others stayed until the end. The WRA gave evacuees twenty-five dollars each—fifty dollars for a family—and enough cash to cover transportation costs. Leaving with little more than they had come with, evacuees began their venture beyond the barbed wire that had separated them from other citizens for the past three years.

Henry Okubo recalls that at first, it was difficult to leave Amache—the friendships made while in camp made departing a bittersweet occasion. For Okubo's parents, the prospect of going out into a hostile America was a rather terrifying one. Regardless of their feelings, Okubo and his parents hopped a Greyhound bus to Denver where his father eventually opened a market on Twenty-Eighth and York. Although his parents would later find their way back to the West Coast, Okubo remained in Colorado where he enlisted in the army and later received an engineering degree from the University of Denver.[559]

Some evacuees chose to stay in Colorado. After the evacuation order had been rescinded, Harry and Kimi Shironaka—who had been on indefinite leave—bought thirty acres of land with the money he had received from selling his farm equipment before the war.[560]

Helene Ioka recalls that she and her husband moved to Denver from Michigan where they had been on an indefinite leave "to help his folks move to Denver from camp." Ioka and her husband found a place to live in Denver, and they opened a body and fender shop on Broadway and Twenty-Third. "Right on the corner there, he had a shop there. Tom's Auto Body—my husband owned that. We ran the business for about, oh, twenty years or so. Maybe twenty-five years… Being honest and doing good work kept his business going."[561]

Unlike Okubo and Ioka, many evacuees moved to Denver for only a short time. Sets Sumikawa recalls, "Most of the people

---

[559] Okubo, interview.
[560] Shironaka, H., interview.
[561] Ioka, interview.

went to Denver and then on to California. I don't think I wanted to go to California, when I was kicked out, my choice was to stay in Denver."[562] But for those who remained in Denver, many settled around the Larimer area of the city. What had once been a community of 323 in 1940 grew to over 3,000 by 1946.

The staff and evacuees of Amache began, bit by bit, to dismantle the "city" they had built over the past three years. The process for the disposal of WRA property had been defined as early as January 1945. Once a complete list of regional WRA items were identified for sale or disposal, it was sent to the Washington WRA office where it would "be submitted to other agencies of the Department of Interior that will requisition items they need." Any property left after this process would then be left to the treasury procurement divisions in Denver for final disposition.[563]

Signs of shutdown were all around the camp. In early February, the center's farm section officially ended with a banquet to honor the work done on Amache's farm project. The farm section had good reason to celebrate. In 1944 alone, the center produced over $290,000 in vegetables, field crops, and livestock. "The success achieved in vegetable production on our farm," remarked John W. Spencer, superintendent of the WRA Amache project farm, "was possible largely because of the ability of evacuee farmers who had past experience with these crops."[564]

Likewise, in March, it was announced that the center's schools would close permanently in June. More than 3,500 students had been enrolled in Amache's school system from its opening. One hundred nine seniors would attend the final baccalaureate service held on June 5, 1945, bringing the total graduates from Amache's high school to over 610 students. A remarkable percentage—22 percent—of these youths would eventually go on to attend college by the camp's closure.[565]

---

[562] Sumikawa, S., interview; WRA, *People in Motion*, 134.
[563] *Lamar Daily News*, 23 January 1945, 1.
[564] *Lamar Daily News*, 3 January 1945, 1.
[565] *Lamar Daily News*, 6 June 1945, 1, 2; 15 October 1945, 1.

AMACHE

April brought great shock and sadness to evacuees in Amache. On April 13, 1945, newspapers around the world announced the sudden death of President Franklin Roosevelt. The stunning news was greeted by genuine remorse and uneasiness at Amache. With Germany's final surrender just a month away, and the surrender of Japan still an uncertainty, the leader who had overseen the details of war was now dead. Amacheans, like the rest of America, mourned the loss of this wartime president. At Amache, the man who had signed the final orders to evacuate and imprison West Coast Issei and Nisei was given a memorial service at the center's high school.[566]

But as America readjusted to the new leadership of President Harry Truman, those inside Amache continued with closure proceedings. Individuals like Dr. E. Viles, Washington educational advisor, J. B. Barge, army engineer, and Colorado congressman Chenoweth arrived to discuss possible sale of the center's land, buildings, administrative and educational equipment, and vehicles. Other individuals from surrounding communities also got in on the action. On April 26, 117 pieces of farm machinery were sold at an auction attended by over 130 bidders.[567]

Outside Amache, in cities like Cleveland and Los Angeles, Boston and Seattle, San Jose and Denver, hostels were established to aid evacuees in the process of relocation. Representatives from the Civil Service Commission and various private organizations were also recruiting evacuees for relocation to western and midwestern states.[568]

Shigeko Hirano took advantage of an employment opportunity in Minnesota in the summer of 1945. "We went to this downtown office where my sister was already working," Hirano recalls. Hirano was one of those students who had participated in Amache's final high school commencement exercises.

> You know those little address labels. We were typing the stencils for them. At the factory the

---

[566] Lindley, "Final Report," appendix IV, 38.
[567] *Lamar Daily News*, 26 April 1945, 1; Lindley, "Final Report," appendix IV, 38.
[568] Lindley, "Final Report," appendix IV, 38, 39.

> going rate was forty-five cents an hour. Jenny, this Norwegian lady, was really a fine, wonderful woman who helped so many of us Japanese Americans that worked there. She knew we needed the money, so she gave us jobs… She let us work there—because we wanted to, sometimes until 10 o'clock at night because we needed the money… She was a very wonderful person who helped us. We needed friends like that. We were only seventeen or eighteen. We were so sheltered in camp. We just didn't know how people would take to us. It was a very scary time.[569]

Hirano's boyfriend from Amache, George Hirano, had graduated in the fall before the evacuation order had been rescinded. After graduation, Hirano left camp immediately for Chicago to find employment. "I was sixteen and a half at the time. I was extremely scared but I knew I had to go. My mother was extremely supportive—she was amazing. Anything was better than staying in the camp."[570]

Hirano, whose parents were still at Amache in the summer of 1945, recalls his parents' final days in Amache:

> Before the camp was closed, they knew the camp was closing and they were told to "Go out and do something—you can't stay here." A number of people were coming into the camp to recruit workers, and we didn't have any money to really go anywhere. We didn't know if we should go back to the West Coast right away. This person came from Utah and recruited my mom. Then we relocated to Utah. I came back to help them do that…me being the world traveler in their eyes.[571]

---

[569] Hirano, S., interview.
[570] Hirano, G., interview.
[571] Hirano, G., interview.

Once outside, Hirano and his parents made their way to a place near Brigham City, Utah, called Bear River. "We were housed in housing worse than the camps. It was much colder in Utah. This place was really a tarpaper shack. We had to go outside and build our own toilet—an outhouse. Water was pumped out of a well in the middle of the street. We were in barracks, but they were not as strong or as weather proof as the ones at camp. We had to cook off a little two-burner kerosene stove. We had to build our beds again, this time to do them double-decker style."[572]

Over time, Hirano's family found that California was beginning to provide safety for those of Japanese ancestry. Because of this, Hirano's parents eventually moved back to Sausalito, where they started a gardening business. George Hirano also eventually returned to California where he married his sweetheart from camp—Shigeko Hamaka—in 1950.[573]

Throughout the spring of 1945, the ebb of evacuee return and relocation slowly reduced the number of residents of Amache. A January census of the center had showed a population of nearly 6,200 residents. By April 1945, the camp population was just over 5,000.

With the movement of evacuees to outside points came the strains of keeping the camp running. The lack of young workers necessitated using skeleton crews throughout the center. The fire department was forced to exist on a minimal crew of about ten firemen per day—five men for a twelve-hour shift. The center's hospital was put on a new time schedule to balance needs of the evacuees and the reduced workforce.[574]

The Amache hospital staff that had worked amazing feats throughout the life of the camp was feeling the strain of closure. The hospital had provided care for over 10,000 residents. An average of 60 patients were hospitalized daily. Over 1,900 patients were treated

---

[572] Hirano, G., interview.
[573] Hirano, G., interview.
[574] WRA, Granada Relocation Center. "Monthly Fire Report," April 1945, 309:0080 L6.92, Japanese American evacuation and resettlement records, BANC MSS 67/14c, the Bancroft Library, University of California, Berkeley.

each month by the staff. Over 400 babies were born in the hospital—eleven of which were born in one night. But as evacuee doctors and nurses began to leave, so, too, did the ability to provide ample medical care. Those hospital staff members remaining continued to provide services for the large number of evacuees left in the center.[575]

By the end of June 1945, a little more than 31 percent of the evacuee population had moved out of the center. Evacuees who remained within the center continued life's activities, as if the approaching day of closure was merely a myth. Support for the war continued. A scrap drive was conducted through March and April. Rationing of gasoline, sugar, and cigarettes continued. The May 8 announcement of the surrender of Germany was greeted with a subdued celebration. Routine tasks of the center were carried on as usual. For those in America and Amache, the war was not over—for the surrender of Japan was still months away.[576]

On June 25, 1945, between 7:50 p.m. and 8:10 p.m., the camp experienced a tornado-like storm that wreaked havoc on the warehouse / motor pool section of the center. On the morning of the storm, the weather had been cool and had warmed by midday with winds increasing from the north. By seven thirty that night, Amache staff members reported that winds had picked up to include "spasmodic characteristics" and gusts of over forty-one miles per hour. Severe lightning and thunder were also present, with the worst of the storm going on for over twenty minutes. As the camp became entrenched in the storm, the freakish winds knocked out the camp's power supply, leaving evacuees and staff completely without electricity and phone service for several hours. The following day, already taxed crews began the task of cleanup. The cost of repairs would total nearly $8,000, with the major damage at the center's garage section. Various center vehicles and equipment also were damaged during the storm.[577]

---

[575] *Lamar Daily News*, 20 December 1944, 1.
[576] Lindley, "Final Report," 6.
[577] Reports Office, Granada Relocation Center, "Report of Storm on June 25," 309:0183 L6, Japanese American evacuation and resettlement records, BANC MSS 67/14c, the Bancroft Library, University of California, Berkeley.

With the advent of summer, the camp's closure picked up momentum. Lindley's weekly reports became "more and more a log of relocation." Lindley and his staff constantly kept the evacuees at Amache informed as to the pace of relocation. There were speeches and assemblies at existing mess halls. The *Pioneer* published articles about the relocation. On June 7, 1945, the first special rail coach left for California. Returning to the Sacramento area, the coach would be the first of many "California specials" to leave the camp for California locations. The *Pioneer* published a special July 12 edition on the closure of the center, which was now scheduled for October 15. By the middle of July, the hospital was operating on an emergency basis only. Mess halls began to close in rapid succession—beginning with the hall at 6E. Over the next several months, as a block's population would dwindle below 150, those remaining would seek services in other blocks nearby.

Although many evacuees from Amache moved to cities, towns, and farms around Colorado and midwestern states, the majority took advantage of California specials and returned to the West Coast. Tom Shigekuni recalls that initially he had gone, as a tenth grader, on indefinite leave to Chicago for work in a defense plant. But when he was told his family was planning to return to California, he came back to Amache to aid in the move.

Shigekuni found the move back to California a rough experience.

> I had to go to school and the principal of the school we lived next to said, "We don't want your kind here." Here I lived right next to the school, I mean fifty feet from the school, and he told me, "Your kind, they go to Oakland Technical High School." I had to ride a half an hour by streetcar to get to school. I didn't have to listen to that guy, you know. I could have insisted—it was a public school after all. But being fresh out of camp, I didn't want to make too many waves and I went to this Oakland Tech. There and then I decided

> that I was getting out of there. So I disenrolled and came back to L.A.[578]

Shigekuni notes that he encountered many of these types of experiences. He recalls one example of "walking down the street going to the street car from where we were living... The firemen would be standing out in front of the fire station. They had a game, 'Is that guy a Jap or is he a Chinaman.' I mean, here I was walking twenty feet from them and they are arguing about what my racial background was. Now that is as rude and crude as I can imagine. That's the kind of thing we were facing."[579]

Even Japanese American servicemen were not immune to racism. Walter Miyao, after his discharge in October 1944, was sent back to Amache because the West Coast would not allow any Japanese Americans to return—even if they had served in the military. After about a month in Amache, Miyao found employment on indefinite leave to Detroit.[580]

Robert Ichikawa, who had fought valiantly in campaigns in Europe, recalls that, at first anyway, he returned as a hero.

> The war ended after a few months and many of us who had enough points were returned to the U.S. for discharge. I was assigned to an aircraft carrier converted to a troop carrier. We arrived in New York harbor on Christmas day in 1945. Through the fog came a tugboat load of WACs playing "Jingle Bells." After a couple of turns around the ship they disappeared into the fog. Later we viewed the Statue of Liberty. We finally docked and we go off that night at around 1:00 in the morning. We were greeted by the Red Cross Gray Ladies in the cold, snow, and rain

---

[578] Shigekuni, interview.
[579] Shigekuni, interview.
[580] Miyao, letter.

with coffee and donuts and a little gift. God bless those ladies.⁵⁸¹

But the celebrations soon ended. After Ichikawa had returned, he notes:

> Later I looked for my family and found them housed in two trailers that were formerly used by the servicemen to house their dependents during the war. I then went to the local office where more permanent apartment type units were rented. I was told it was for navy discharges only. I asked, "Doesn't the army count?" I went back the second time and was asked if I worked in the naval shipyard. In disgust, I went to the local VA office and asked about housing. They gave me a letter requesting housing for a vet. I was finally given a place.⁵⁸²

Evacuees like Miyao, Shigekuni, and Ichikawa even became the targets of professional patriots who continued to stir up racial hysteria in West Coast states. Some branches of the Foreign Legion were urging evacuees to not return to coastal areas. The Native Sons of the Golden West had even proposed legislation that would limit the actions of those Japanese aliens returning to the West Coast.⁵⁸³

In spite of the external pressure, evacuees found employment and began to construct new lives. Ichikawa remembers getting a job at the Long Beach Naval Shipyard shortly after returning to the West Coast:

> I started as an apprentice optical instrument maker. At the time there was only one job opening

---

⁵⁸¹ Ichikawa, letter.
⁵⁸² Ichikawa, letter.
⁵⁸³ Lindley, "Final Report," appendix IV, 35, 37.

and many vets wanted the job. I got it because I was a ten-point vet, which upgraded my test score by ten. Mr. McDonough, a retired Navy vet was in charge of the lab and of teaching apprentices. He instructed me about repair and overhaul of Rangefinders, telescopes, binoculars, gun sights, navigational instruments, and cementing and coating of optical lenses. I also was taught how to work in the machine shop making replacement parts for the instruments. "Mac" had a son who was killed in the South Pacific during World War II, but he showed no animosity toward me, for which I shall be forever grateful.[584]

Starting from scratch, many like Ichikawa found prosperity in places where they once were denied access.[585]

The State of Colorado seemed like no safer haven than that found on the West Coast. In October 1944, a measure had been placed on the Colorado ballot to stop Japanese aliens from owning land in the state. Although it had passed the Colorado House, the bill was eventually defeated in the state's senate. The measure was originally placed on the ballot because it was reported that over three thousand aliens already owned land in Colorado. In reality, however, only sixty-two Japanese aliens were in fact landowners within the state. Although Colorado voters defeated the measure to amend the state's constitution on November 9, 1944, evacuees at Amache were given the signal that they weren't overwhelmingly welcomed by citizens to resettle in Colorado.

Leo Goto, whose family had moved to Colorado during the voluntary relocation period, feels that the harassment intensified for his family after the war. "We didn't suffer any real harassment until after the war had ended and we moved to Denver. In Denver, when we started to school… I remember having a talk about how the Japs

---

[584] Ichikawa, letter.
[585] Ichikawa, letter.

were enemies and we were evil people—just a whole variety of things. For me I just laughed at it, I was just in grade school at the time. But for my parents, older brothers and sisters, it was a difficult time. It wasn't really until the Korean War that it eased off."[586]

With the dropping of an atomic bomb on Hiroshima on August 6, 1945, and a second on the city of Nagasaki three days later, Americans began to realize victory was finally at hand. The official announcement of victory on August 14 gave Americans the right to celebrate. Those who still resided at Amache—over three thousand evacuees still remained by V-J Day—also celebrated the victory. Beginning August 15, a two-day camp wide celebration was held. Offices were closed. A special service was held honoring President Truman's request for a nationwide day of thanksgiving. And cheers went up when they heard that Italy had chosen Nisei soldiers to lead a victory parade of over fifteen thousand GI troops.[587]

Amache itself was beginning to look less like a military institution. By mid-September, the MP guards patrolling Amache had left the center. With the exception of the barbed wire fences encircling the camp, Amache began to look less like a concentration center and more like a dying town.

At times, the death of the camp was pushed along by force. In late August, the staff of Amache firmly stated their resolve to close the camp by forcibly ejecting an elderly individual from it. In a letter to the evacuee-run community council, Lindley defended his position:

> There is no use in explaining to the Council the reasons for [his] forcible removal from the center. He refused to carry out the regulations of this center and the laws of this country. He was told to make his plans for relocation, he refused, and in a loud, blustering manner, stated that he would not leave the center even on October 15 and would make no plans. We then gave him the necessary

---

[586] Goto, interview.
[587] Lindley, "Final Report," appendix IV, 43.

three-day notice to leave on Saturday night. He was visited by the Chief of Internal Security on Saturday and then reiterated his statement that he would not leave the center and would stay and go to Japan. He was told that there were no plans made by the WRA to send individuals to Japan and that we would give him until Monday, and if he had not made plans to leave Monday night we would remove him from the center.

This was accordingly done, acting under my orders from Dillon Myer, who has his authority under the president of the United States. Any individual who refused to leave the center on schedule will be forcibly removed. As has been many times explained, this is not done as a punitive measure. We have been ordered to close the center. People have had full time to make their plans and will continue to be given all the help WRA has available.

I regret the necessity of using force but when dealing with an individual who will not respond to any other argument, force will be used.[588]

This removal by force was meant to be a signal to others who might have entertained notions to fight the decision for reverse evacuation. Lindley and his staff were sending a clear warning that their resolve to close the center was much greater than any evacuee's resolve to stay.[589]

To encourage evacuees to move out quickly, Lindley's staff had relied heavily on the *Pioneer* as the principle vehicle of information. However, the *Pioneer*, too, was forced to close its offices on September 15. Over its lifetime, the free publication had a circulation of 3,500

---

[588] James Lindley, letter to Amache Community Council, 288:0188 Ll.15, Japanese American evacuation and resettlement records, BANC MSS 67/14c, the Bancroft Library, University of California, Berkeley.

[589] Lindley, letter to Amache Community Council.

and had served as the center's primary source of news. The paper had been staffed by some of the finest Japanese employees in the country, including six editors, two former Disney artists, and a handful of writers and illustrators—all working for nineteen dollars a month.[590]

Along with the closure of the *Pioneer* came several major spasms of evacuees leaving Amache. A California Special, including 7 coaches and 3 Pullmans, left the center on September 22 with over 400 evacuees headed for the West Coast. Within 3 days, more than 130 others would leave for California.[591]

The sudden increase in departures and the subsequent decrease in evacuees available to freight personal belongings began to wear on the center's staff. In late September, evacuee families returning to Cortez, Livingston, and Walnut Grove were asked to organize and crate their own belongings for shipment. They also loaded freight cars and assumed all responsibility for their own shipments. The evacuee property section noted that this shipment was just part of the over 1,161,000 pounds of goods shipped out by freight, express, and WRA in the month of September alone. Many of these shipments were handled by appointed Caucasian personnel due to the lack of evacuees.[592]

In the nation, October 1945 found Americans celebrating victory while trying to pick up the pieces war had left behind. Soldiers found themselves on ships and trains on their journeys home. Chevrolet resumed automobile production at its Leeds assembly line. America was at the end of a great and taxing war—and it was ready to begin anew.

But at Amache, curtains were closing on what had once been a thriving community. As evacuees were venturing into the far reaches of America, darkened barracks and silent mess halls became bittersweet reminders of a life once filled with joy and sorrow, friend-

---

[590] *Lamar Daily News*, 7 September 1945, 1.
[591] Lindley, "Final Report," appendix IV, 44.
[592] WRA, Granada Relocation Center, Property Section Monthly Report, September 1945, 306:0317 L6.31, Japanese American evacuation and resettlement records, BANC MSS 67/14c, the Bancroft Library, University of California, Berkeley; Vatcher, "Granada Final Report."

ship and opposition. Photographers, writers, and WRA specialists descended on the camp, attempting to capture the final moments of a city destined for death.

On October 2, a special train with ten coach cars, two Pullmans, and two baggage cars departed from Granada carrying the largest group of evacuees—578 people—of the entire process of reverse evacuation. Home for these people were destinations like Walnut Grove, San Francisco, Colusa, and Los Angeles.

Within days, more coaches would once again dislodge evacuees who, by now, knew the process of moving only too well.[593]

Closing came as scheduled. On October 15, 1945, the city known as Amache became a ghost town. At 3:00 p.m., 126 people left the Granada railway station on California specials and other coaches for points around the state and nation. A photographer was on hand to catch a photo of the last evacuee to leave.

Where once stood a people intent on making the best out of captivity now stood piles of tables, dressers, and furniture made of scrap lumber left behind by evacuees who no longer needed them. Dogs and cats that could not be taken were left behind to roam the project until they could be taken to local shelters.[594]

The chapter of evacuation, concentration, and relocation had at last ended in Colorado. What had once been a chapter filled with hatred and paternalism was now closed. Echoes of its history would resonate into future decades. But for the Japanese community housed at the Colorado center called Amache, the conclusion was finally at hand.

Amache was a grandiose governmental experiment in paternalism. At its peak in October and November 1942, the population of the center was 7,567. During its 1,146 days in existence, the center saw 10,331 evacuees filter through its gates. Of this number, Lindley noted that perhaps 1,000 people were "inductions, transfers, or visitors who forgot to leave." Only a little over a third of those who entered Amache—approximately 4,000—left on indefinite leaves.

---

[593] Lindley, "Final Report," appendix IV, 44.
[594] Lindley, "Final Report," appendix V.

Four hundred fifteen new lives were born into the camp. One hundred seven died while on Amache's roles. Nearly 1,000 men and women were inducted into military service from Amache. Thirty-one of these gave their lives while fighting for what they regarded as their country.[595]

By March 20, 1946, with the closure of Tule Lake, all of Dillon Myer's way stations were empty. With the closure of Tule Lake, one of the darkest dramas in America's history had finally ended. Never before had concentration camps been set up in a nation built on constitutional rights. Never before had so many American citizens been evacuated from their homes and legally interned. Few today vividly remember these American concentration camps, but if Americans are to avoid similar mistakes in the future, they must never be forgotten. Camps like Amache are clear reminders of how even a government built on principles of democracy can fall prey to economic greed and racial injustice. If we are to maintain a government based on equality, we must remember the voices of the past. Only then will camps like Amache have purpose and meaning.

---

[595] Lindley, "Final Report," appendix IV, 38, 44; appendix I, 3–4; *Lamar Daily News*, 15 October 1945, 1.

CHAPTER 10

AFTERMATH

Jackrabbits and rattlesnakes again dominate the landscape of Amache. Gone are the wooden barracks housing a people displaced. Gone is the clank and clatter of pots and tin plates at the camp's mess halls. Gone are the shouts and chatter of young children making their way home from school. Mess hall and barrack foundations are fighting a battle against sagebrush, blowing sand, and time. Where victory gardens, baseball fields, and school playgrounds once stood, cottonwoods and cactus now reside.

Nowadays, it takes great imagination to picture the once-teeming site of Amache. Perhaps time is undoing something that never should have been. However, there are many things at the site of Colorado's relocation center that have remained remarkably intact.

Roadways are the most readily visible reminders of the community. Spaced in north-south and east-west directions, these lightly traveled roads—many of which rise slightly above or slightly below the blocks they surround—section off the center into the administrative and support areas as well as the orderly grid of the evacuee living areas.

Concrete foundations of mess halls, latrines, and laundry rooms are visible reminders of their roles in the past. Twisted steel bolts and rebar occasionally surface from stone to signal where walls of wood,

Celotex, and gypsum board once stood. Small holes and protruding pipes still give the appearance of plumbing.

With a little imagination, the sounds of musicians playing slightly off-key swing tunes might still be heard. One can almost catch the aroma of an evening meal wafting from a mess hall kitchen, all of it mingling with the sights of MPs in watchtowers and the sounds of wind whistling through the barbed wire. Only when one pictures the entire picture can one truly begin to empathize with those who lived in Colorado's WRA concentration camp.

The even and orderly patterns of barrack perimeter foundations still provide ample evidence of twenty-nine evacuee blocks. Walls were long ago taken away for use in buildings around the west. The brick flooring is visible in some of the blocks situated at higher elevations. Most of the barrack's flooring, however, has disappeared under vegetation and layers of sand and silt. Full-grown Chinese elms and cottonwoods still remain as testaments to evacuees' determination to overcome dismal living conditions.

What Dillon Myer once called "the most famous high school in America" is now nothing more than a vacant lot strewn with myriad concrete slabs. The concrete foundations of the school have been removed. A slight depression in the land is the only indication of what was once the school's auditorium. Concrete remnants that supported the school's heating plant are still intact in this area.

Several earlier landmarks still remain around the center. A water reservoir structure still stands just north of the evacuee block section. The twelve-by-twelve-by-nine-foot concrete storage vault built and used by the center's co-op still remains at block 9F. A rock garden also has recently been unearthed on Fumiye Nishizaki's block of 6F.

Granada's current town landfill is situated atop the spot where the Amache sewage treatment plant once stood. Remains of the relocation center's landfill, a root cellar, and the coal storage areas have been left, for the most part, untouched by local residents. All remnants of coal left at the coal storage area have been taken away or covered over time.

The cemetery, located in the southwest corner of the center, has become the focal point of Amache in recent years. Every May, former evacuees and members of the Denver Central Optimist Club make a pilgrimage to the center's cemetery in an attempt to keep the memory of Amache alive. Located at the cemetery site are nine small grave sites and a larger ten-foot-tall memorial with the inscription "Amache Remembered" at the top. The Denver Central Optimist Club placed the memorial at the site in 1983 to honor the thirty-one Amachean soldiers who gave their lives in battle as well as to remember those who lived and died in the relocation center. Also within the cemetery's perimeter are numerous benches and trees and a small brick building used for storage.

The fields once devoted to agriculture at Amache have long since changed hands. Sugar beets are no longer the dominant crop in the Granada area. The sites where Amache's hog and chicken farms once sat have now been converted to local farming endeavors. Many of the buildings once used by evacuees are currently used in other areas of the state. Likewise, most of the canals used for irrigation in Amache are still in use by local farmers. Most of these buildings and canals were not built by the WRA or evacuees but were taken over along with the land at point of purchase in 1942. When the land was sold in 1945, so, too, were the buildings and canals.

The discussion of what to do with the Amache property began in late January 1945 when E. H. Reed, Washington WRA chief of agriculture, arrived at the center to outline the process for disposal of excess farmland and machinery. Over the next three years, the center's land, buildings, and machinery were sold to various interests around the west. The land on which the main portion of the center was located—the land in which evacuees and staff lived and worked—was sold to the town of Granada for $2,500. Land around the center was eventually sold to various farmers and ranchers.[596]

The process of selling off the center's buildings was accomplished primarily in 1946 and 1947. The War Assets Administration (WAA) disposed of the center's buildings and contents through sales held in the fall of 1946 and the spring of 1947. Advertisements announcing these sales appeared in Colorado newspapers such as the

---

[596] Lindley, "Final Report," appendix IV, 36.

Rocky Mountain News, *Denver Post*, *Lamar Daily News*, and Trinidad's *Chronicle News*.

The targets of the WAA were initially government agencies, small businesses, state and local governmental agencies, and nonprofit organizations. Many of the buildings and contents of Amache were demolished for salvage or sold to local residents on farms, homes, and businesses. However, a few buildings were sold intact to buyers around southern Colorado.

The Otero County School District 11, which includes the city of La Junta, was the largest buyer of property from Amache. The district bought the auditorium/gymnasium, thirty-two barracks, three mess halls, three recreation centers, and three bathrooms / laundry rooms to use in the construction of a new junior college and two elementary schools. Other school districts to purchase Amache's property were the Bent County School District 6, Bristol consolidated schools, Hartman consolidated schools, Holly public schools, and Granada public schools.

Sales to school districts were greatly reduced in price. For instance, barracks that had, in 1942, cost over $4,100 each to build were sold in 1946 and 1947 for an average price of between $21 and $200 per barrack. This final cost was arrived by giving discounts of 80 percent above and beyond the fair market value already assigned. Hartman consolidated schools purchased an administration building that had been built for just over $6,000 in 194—-having a fair market value of $310 attached in 1946—for just over $60 in 1947. Likewise, the Otero County school district purchased barracks that had originally been built for over $4,100 in 1942 for as little as $21 per unit after fair market value and an 80 percent discount.

The University of Denver also purchased a large number of buildings for use at its Denver campus. Purchasing over fourteen buildings, the university used the buildings as classrooms, offices, laboratories, and maintenance shops. The university also used buildings from Amache as women's dormitories. Two buildings were even linked together for use as a thirty-two-bed hospital and medical clinic for students of the campus.

The McMurtry Land Company purchased the camp's gas station, gatehouse, and blacksmith building. The garage in the motor pool area was sold to the West Adams County Fire Protection District. Much of the water and sewage pipes were sold to the town of Rangely.

Surrounding community governments also purchased buildings from Amache. The city of Lamar bought twelve barracks for just over $5,000 as well as a recreation building and a laundry/bath building for just over $650. Likewise, the towns of Granada and Holly and the counties of Prowers and Bent purchased staff offices, warehouses, and other buildings for administrative and storage purposes.

Farmers around the area also bought warehouses and barracks for use on farms and ranches around the Granada area. The WAA had tried to persuade farmers to build grain and silage storage facilities around the already existing concrete slabs of Amache's mess halls and administrative buildings. However, no such storage facilities were ever constructed on these sites.[597]

After his short tenure as director of the WRA, Milton Eisenhower—the first national director of the WRA—worked as associate director of the Office of War Information until 1943. In July of that year, Eisenhower was offered, and accepted, the position of president at Kansas State College. In his lifetime, Eisenhower would serve as president of Pennsylvania State University and John Hopkins University as well as special presidential ambassador to Latin America.

Toward the end of his life, Eisenhower spoke candidly of the evacuation process and how such an event could have taken place within the United States:

> I have brooded about this whole episode on and off for the past three decades for it is illustrative of how an entire society can somehow plunge off course.

---

[597] Records of the War Assets Administration, Real Property Case Files 1940–1946, Federal Archives and Records Administration, Lakewood, Colorado, Record Group 270-NN-372-195, 270-57 A542, 270-62A757.

It would be comforting to heap the blame for the evacuation on some individual or group of individuals. General DeWitt is a likely candidate, as is the unyielding Colonel Bendetsen. Perhaps General Gullion, the Provost Marshal General, or Assistant Secretary McCloy. Or even Secretary Stimson. President Roosevelt signed the fateful order and must be ultimately responsible; perhaps he should bear the blame. Certainly his approval of the evacuation was a glaring example of how a busy president often makes a decision on inadequate evidence, simply because he is preoccupied with seemingly more pressing matters.

All these men—and many more—played key roles in the tragedy and all must share the responsibility. But I am convinced that no one fully understood at the time, or even knew about, all of the events that transpired between December 7, 1941 and March 1942, which led ultimately to the evacuation.

Only after the events had taken place could historians work their magic and reconstruct chaos into neat, logical, linear chronology. But, at the time, many forces were at work—military, political, economic, emotional, and racial. The principal actors in the drama frequently acted independently of each other. Often they were unaware of what the others were doing or thinking or how their decisions or actions related to other decisions or actions. I doubt that anyone saw the overall pattern that was emerging or how his actions contributed to that pattern.[598]

---

[598] Eisenhower, *The President Is Calling*, 125–126.

Whether Eisenhower's claims are true, only history can decide. Certainly, those evacuated from the West Coast might disagree with some of his statements. Moreover, those who played major roles in evacuation probably never saw their actions as anything more than patriotism at its highest.

For example, Eisenhower's successor—Dillon Myer—continued the paternalistic role he developed when, in 1950, he was named as commissioner of the Bureau of Indian Affairs (BIA). Convinced by his experiences in the WRA that ethnic minorities could be assimilated into the general population, Myer worked to end all cultural pluralism within the BIA. Under Myer's stint in the BIA, American Indian children were phased into Anglo schools. By doing this, Myer hoped to repress all learning that had been associated with tribal ways. Myer consistently denied that American Indians possessed "legitimate cultures."[599]

Throughout his tenure as commissioner, Myer worked to relocate residents of reservations into communities outside, much like he had done in the WRA. In moves representing his past work with Japanese Americans, Myer's BIA offered housing assistance, job placement, travel expenses, and free job training. It also set up relocation offices around the country to aid those who sought removal from reservations.[600]

To some, the legacy of Myer is one of darkness. In his book *Keeper of Concentration Camps*, Richard Drinnon notes that Myer and the WRA served simply as an "employment agency for domestics." In his haste to relocate Japanese Americans into outside communities, Drinnon claims that Myer became a part of a process in which "many Anglo-Americans evinced much greater eagerness to have the impounded people as servants than as free equals."[601]

To others, Myer's legacy is that of sympathetic champion for human rights. On May 22, 1946, the JACL presented a testimonial scroll to the former national director at a banquet in New York City.

---

[599] James L. Rawls, *Chief Red Fox Is Dead* (Fort Worth: Harcourt Brace, 1996), 40.
[600] Rawls, *Chief Red Fox Is Dead*, 47.
[601] Drinnon, *Keeper of the Concentration Camps*, 282.

In this banquet, the JACL thanked Myer for his accomplishments "against war hysteria, race prejudice, and misguided hate, as well as economic greed draped in patriotic colors." In the opinion of the JACL, Myer had been the one who "so capably and ably administered the War Relocation Authority under the most difficult of circumstances and against the most vicious of opposition in a manner which commended him, the American people, and the evacuee population."[602]

Myer saw himself as being a comforter to the inflicted. In later years, Myers defended the camps by stating:

> The centers were not prison camps. The War Relocation Authority looked upon the centers as way stations at which the people who had been evacuated could be provided with quarters, food, and other basic necessities temporarily until they could be resettled in normal communities either throughout the United States outside of the evacuated area or back on the West Coast whenever the exclusion order could be lifted.
>
> A large number of the evacuees looked upon the centers as havens of rest and security. This was especially true of many of the elderly Issei, particularly during the months after the turmoil of the evacuation and the period of adjustment to community living had been pretty well accepted.
>
> It must be remembered that here was a minority group who over the years had become inured to discrimination and race-baiting. In spite of this, many had done well economically, but many others had worked hard to secure a mere minimum subsistence.[603]

---

[602] Myer, *Uprooted Americans*, 291–292.
[603] Myer, *Uprooted Americans*, 291–292.

Most in Amache knew little of Myer. But many did know James Lindley, Amache's camp director. Most of the evacuees who knew Lindley felt he was an able administrator with a deep regard for fairness.

Lindley likewise had fond feelings for the evacuees under his watch. In his final report, Lindley admitted, "It is hard for one to visualize any other group of people who would be so well behaved under similar conditions. In close contact with them for over three years, I can only admire their cheerful acceptance of unfair treatment; their overcoming of fear, resentment and frustration; their willingness to give their time and effort to make various phases of the WRA program work."[604]

However, Lindley could also be very blunt about his own personal feelings toward the Japanese people he had come to know. "Just," Lindley remarked, "as much as I am convinced that the Japanese, as a people, do not have a corner on treachery, cruelty and other attributed racial characteristics, I am also of the opinion that in their racial reputation for smartness they are somewhat overrated. I question their ability to think things through, to listen to and apply logical reasoning. They are more stirred by sentiment than by reasoning; they are definitely emotional."[605]

Still, he saw those under his protection as a "people—even as you and I. Capable of assimilation into our western civilization, they bring to it a love of beauty, a time factor which we westerns are in danger of ignoring, a recognition of the need of courtesy and politeness in our everyday dealings." In the end, it was Lindley's hope that as the evacuees would become dispersed throughout the country, they and their neighbors would "benefit by mutual association and that something good will come out of this 'piece of wartime folly.'"[606]

By the 1950s, racial barriers were disappearing for Japanese Americans. Legal restraints keeping Issei from owning land were disappearing from statute books around the country. Issei were becom-

---

[604] Lindley, "Final Report," 6.
[605] Lindley, "Final Report," 6–7.
[606] Lindley, "Final Report," 7.

ing eligible for the process of naturalization. And for the first time in American history, the admission of Hawaii brought a state into the union that was made up of an Asian majority.

Likewise, through the 1970s and 1980s, a drive was begun and maintained for governmental recognition of wrongdoing in the evacuation of Issei and Nisei from the West Coast. On February 19, 1976, President Gerald R. Ford issued a formal apology to Japanese Americans on behalf of the United States for the internment process. With this apology, the path to redress was opened. In 1980, a nine-man commission—the Commission of Wartime Relocation and Internment of Civilians (CWRIC)—was established to hear testimonies and review wartime documents. The goal of the CWRIC was to make a conclusion as to the validity of reparations to evacuees.

By 1983, the commission reached a conclusion. The commission's report, *Personal Justice Denied Part 2: Recommendations*, stated that Executive Order 9066

> was not justified by military necessity, and the decisions that followed from it—exclusion, detention, the ending of detention, and the ending of exclusion—were not founded upon military considerations. The broad historical causes that shaped these decisions were race prejudice, war hysteria, and a failure of political leadership… A grave personal injustice was done to the American citizens and resident aliens of Japanese ancestry who, without individual review or any probative evidence against them, were excluded, removed and detained by the United States during World War II.[607]

According to the CWRIC, the economic losses of those evacuated from the West Coast was staggering. The commission noted

---

[607] The Commission on Wartime Relocation and Internment of Civilians, *Personal Justice Denied Part 2: Recommendations* (Washington, DC: June 1983), 5

that in 1945 dollars, it was estimated between $108 and $164 million was lost in income, while another $41 to $206 million was lost in property. The commission calculated that in 1983 dollars, the damage could be estimated as high as $2 billion.

The commission stated clearly that should any monetary payment be given, it could never "fully compensate the excluded people for their losses and sufferings. History cannot be undone; anything we do now must inevitably be an expression of regret and an affirmation of our better values as a nation, not an accounting which balances or erases the events of the war."[608]

Therefore, the CWRIC concluded that the US government should show penitence for its actions toward the Japanese Issei and Nisei during the war by acting on five distinct recommendations. First, it was recommended that Congress pass a joint resolution, signed by the president, recognizing the injustice of evacuation and apologizing for the "acts of exclusion, removal, and detention." Second, the commission recommended that presidential pardons be given to those who were charged with violation of curfews, relocation laws, and general protests. Next, the CWRIC recommended the United States allow Issei and Nisei the right to "apply for the restitution of positions, status or entitlements lost in whole or in part because of acts or events between December 1941 and 1945."[609]

The CWRIC's fourth recommendation was for Congress to establish a fund designated specifically for "educational and humanitarian purposes." Finally, the commission recommended that Congress establish a $1.5-billion fund to provide personal redress. The commission recommended this fund be used "to provide a one-time per capita compensatory payment of $20,000 to each of the approximately 60,000 surviving persons excluded from their places of residence to Executive Order 9066."[610]

---

[608] Commission on Wartime Relocation and Internment of Civilians, *Personal Justice Denied*, 6.

[609] Commission on Wartime Relocation and Internment of Civilians, *Personal Justice Denied*, 8–9.

[610] Commission on Wartime Relocation and Internment of Civilians, *Personal Justice Denied*, 9–10.

AMACHE

In 1988, Congress passed a bill meeting the recommendations of the CWRIC, and in his final days in office, President Ronald Reagan signed the bill into law. The reparation program went into effect in 1989 with the signature of President George Bush.[611]

Some in America resisted the idea of reparations. Shigeko Hirano is reminded of these issues very clearly.

> They had the subject on talk shows—on radio talk shows—and there was a fellow in Los Angeles. He would get more calls saying how we shouldn't get the money. "After all," one lady would say, "My brother-in-law was in a Japanese prison camp." And he would say to her that he wasn't talking about the Japanese from Japan, "I'm talking about the Americans that were Japanese." …I know she heard him, but she still would not admit that [our situation] was different.[612]

Likewise, historian Roger Daniels notes that editorials and letters to the editor mentioned "that since Japan had bombed Pearl Harbor the now rich Japanese government should make any payments that were due." Daniels also adds that "more frequent were arguments that the United State couldn't afford it or that the Japanese didn't need the money."[613]

Even some Japanese Americans who were interned during the war felt reparations were unnecessary. "It was a war," states one Amache evacuee. "I felt everyone was going through a hard time. I didn't think we should get anything. Because I didn't think anybody owed us anything. It was war. Everybody loses in a war. This is my idea. So [my husband and I] never fought for any money. I think the older people felt that way. But the younger people had different

---

[611] Commission on Wartime Relocation and Internment of Civilians, *Personal Justice Denied*, 5–9.
[612] Hirano, S., interview.
[613] Daniels, "Japanese Relocation and Redress," 390.

ideas—'we were citizens, we should demand it.' I think younger people requested it."[614]

But most today feel the process of reparation was justified. "I think we had it coming to us," states Art Yorimoto. "What we went through was quite a bit."[615]

George Hirano feels

> rather ambivalent about it. I feel that our government and our people are very monetary oriented and that if it had been a simple apology, it wouldn't have carried any impact at all. I feel from that viewpoint, it was something that rightfully needed to be done. As for the amount, I'm not really sure that has anything to really do with it… My mother, God rest her soul, died at 101 and 7 months about four years ago, and she said, "I don't want it. I want that apology from the president of the United States." So she just divided it among the grandchildren, because she didn't want any part of it. In the long run the apology remains clear in our minds, but whatever people did with the money is gone.[616]

Grace Kimoto agrees. "I don't think any [amount] of money would be enough. The written apology is good, and I'm glad there was some money because with Americans, if anything is worth it, it seems to cost money. But I don't think any amount of money would pay for what we had to go through."[617]

"To tell you the truth," Shigeko Hirano remarks, "I really didn't expect that it would finally go through where we would get it. I couldn't believe we would get it. I told some Caucasian friends 'I'll believe it when it's in my hands.' I'm grateful they did, I'm just sorry

---

[614] Nishizaki, interview.
[615] Yorimoto, A., interview.
[616] Hirano, G., interview.
[617] Kimoto, email.

that my parents didn't get it, you know, they were gone by then; and my sister—one of my sisters had died by then. I think who really should have gotten it were the Issei—because they really suffered a lot. You know, we lost a lot, but we were still young."[618]

Like Hirano, many evacuees feel that reparations came too late. "I think it was very nice," Yoshi Tanita comments. "But most of the Issei, you know our parents, were gone by the time the money came around to us. They were the ones who really deserved it."[619]

Sets Sumikawa adds, "I think I would be very happy if reparations were given to my parents—because they were the ones who went through this. They didn't have any passports or citizenship papers. They also couldn't own anything. Now things are different. You can be a citizen, you can even own a business if you want—if you have the money. The money should have been given earlier."[620]

The effects of evacuation are much more costly than any amount of redress. Michi Nishiura Weglyn, in her book *Years of Infamy*, writes that some evacuees have emotional scars similar to those found within survivors of sexual assault. Some suffer from survivor's guilt. Others suffer from flashbacks and depression. Still others feel disgraced or shamed by the experience. Because of these emotions, memories associated with the camp experience have been repressed over the years. Many have chosen to remain silent about their experiences until only recently. Only within the last few years have many Japanese Americans even begun speaking of their past to those wishing to listen.[621]

The phrase "Shikataganai," meaning "It cannot be helped," was a fitting stance for some Issei and Nisei who endured the evacuation process. "The government was too strong," notes Sets Sumikawa. "They would not allow us to do anything different." Most evacuees simply endured and persevered in the face of evacuation, much as

---

[618] Hirano, S., interview.
[619] Tanita, interview.
[620] Sumikawa, S., interview.
[621] Weglyn, *Years of Infamy*, 273.

rape victims are forced to endure and recover from their memories. Today, many evacuees have chosen to forgive.[622]

But Issei and Nisei alike are not willing to forget the past. Today, older generations of Japanese Americans are beginning to speak out against the actions of the US government. Today, those who experienced evacuation remind America that its federalist democracy is not immune to concentration camps and selection of worth by race.

Today, when asked about evacuation, Tom Shigekuni answers,

> [The camps] were the same as Hitler's, except Hitler killed the people and they didn't kill us. That was the only difference. The intent was exactly the same. It was an act of war against the Japanese Americans in that it was—if you want to say so—a socialistic reallocation of wealth from one group of people to another. The Japanese controlled most of the farmland around California—wholesale produce, wholesale flower, wholesale nursery business, and the fishing. All that changed overnight to another group. That's what this evacuation was all about. This thing about loyalty and war and all that is a bunch of baloney. It was really an economic act—a reallocation of wealth. They should call it what it was instead of dancing around and talking about loyalty and national security and all that stuff. It was baloney.[623]

Today, when asked about evacuation, Sets Sumikawa answers:

> Probably most [evacuees] say good things about the Japanese in the camps, but I'm one of the few that have some problems. I'm telling you these

---

[622] Sumikawa, S., interview.
[623] Shigekuni, interview.

things so that a lot of people will understand what we went through. I think that for the most part the camp was nice—it was very quiet…we didn't have to pay out for breakfast or lunch or dinner. We were treated really nice there. So I have nothing to say against the government—but we went to camp, for what reason? The government can answer that. What we think is different than what the government says. I'm very bitter about what their attitude was toward the Japanese.[624]

Today, when asked about evacuation, Grace Kimoto answers:

My feelings during camp was as a child's, but now as I learn the truth of what happened, I hurt. Today, I was told I might have been evacuated for my safety. Whew, I can't believe it. That really hurt. How can we be so ignorant? I am so glad we have some public education money to teach teachers about the evacuation, hoping this kind of stuff is never done again. The lessons have to be equality for all Americans. We have to learn to love and respect all Americans alike—kindness and acceptance of differences. The internment process is not in our government's vocabulary and never is a solution. Can't we get together?[625]

Amache is a reminder of the past. Named a National Historic Site in 2022, the Amache site was once one of Colorado's most endangered historical sites. However, in the 1990s, students at the Granada High School, under the direction of then-teacher John

---

[624] Sumikawa, S., interview.
[625] Kimoto, email.

Hopper, toured the state, making others aware of Amache's existence. "When we first started this project," Hopper recalls,

> it was a research project, and we were just trying to gather as much information as we could on Amache… Then we decided to make a scale model of the camp, and make presentations to the community. That just escalated to presentations to all over the state. We've done presentations to colleges and other schools and clubs. That's where we started. Then in the latter part of 1997, we started sending out newsletters to people telling them what we were doing.[626]

Over time, Hopper and his students also actively restored portions of the Amache site. They created signs and placed them around the site, directing and informing visitors. They planted trees and grass at the cemetery site and, over the years, have actively been involved in its upkeep. Hopper and his classes filmed documentaries describing how the camp affected the local community. Students even worked on the excavation of a Japanese rock garden and the center's dumpsite.

Also in the 1990s, the Denver Central Optimist Club, as well as members of the Amache Historical Society, provided some of the funding and volunteer help needed for the upkeep and restoration work done at the site. But according to Hopper, the lack of sufficient funding and the small pool of volunteers were never truly enough to make an overwhelming impact.

However, things changed greatly in 2022 when President Biden signed the Amache National Historic Site Act, designating the Amache site as part of the National Park System. The designation of the Amache National Historic Site will not only protect the remaining structures and property for generations to come but will also bring attention to a site that continues to require funding for upkeep and renewal.

---

[626] Hopper, interview.

In the last few years, several structures have been built to provide a sense of what the evacuees once saw. A replica of a barrack building and mess hall have been constructed in the southern portion of the camp. Nearby stands a guard tower and a replica of the original water tower. "I'd really like to see one of the center's blocks be totally reconstructed," said John Hopper. "It would be great for visitors to see the structures, just to get a sense of what internees were experiencing."

In the town of Granada, Hopper and his students have established a large museum that showcases artifacts once belonging to former Amache evacuees. Clear, concise exhibits give witness to what life was like in the camp. Photo scrapbooks allow visitors to see images available nowhere else. And student guides are available to help visitors who are wanting additional information on the relocation process.

There has been great progress at what has become the National Historic Site of Amache. However, there are still obstacles to be overcome—primarily finances and communication.

"Money is always tight," remarks Hopper. "Primarily the funding for taking care of the site comes from private donations that we get throughout the year."

Some funding has been made available through the help of grant writers at Colorado Preservation Inc. Hopper notes that "we have successfully applied for grants to help offset some areas. The funding that erected the structures was from the Federal JACCS grants and supplemented by the State Historical Fund and other funding sources. The barracks were done with JACCS and some State Historical Funds, but we received a check from the Hilton Foundation as well. We have also gotten several grants from the El Pomar Foundation, and we used their funding to erect the kiosk at the main entrance of the site." Despite these funds, however, Hopper notes that "all of the funding we use to operate on a daily basis comes from private donations."[627]

---

[627] John Hopper, interview, 2022.

Possibly an even larger task might be that of communication. The average American knows very little about the internment process, and fewer still are aware of relocation centers in western states like Wyoming, Utah, and Colorado.

"Most [people] don't know that we were in camp," Fumiye Nishizaki says. "They don't know a thing about the Japanese. They don't know who the Japanese are, or they don't know anything about the war. Nothing. It hasn't been printed, and unless you're a Japanese, I don't think you read anything about these things. Now it should be in history books."[628] But very little has been included in contemporary history books, leaving most Americans with only the most superficial information. This is one of the largest hurdles facing the preservation of Amache. Without the knowledge that an internment camp once existed within their state, contemporary Colorado citizens will never feel the need to save such a site.

And saving Amache is vital to America's future. Today's citizens are haunted by Santayana's caution that those who forget the past are doomed to repeat it. If the memory of Amache fades away, then the lessons learned there may likewise die.

This is the reason Robert Ichikawa feels Amache should not be forgotten. He warns, "I hope the leadership of our country will remember that Americanism should not be based upon color or national origin."[629] Through the examples of what has happened in the past, perhaps governmental and military leadership will be slowed in their judgment of Americans and aliens with ties to enemies of war.

Indeed, John Hopper is haunted by the ease in which the American government once abandoned the nation's principles of democracy.

> I think it was a travesty… I feel that by putting these Japanese Americans into internment centers, nobody is really safe within our federalist

---

[628] Nishizaki, interview.
[629] Ichikawa, letter.

> democracy. I wonder how, just because something happens, we can throw our constitution away and do this to people. What this symbolizes to me is that the constitution is a matter of convenience... We would like to say that we are above everyone else in our federalist democracy but it's not always that way. So I think it can happen again. I mean at this scale, I have no idea... I would hope not. Over a hundred and some thousand people, I would hope not.[630]

But Yoshi Tanita remembers just how easy a modern America can be swept into hysteria like the one she endured. Tanita recalls that there was serious talk in the late 1970s of imprisoning Iranian Americans in an attempt to gain release of American hostages held in Iran. "I thought that was really frightening to think that it could happen again," Tanita remarks.[631] And Tanita's thoughts of the past are, today, recalled again in the actions of Americans against Afghan Americans and Iraqi Americans. Every time a report of violence against a citizen with a Middle East heritage comes to light, we must remember how similar actions against Japanese Americans in the 1940s led to the even greater abuse of internment.

George Hirano agrees:

> Our government has a constitution and no matter what the circumstances are, we have to abide by it. I believe that is the moral essence of our country, and when we depart from that because of circumstances, then we become amoral. I believe in and love my country. All citizens regardless of color and creed are equal to one another. When we take action against a certain segment of the society, and we don't do anything about it or raise

---

[630] Hopper, interview.
[631] Tanita, interview.

up objections, then we are part of the people that are causing the problem.[632]

In later years, Milton Eisenhower claimed that the 1940s were filled with misunderstanding, rumor, fear, misinformation, prejudice, and ignorance. Like "dark winds that blew across the land," these actions and reactions whisked over America, infecting the very souls of its citizens and leaders. In Eisenhower's view, the rumors, slander, political moves, and military decisions "fell like pieces into a mosaic that no single individual could perceive or had created."[633]

In many ways, Eisenhower's perceptions of the events leading up to evacuation were accurate. Many distinct and varied ideologies and reactions converged to create one of America's most horrific events. But if one individual's cry had united a chorus of voices against such actions, the evacuation process might have never happened. If one powerful leader had refused to sign—because of personal conviction—that which others deemed necessary, evacuation might never have happened. If citizens of the United States had looked less to political cheerleaders and professional patriots, and more to the constitutional democracy they were fighting to save, evacuation might never have happened.

Today, Grace Kimoto visits schools in her community to tell kids of all ages about Amache. She speaks of personal responsibility. She speaks of the pain caused to others when this responsibility is ignored. And she speaks of forgiveness. "We need to remember that the Constitution is only a piece of paper; and it's a wonderful Constitution if we abide in it. I tell the kids, you are so lucky to be in the best country in the world. What country would apologize—the president sign an apology—when something wrong was done. So I really lay it on the kids, picture it in a way that they are really lucky to be Americans."[634]

---

[632] Hirano, G., interview.
[633] Eisenhower, *The President Is Calling*, 125–126.
[634] Kimoto, email.

AMACHE

The memory of Amache reminds us today of perseverance in the face of tragedy and loyalty despite persecution. Amache does not remain in our memory to open old wounds, but to stop such wounds from being repeated. Amache must be remembered. From freedom to personal safety to constitutional rights—survivors of Amache understand better than anyone else what these treasures of democracy mean. Having been without such rights herself, perhaps that is why Grace Kimoto can now tell children how lucky they are to be Americans.

INDEX

Agriculture:
    Amache's, 169–170, 173–174, 270
    need of laborers in, 66–67
    Southeast Colorado's 169–170, 214
Alamosa Daily Courier, 72
alien registration, 20
Amache:
    area around, 81
    building of, 90–92
    check-in procedures at, 104–105
    climate at, 178–180
    closure of, 275
    crime at, 137–139
    disposal of buildings at, 286–288
    disposal of land at, 286
    disposal of property at, 286–288
    excavation of, 300
    first arrivals to, 104–106, 242–243
    landscape of, 121
    nutrition in, 181–182
    operations area of, 114–115
    peak population at, 282
    segregation from, 234–241
    statistics, 282–283
    transportation to, 100–104
Amache Bulletin, 170, 171
American Legion, 24, 222, 247, 249
assembly centers:
    atmosphere at, 56–60
    definition of, 50
    facilities at, 56–60
    leaving, 63
    Merced as an, 55–60
    Santa Anita as an, 53–55
    schools at, 60

Bendetsen, Karl R., 18–19
Betz, Ava, 84
Biddle, Francis, 25–27, 28, 29, 30
block managers, 128, 130–131
Bocher, Robert E., 246–247
Boy Scouts, 133, 154–155, 194, 261

Boyer, S. J., 245
Bush, George, 295

Camp Fire Girls, 154
Camp McCoy, Wisconsin, 252
Camp Savage, Minnesota, 253
Camp Shelby, Mississippi, 253–254
Carberry, Jack, 162–165
Carr, Ralph, 41, 47, 65, 69–76
curfews, 10, 36
Chandler, A. B., 250–251
Chenoweth, J. Edgar, 145–146
Chinese immigrants, 8
Civil Exclusion Order No. 1, 33
Civilian Conservation Corps, 45–46, 111
    Colorado camps of the, 69, 76, 154–155
coddling charges, 182, 204–207, 245
Colorado, 206, 210, 233
    attitudes of citizens of, 68, 71–73, 206–207, 210, 214, 222–223
    governmental legislation in, 278
    Japanese population in, 73
    migration of Issei to, 5–6
    need of labor in, 67–68, 214–215
    participation in war effort by, 69, 171
    relocation by evacuees from Amache into, 212–214, 216–219, 269–270
    rumors of voluntary evacuation to, 68–69, 82
    speculation of WRA sites in, 68–69
    train ride to relocation center in, 105–106, 108
Colorado Council of Churches, 244
Colorado River relocation center, 113
Commission of Wartime Relocation and Internment of Civilians, 293–294
    recommendations of the, 295
community council, 128–130
conference of ten western states, 46–47
    see also Carr, Ralph
Cub Scouts, 154

Daniels, Roger, 11, 15
Delano, California, 1, 3, 6, 13
Delta, Colorado, 5, 39, 40
Denver, Colorado, 6, 67, 73, 92, 203, 214, 215–219
    disposal of Amache property in, 270, 287
    relocation by evacuees from Amache into, 269–270
    war effort of, 65–66
    evacuee population in, 270
Denver Building and Trade Council, 146
Denver Central Optimist Club, 286

Denver Civilian Defense Corp, 203
Denver Post, 69, 162, 286–287
Department of Justice, 234
DeWitt, John L., 16–20, 29–30, 32–33, 37, 41–42, 45–46
Dies, John, 24
Doi, Satera, 265, 267
Drinnon, Richard, 235, 290
Durango, Colorado, 155
    education program, 142–145
    closure of, 270
    enrollment in, 148
    high school for, 145–147
    subjects taught at, 149–150
    teachers in, 142–144

Eisenhower, Milton:
    appointment to WRA of, 42–43
    evacuation opinions of, 45–46, 48–50
    governors resist ideas of, 76–77
Ellwood oil refinery, 31
emergency services:
    fire department as, 132–134
    internal security as, 135–139
    medical facilities as, 139–141, 142
    reasons for, 131–132
Emmons, Delos C., 20
Endo, Russell, 5
evacuee government, 129–131

evacuee property:
    storage of, 51–52, 185–187
    transportation of, 51, 185
    vandalism of, 183–185
evacuation, forced:
    governor's resistance to, 45, 46–47, 76–77
    loss of property due to, 183–185
    registration for, 27–30
    rescission of 263–264
Examiner, 247
Executive Order 9066, 30

442 infantry, 253
442 Regimental Combat Team, 253–260
552 artillery battalion, 253
FFA, 154–155, 261
fair play chapters, 26
farm program, 169–170, 270
FBI, 2, 11–13, 26–27, 40, 56, 207
fire department, 132–134
Florin, California, 7
Freier, Paul H., 120–121
Ford, Gerald R., 293
Ford, Leland, 24–25
Fort Lincoln, North Dakota, 111
Fort Missoula, Montana, 111
Fort Snelling, Minnesota, 253
Fortune Magazine, 236, 248

Garrison, Lloyd A., 142, 153
Garrison, Mildred, 177, 181, 182
German nationals, 12

Germany, 271, 274
Gila River relocation center, 81, 112, 206
Goto, Leo, 39
Grand Junction, Colorado, 5
Granada, Colorado:
  attitudes of residents in, 206–207
  FBI in, 207
  history of, 80, 88–89
  Koen Ranch near, 80–81
  proposed site in, 78–80
  shopping in, 88, 174–175
  XY Ranch near, 79–80
Granada High School, 299–300
Grandstaff, George H., 257, 259–260
Gannon, Chester F., 246
Gullion, Allen W., 11, 18–19

Hanley, James M., 257–259
Hawaii:
  army command in, 10–11
  attack of, 10
  Emmons' fifth-column report of, 20
  immigration to, 3, 4
  martial law in, 10
  percentage of Issei in, 20
Hearst Publications, 9, 21
Heart Mountain relocation center, 204
Heart Mountain Sentinel, 205
Hirano, George, 52, 101, 102, 103, 106, 121, 123, 150, 151–152, 178, 296, 303
Hirano, Shigeko, 1–3, 6, 12, 13–14, 179, 180, 271, 272–273, 295, 296

Holly, Colorado:
  agriculture of, 85, 87
  history of, 85
Holly Chieftain, 213
Hosokawa, Bill, 205
Hospital, 139–141, 142
Hopper, John, 81–82, 169, 299–301, 302–303
House Un-American Activities Committee, 24
housing area, 117–118, 120
  bath facilities in, 123–124
  living quarters in, 118–119
Hughes, John B., 23–24
Hull, Cordell, 21

Ickes, Harold L., 48
Ichikawa, Robert, 51, 57, 62, 101, 254–255, 276–278, 302
Immigration Act of 1924, 8
indefinite leaves, 128, 211, 215, 220, 221–222, 263, 282
internal security, 135–139
internment camps, 111
Ioka, Helene, 140, 269
Ishi Koen Kwai, 141
isolation centers, 111
Issei, 4
  as block managers, 128, 130–131
  economic losses of, 183–185, 186–187
  FBI records of, 11, 13, 73, 222
  Hawaiian, 11–12, 13, 20
  loyalty questionnaire and the, 111, 237–231

nonviolent resistance of,
  165–166
relocation centers and the,
  49, 77, 111–114, 167,
  216, 260
rescission and, 221–222,
  263–264
Italian nationals, 11, 12, 32–33,
  70, 165
Itano, Cecil, 183–185

Japan, 4–5, 7, 12, 70, 224, 279
Japanese American Citizens
  League (JACL), 35–37
Jerome relocation center, 112,
  113, 261
    movement of evacuees to
      Amache from, 261
Johnson, Ed C., 73, 75, 76, 78,
  79–80

Keeper of Concentration Camps,
  235, 290
Keetley Farms, 38
Kibei, 7
Kimoto, Grace, 59, 151, 187,
  296, 299, 304–305
Kjeldgaard, Enola, 144, 148
Knox, Frank, 17
Kuruma, Itsako, 119, 178

Lamar, Colorado:
  attitudes toward Amache
    in, 87, 137, 177, 231
  history of, 80–82, 86–87
  shopping in, 124, 137,
    174–175
Lamar Daily News, 80, 102, 146
Lamar Register, 91, 206

Leupp isolation center, 111, 242
liberation of Dachau, 256
Life Magazine, 21, 247
Lindley, James:
  community council and,
    279–280
  construction of high school
    and, 147, 285
  legacy of, 292–293
  loyalty questions and,
    228–230
  segregation and, 239, 244
  setting up camp by, 92,
    104–105, 110
  Spanish Embassy and, 131
  Tuleans and, 242–243,
    253–254
Lippmann, Walter, 29
Livingston, California, 281
Lordsburg, New Mexico, 14
Los Angeles, Times, 15, 29, 247
loyalty questionnaire, 111,
  227–228, 239

Mancos, Colorado, 154
Manzanar, 50, 112, 125
Marshal, George C., 252
Masamori, Frank and Terri, 34,
  113
Masaoka, Mike, 35–37
McCloy, John J., 19, 29
McFarling, Ralph, 265–266
McIntyre, John J., 204–205
McLemor, Henry, 21
Meiji Government, 4–5
mess halls:
  in assembly centers, 56,
    58–59

in Amache, 105, 122–123, 173, 275
  operations for, 107, 109, 181–182
Merced, 55–60
Military Area No. 1, 32, 45
Miliary Area No. 2., 32
military exclusion, 224–225
military guard:
  assembly center, 54, 56, 62–63
  Amache, 92–93, 127, 135, 136–137, 158–160
  dismissal of, 279
  transportation to Amache and the, 101, 102
Military Intelligence Service Language School, 252–253
Minidoka relocation center, 81, 113, 134
Miyao, Walter, 7, 9, 276, 277
Momii, Chcz, 55, 60, 108, 178, 179, 180, 187, 218, 219
Monitor, 182, 207
Montrose Daily Press, 80
Muranaga, Kiyoshi, 260
Myer, Dillon, 141, 142, 160, 263–264
  evacuation opinions of, 210–211
  legacy of, 290–291
  vision for WRA of, 82, 107, 210–211, 263
  way stations of, 107, 108, 291
  WRA appointment of, 49–50
Mydan, Carl, 247–248

Nagasaki, 279
Nakano, Akiko, 202
Namura, Emory, 57, 139–140, 168, 173, 177
Namura, Tae, 57, 170–171
Native Sons of the Golden West, 24, 277
Naturalization Stature of 1870, 6
Newman, Bruce, 89–90, 132, 173, 174–175, 207
Nichiren Church, 184–185
Nisei, 164–166, 190–191, 222, 248, 249–250
  community councils and the, 128–130
  loyalty questionnaire and the, 226–228
  military and the, 224–227, 228, 229–230, 232–233, 253–260
  relocation center and the, 190–191
  work ethic charges against the, 155, 165, 232
Nishizaki, Fumiye, 51, 56, 60, 104–105, 124, 128, 130, 182, 186, 238, 264–265, 285, 302
no-no boys, 230

100th infantry battalion, 252, 254–255, 256
Ochinee, Amache, 168, 184
Odum, Katherine, 143–144
Okubo, Henry, 102, 109, 138, 175, 260
Okubo, Mine, 248

Otero County School District, 287

Pacific Coast Committee on American Principles and Fair Play, 246
pampering charges, 145, 164–165
Pearl Harbor, 10–11
Persistence of Ethnicity: The Japanese in Colorado, 5
Personal Justice Denied, 293
Pioneer, 152, 171, 202
    closing of the, 280
    portrayal of evacuees by, 176, 190
    report of Polio by, 183
    report of segregation by, 238
    report on closure of Amache by, 263–264, 275, 280
    WRA use of, 171, 221
Pitts, Malcom, 205, 223
Platteville, Colorado, 208, 209
polio, 182–183, 243–244
postal service, 168
Poston relocation center, 34, 81, 113, 125
psychological effects of internment:
    adult, 187–191
    children, 155–160
Provision Infantry Battalion, 252
Prowers County, 79–85
Prowers, John Wesley, 168
Public Proclamation number 1, 32

Public Proclamation number 2, 32
Public Proclamation number 3, 32–33
Public Proclamation number 4, 45
Public Proclamation number 21, 263–264
Pueblo Chieftain, 245

question 27, 227–229
question 28, 227–229

Rademaker, John, 188, 190, 221, 231, 232
railroads, 5, 8
    transportation of evacuees using 100–104
Rankin, John E., 224
Reagan, Ronald, 295
recreation:
    adult activities for, 172–174
    dances for, 150–151
    sports for, 152
    youth clubs for, 154
redress, 293–294, 295
relocation:
    applications for, 220–221
    applying for, 222
    financial assistance for, 217, 264
    reactions to, 217–218
    request for evacuees in, 220
relocation centers:
    location sites for, 111–114
    proposed Colorado sites for, 80–81, 114–115

removal of evacuees from, 279–280
rumors in Colorado about, 68–69, 82
Reynolds, Robert R., 204, 205
Rocky Mountain News, 65, 76, 80, 129, 164, 203, 207, 208, 287
Rohwer relocation center, 81, 113
Roosevelt, Eleanor, 26, 112–113, 206
Roosevelt, Franklin D., 42, 126
    activation of Nisei military units by, 225–226, 253
    comments on past Nisei military service by, 246
    death of, 271
    request for Nisei military units by, 225
    speeches of, 31, 34, 126
rubber production, 64–65, 126

sabotage charges, 16–17, 18, 20, 70–71
    Colorado and, 79, 207
Sacramento, California, 55, 181, 275
Sand Island Detention Center, 11
San Francisco, California, 252, 282
San Francisco Chronicle, 9
Santa Anita, 53–55
Santa Fe, New Mexico, 14, 111
seasonal leaves, 46, 81, 110, 212–215, 245

segregation:
    Amache as a site for, 236–240, 242
    American states constituted, 6
    viewpoints against, 231
    WRA camps of, 111, 234–235, 243
segregation centers, 112, 234, 236, 243
Shigekuni, Tom, 23, 54, 58, 61, 100, 101, 104, 108, 116–117, 148, 155–158, 165, 187, 188, 208, 275, 276, 277, 298
Shigekuni, Tunney, 186
Shikataganai, 57, 297
Shironaka, Harry, 52–53, 110, 172–173, 177, 187, 212, 214, 269
Shironaka, Kimi, 175, 212, 269
Short, Walter, 10, 16
short-term leave, 183, 211–212
silkscreen industry, 122, 260–261
Smart, Joseph, 205
sociological problems of Amache, 187–193, 232–233
Spanish Embassy, 131
Spencer, John W., 270
Stimson, Henry L., 18, 29–30, 225, 253
storms, 118, 121, 178, 179
sugar beets, 25, 67, 85–86, 169
Sukura Square, 71
Sumikawa, Henry, 39–40

Sumikawa, Sets, 56–57, 60, 137, 159–160, 187, 231, 269–270, 297, 298–299

232 Engineers Company, 253
Tanita, Yoshi, 51, 151, 180–181, 187, 216–217, 218, 297, 303
Taniwaki, Oski, 87–88, 171–172, 176, 191, 202–203
Tateishi, John, 256
Terminal Island, 27–33
Terry, Paul J., 147
Texas battalion, 255
The Decision to Relocate the Japanese Americans, 11–12
The Japanese in Our Midst, 244
The Seattle Post Intelligencer, 15
Thomas, J. Parnell, 204
Time, 246
Tokugawa Government, 4
Topaz relocation center, 113, 134
Truman, Harry S., 271, 279
Tule Lake relocation center, 111, 112
Tule Lake segregation center, 111, 230–231, 234–236, 242, 246, 247–249, 283

University of Denver, 287

Voluntary evacuation, 32, 36
 Colorado as a place for, 39–40, 71–72
 estimates relating to, 41
 relocation offices roles in, 251–252

 resistance to, 44–45, 72
 the failure of, 37
Vosges Mountains, 255, 256

wages, 133, 140, 141, 144, 204–205, 216
Walnut Grove, California, 101, 267, 281, 282
War Assets Administration, 286
War Relocation Authority:
 employee living quarters of the, 114, 119–120
 employees at Granada of the, 141–142, 167
 establishment of, 42
 relocation offices of, 215
 selection of sites by the, 44–45
 types of camps in the, 111–114
Warren, Earl, 28, 204
Watada, Alley, 208, 214
Watada, Albert, 209, 210
Watada, Yoshimi, 40, 41
Weglyn, Michi Nishiura, 8, 82, 129, 159, 297
West Adams County Fire Protection District, 288
Wiley, Colorado:
 football matchup between Amache and, 152–154
 the history of, 86
World War II:
 attacks on the continental U.S. during, 28, 31
 homecoming of military from, 276–278

production during, 64–65,
    126–127, 181
rationing for, 65–66
sacrifice during, 65,
    126–127, 251
scrap drives in, 104–105,
    126

YMCA, 154, 157
YWCA, 154
yellow report, 24
Yorimoto, Art, 13, 53–54, 55,
    58, 61, 62, 103, 213, 215,
    216, 296
Yorimoto, Kana, 59

zoot suits, 187, 189, 190, 201

ABOUT THE AUTHOR

Robert Harvey is the author of *Amache: The Story of Japanese Internment in Colorado During World War II*, a work written to preserve the voices of Amache internees. Now a teacher in Douglas County, Colorado, he and his wife call the Denver area home.

www.ingramcontent.com/pod-product-compliance
Lightning Source LLC
Chambersburg PA
CBHW031406290426
44110CB00011B/282